Surviving Ellen

❖

A Memoir
by Greta Eichel

Neshui Publications
45 Aberdeen Place
Saint Louis, MO 63105

ISBN 1-931190-15-1

Distributed by Ingram Books
1 Ingram Blvd.
P.O. Box 3006
La-Vergne, Tennessee
37086-1986

*This book is dedicated to
my husband Stuart
my son Steven, and the
memory of my daughter Ellen*

Contents

Acknowledgments

I started writing this book in 1995, two years after Ellen's death. Its original title was *Easy Street*. I asked a number of friends and relatives for help and advice, which they generously gave. Many of them encouraged me to write more about Ellen. At first this was too hard for me to do, but as the years went by I was able to take their advice. *Surviving Ellen* is the result. I thank them for their help and encouragement.

They are: Alan Arnold, Gloria Arnold, Jean Drennen, Steven Eichel, Belinda Eichel, Murray Evans, Florence Ferris, Marilyn Flam, Samuel Flam, Billie Friedman, Jane Garron, Dorothy Hirsch, DJ Jessee, Jim Kelly, John Kettlewell, Bernice Krol, Sonia Linke, Vincent Melomo, Dee Montie, Barbara Moore, Mary Novotny, Betty Peabody, Linda Rosenbluth, Susan Sameroff, Sandy Schwartz, Joan Boyd Short, Sonia Taub, Barbara Volin, Briget Wandruff, Arnold Werner, Elizabeth Werner, and Melinda Winters.

Writer Stephanie Piper, who read chapters as I wrote them, gave me to courage to continue. Writer Nancy Seid read my first draft. Her enthusiasm for the manuscript encouraged me greatly. Writer David Hunter was the judge for the Tennessee Mountain Writers Conference in 1997. He gave me a first place award for a portion of *Easy Street* in the first contest I had entered and said, "Now get published."

Parade magazine's managing editor, Larry Smith, who read my first draft, liked the content, and told me to take some classes to learn how to put a book together. Poet Marilyn Kallet, in her "Dreamworks" class at the University of Tennessee, taught me to write poetry, which freed me to reveal emotions that were, at first, too hard to express in prose. She introduced me to novelist Allen Wier, who with inspiration and patience helped me turn my stories into a book. The New York State Summer Writers Institute's Joanna Scott, who was my teacher, and Douglas Glover who read my book; they both encouraged me to seek publication.

Jacqueline Volin edited both *Easy Street* and *Surviving Ellen* and gave me thoughtful, sensitive, and professional help. Jeff Linger, a person of talent and insight, served as a literary consultant. Special thanks to Nancy Goldberg for the final edit of *Surviving Ellen*.

Note: All of the events that take place in this book are true and all of the people are real. I have, however, changed some of the names where their inclusion might cause embarrassment.

Foreword

Three years after her daughter's death, Greta Eichel handed me a manila envelope. I've started to write about my family, she said. I've never done anything like this before.

I read the pages with wonder. Greta had discovered what most writers spend a lifetime trying to find: an authentic voice.

It was a voice I had come to know well since we first met at the University of Tennessee. Both transplanted New Yorkers, we were alternately charmed and baffled by life in Knoxville. We shared a keen sense of the ridiculous, an intolerance of bureaucracy, and a preference for long lunches. We laughed a lot.

And then, a month after our first meeting, Greta's daughter Ellen committed suicide. I had never met Ellen, but I was shattered by my new friend's loss. I labored over a letter of condolence and kept a respectful distance.

Greta returned to work six days later. Our lunches and long talks continued. Gradually, she began to talk about Ellen.

The stories spilled out in no particular order—the quirky little girl who made friends with random-dialed strangers on the phone; the curly-haired beauty who made her parents lives a misery. Some days, the stories weren't about Ellen at all, but about Greta's parents, or her Brooklyn childhood. She turned the pages of an invisible album, framing verbal snapshots in the clear light of total recall.

Greta did not ask for comfort. She went dutifully to therapy and stopped when it felt like enough. She designed publications and won awards. One day, abruptly, she announced her retirement. Then she went home and began to write.

The stories seemed to leap off the page. Greta's voice—sometimes reflective, sometimes funny, always uncompromising in its honesty—demanded attention. When she showed me the early drafts, my only suggestion was to keep at it, to fill the album and leave no blank spaces.

Surviving Ellen is complete. The snapshots, arranged with compassion and humor, trace a personal history. Each picture tells its own story. Together, they present a powerful image of courage and healing which will speak to anyone who has suffered loss.

—Stephanie Piper

PROLOGUE

I can't fight what I've done.
I can't change where I've been.
I *can* fight for my future.
God, I hope I win.

The last entry in a book of jokes Ellen was writing for her act as a stand-up comedian.

. . .

Ellen, my daughter, killed herself when she was twenty-nine. Her suicide was the defining moment in my life. I was fifty-five when it happened. I had lived twenty-six years before she was born, and now I can't help separating my life into the time before Ellen died and the time after. I think I should talk about that right from the start, but this book is not about her death only. Someday, when I'm stronger, I may write a book about Ellen.

My husband, Stuart, and I had worried about our daughter ever since she was fourteen, when she changed from a wonderfully weird child into a hostile stranger. After Ellen graduated from the University of Tennessee in Knoxville, where Stuart and I live, and moved to Nashville, I thought about her only when I got a letter, a funny card, a phone call, when one of her

1

many ex-boyfriends called us, trying to track her down, or when Stuart and I occasionally wondered aloud to each other where she might be the next year. Now that she is dead, I think about her every day and wonder, if she knew that, would it make her happy?

Eight months after Ellen's death I went to a psychologist for the first time in my life. My friends almost forced me to go. They said they didn't even know me anymore, that there was nothing behind my eyes, that I was just going through the motions. After six months I asked my therapist, "Am I done yet?" and she said, "No, you're not done." But I told her I was; I didn't want to talk anymore. I don't really know if the therapy helped me. I have never written a story before and I must admit, it has been kind of therapeutic.

In 1991 Ellen moved to Seattle. She decided to leave Nashville because an ex-boyfriend was stalking her. I wonder why she chose that city of rain and gray mist? She got a job as a secretary for INCA, a structural engineering firm, and was moonlighting as a stand-up comedian. She sent us a videotape of her act. "The most exciting part of my day," she said on the tape, "is when I get to type the words *steel erection*. There's actually a position opening up for 'erection inspector.' I thought maybe I'd get a promotion . . . but I'm not a morning person."

Ellen killed herself sometime Monday morning, March 29, 1993. I didn't find out that she was dead until thirty-six hours afterward. Our address and phone number were not written in her book; but then why would they be? It was the same house she had lived in for twelve years. For a day and a half after her suicide, my life hadn't yet changed. The Seattle police called our son Steven in Boston and he gave them our number. The police entered her apartment Tuesday morning after she didn't show up for work on Monday and didn't answer her phone. Her boyfriend Brian kept trying to call her all Monday night, leaving ever more frantic messages on her answering machine. The last message asked, "Ellen, are you *alive?*"

That same Monday I got a letter from Ellen written on the inside of a Gary Larson "Far Side" card that showed a sheep sitting in an easy chair in front of a TV, watching another sheep reporting the news: "And this report just in . . . Apparently the grass *is* greener on the other side." Ellen thanked Stu for the letter and money he had just sent her; she said she had already invested it in the card and some candy. She talked about her job and the guy who sat next to her whose wife had just had their first baby. People were coming by all day to congratulate him and talk about the color of the baby's shit. Stu and I both read it, and although I always saved Ellen's letters, I threw this one away. I don't know why. I didn't know that as I read her words, she was already dead. The next night I took the stained card out of the garbage. I'm looking at it now.

On Tuesday we got an Easter card from Ellen that showed a fat cat sitting on some Easter eggs and saying, "What bunny?" Inside the card it read, "Yes, Virginia, there WAS an Easter Bunny." On the left side, in a large, unfamiliar scrawl taking up the whole page, Ellen had written, "Mommie, I almost sent you headless marshmallow chicks." Ellen, when she was living in Nashville, once sent me an elaborately wrapped box of those bright yellow, sugar-coated marshmallow Easter chicks called "Peeps" with their heads cut off and a note saying, "Mom, I know how much you like these, but how you always hated biting off their heads. So I thought I'd do it for you." On the right side she wrote, "Daddy, do you celebrate the day Jesus Carutherford Christ rose from the dead?" I laughed, because Stu sometimes shouts "Jesus Carutherford Christ!" when upset. Steven and Ellen had learned early on not to comment on their artist daddy's pencil rolling off the drawing board or any other small catastrophe—misplacing his car keys, losing his comb—that prompted his outbursts.

Before our phone rang Tuesday night, March 30, 1993, at exactly 9:30 P.M., Stuart and I thought we were the family that now had everything. Well, almost. I had been diagnosed with multiple sclerosis in 1977, but I had experienced long periods of remission and was still working as a graphic artist, designing publications for the University of Tennessee.

Stuart and I had been married for thirty-six years and were still deeply in love. The year before he had quit the advertising business and was now a painting student at the university. Steven, an attorney, was happily married. And Ellen, our troubled daughter, seemed happy at last. She had met Brian, an aspiring actor, and they had fallen in love. They were planning a visit to Knoxville so that Stu and I could meet him, and they were going to travel to Greece the next year. Then, just when I thought Ellen had gotten her life together, Jerry Webster, the medical examiner from Seattle, called to tell us that our daughter had killed herself. She didn't leave a note. I was horrified but not shocked. Ellen had always lived on the edge, and I thought, crazily, that when she got older she would calm down and find some peace. If she could only make it to thirty, she might be OK. Ellen died five months before her thirtieth birthday. The night the call I had always dreaded came, Stu put his arms around me and said, "I don't know how, right now, but I promise you we'll get through this."

I feel no guilt, but oh, such sorrow, knowing she will never see the sun rise again or write another poem or marry Brian, who sounded so sweet and so devastated by her death when we talked to him afterward. And I feel sorry for *myself*, knowing I will never be the mother of the bride. And such pain for Stuart, who can't bring himself even to talk about it. And such anger at her for murdering our child. And what about Steven, who went to Seattle to send us her papers and still worries that he may have been too mean to her when they were children? And what about the braces for her teeth and the dancing lessons and the private school we couldn't really afford but gave her anyway? What about all the friends who loved her? And her Grandma, who said she wished she had died first? I keep telling myself that Ellen must have been sick and in pain, and probably she took after my mother, who suffered from depression. I now wonder why no one ever made that connection until *after* Ellen's death. Not me. Not her doctors. Maybe that's because her act was so good.

Was her death planned or an impulse? I wonder what her last words were, if any, right before she pulled the trigger. Words were so much a part of my family's life—everyone writing poetry and volumes of letters and always talking talking talking—that I'm sure she must have said something. Was she just tired of going to work for "thirty-five of the biggest geeks on the planet" that day and simply sighed, "Ah, fuck it"?

After her death Stu and I kept getting letters from the coroner's office in Seattle, asking for instructions on what we wanted done with the gun. We threw the first two letters away. We couldn't bear to look at them. A third letter arrived because a gun is an expensive piece of property, after all, and the coroner's office needed something official from the family of the deceased to tell them what to do with it. So we signed a form that told them to destroy it.

When Ellen was an uncontrollable teenager and the phone rang late at night, I always expected it to be the police or the morgue. She took drugs, got drunk, and was sexually promiscuous. During her teens Stu and I argued with her, and with each other *about* her, much of the time. During one of those battles, when she was sixteen, Stu told me I had to choose between him and Ellen. He couldn't stand watching her outrageous behavior and wanted her out of the house. Given that choice I said I would have to choose her, that he was a grown man and could take care of himself but she was still a child. I knew he didn't mean it, though, and that it was a cry of pain and frustration at our inability to change her. He never spoke of leaving again. Though I couldn't stop loving my child, I didn't *like* her very much.

Nothing we tried to do helped her, not our talking to her or taking her to a therapist when she was fourteen. "Does she eat a lot of chocolate?" her therapist asked Stu and me in his first interview with us, before Ellen started her twice-weekly visits. When I told him she did, he said that was a sign of an addictive personality. "Just like her daddy," I told him. (Stu calls *his* addictions, such as long-distance running, "positive addictions.") After a month of visits the psychologist said, "Ellen has a low tolerance for frustration." *Just like her daddy*, I thought. Ellen made fun of her therapist, saying he told *her* to call him by his first name, but that Stu and I had to call him Doctor, implying that *he* was her friend and *we* were the enemy, and Ellen was smart enough to see right through that obvious ploy. Ellen said she thought he was a jerk. We thought so, too, but not knowing who

6

else to turn to, we kept her in therapy with him for six months.

After Ellen overdosed on drugs when she was fifteen, her next doctor, a psychiatrist, suggested "tough love." We never learned how to do that though, and he did not seem able to tell us. Should we chain her to her bed? Keep her from going out with her friends? Commit her to an institution? Quit our jobs and stay home all the time to watch her?

Hating it, I turned into a spy during Ellen's teens. I opened her letters, listened in on her phone calls, and searched her room for drugs when she wasn't at home. When she was almost seventeen, I confronted her after I found what I suspected was marijuana and flushed it down the toilet. I wasn't even sure that it *was*, because I had never seen marijuana before. Ellen angrily asked me if I understood how much it had cost her. She worked at Burger King after school and it was *her* money she informed me. I slapped her face. Now *I* had become the enemy. She said she planned on smoking pot for the rest of her life. This was before all the TV commercials about talking to your kids about drugs and all the billboards telling them to "Just Say No." We were simply overwhelmed and didn't know how to get help. Maybe Stu was right and we should have kicked her out. I was sick a lot with MS at that time, and my limited store of energy was becoming dangerously depleted. Nothing could stop her, it seemed, as she hurtled down the path to self-destruction. To almost everyone else, however, Ellen seemed fine. She was pretty and charming and got good grades. She graduated from high school and moved into a dorm at the University of Tennessee, meaning we would no longer have to watch her behavior. To tell the truth, we thought it was going to be a relief.

But relief was an illusion. In Ellen's first year of college she moved out of the dorm and into a boyfriend's apartment. I got a call from someone in charge of the dorms. She said that Ellen had told them she was leaving the dorm because she had lupus and needed to live at home. I told them it wasn't true, that she was moving in with her boyfriend.

One day her boyfriend came to my office and introduced himself. He said his name was Erik and that he was in love with my daughter, but she was breaking his heart. I told him I didn't think I could help him; she was breaking *my* heart too. During that time Stu and I were barely speaking to her. When she was in her third year at the university, Ellen came to my office to let me know she was going to work as a nude model for the art school. I asked her why she wanted to do that. Ellen said, "I'm not asking for your permission, Mom, I'm asking for your blessing. Didn't you once tell me that Grandma was a nude model?" "Yes," I said, "but it was during the depression and she was desperate. Are *you* desperate?" "Not really," she answered. "I just think it would be fun. Maybe Grandma *liked* posing naked. Did you ever think of that?" Actually, I never had. I wonder if Ellen took after my mother in more ways than one? "You're a grown woman," I said. "I can't give you orders—as if I ever could—but you don't have my blessing." Later she worked as a topless dancer.

I am the daughter of nonreligious Jewish parents and grew up in Brooklyn, New York. My loving family ran the gamut from eccentric and dishonest to suicidal and crazy. Three years after Ellen died, I told a friend whose son had committed suicide that I didn't feel any guilt about her death. He said, "You have to feel guilty, for a whole bunch of reasons. She was your daughter, she inherited your crazy family's genes, you got mad at her, couldn't help her, gave up on her, she died." He told me that he thought there was a lot remaining for me to confront about my daughter. He *knew*, he said, because he still felt so disappointed in himself that he hadn't done more to prevent his son's death. Then he said ruefully, "Advice talk is cheap and a lot of bullshit anyway. Besides, you need something like a dream search sometimes to even *get* at the guilt."

The first year after Ellen's suicide I cried every day whenever I thought of her. I didn't know how I could endure her birthday or the anniversary of her death. It was impossible to keep my composure when I had to tell someone, who didn't know, that she was dead. I woke up and went to sleep (when I could sleep) with a hard knot in my stomach.

I cried for the stupidest reasons. I cried passing a "Dead End" sign when I went for a walk. I cried hearing a woodpecker tapping on a tree because I remembered the way Ellen, from the time she was seven until the last year of her life, made everyone laugh imitating Woody Woodpecker; she pulled her upper lip over her teeth with one hand and the front of her hair straight up with the other and made that "eh eh eh *eh* eh" sound. I cried seeing the weather report on the CNN nightly news claiming it was raining in Seattle. Once I broke into tears at Food City when I saw an Easter display of marshmallow Peeps.

My mother wrote poetry. Whenever she came to our house, she said to Steven and Ellen, "OK children. It's time to write a poem." She handed them each a sheet of lined yellow paper and a sharp yellow pencil and told them to write down what they were feeling, but to make sure it rhymed. My mother typed out their poems on good white paper and put them in a loose-leaf notebook, as she had done with my poems when I was a child. When Ellen was seven she wrote a poem, carefully printed, perfectly spelled, that talked of suicide—but who would have thought a child that age, so sunny, so funny, so bright, could be serious? Didn't we all, at one time or another, imagine ourselves dead and our parents grieving?

THE BAD DAY
by Ellen Eichel (age seven)

The sun is shining bright
But my shoes are too tight.
Everything's going wrong
And my pants are too long.

I wish I could jump in the seven seas
But to do that I'd need six more me's.
I think I'll draw six more me's
So I can jump in the seven seas.

And when I did I drowned.
The drowning me was never found.
I'm glad that story isn't true, aren't you?

I'm glad I didn't die so soon
Because I'm planning to go to the moon.

The drowning Ellen was never truly found. But I am surviving, and Stuart was right that first awful night. Somehow we are getting through it. Now I want to go back to the beginning and try to understand what events led to this awful conclusion. Even though I come from a family that told lies and had secrets, I have not lied in this book. When I look back, I wonder if Ellen was doomed from the day she was born.

NOT EVEN THIRTY-SOMETHING

The numbers kept going around in my head all night on August 15, 1995. It would have been Ellen's thirty-second birthday. Two years before, she had shot herself in the head with a .32-caliber handgun. We had moved to Knoxville twenty-six years ago that month. I was twenty-six years old when I gave birth to Ellen. Stu and I had been married for thirty-six years when Ellen shot herself, and we didn't find out about her suicide until thirty-six hours afterward.

When we moved to Knoxville I was thirty-two years old and felt like a grown-up. Ellen, who did not live to be thirty-two, will always be a child to me, even though I know she was an adult when she died.

Ellen used to think about numbers a lot. When she was a kid she told me she wanted to get married at the same age that I did—nineteen. She never married, though she was beautiful and always had a lot of boyfriends. Sometimes men used to walk up to her on the street and tell her they were in love with her. She never loved herself, though.

When she was a little girl, we bought Ellen a digital clock. She told Steven that she liked to stay up until thirty-four minutes after twelve so she could see the clock read 12:34. Now when I see that number on the clock, I look away. The night of her birthday I watched 12:34, 1:23, 2:34, 3:45, and 4:56; then I got up and took a walk before the sun rose.

Because she was only six years old when we moved to Tennessee, Ellen had a beautiful, slightly Southern drawl. When we got an answering machine in 1985, Stuart's voice gave the message that we weren't at home and at the sound of the beep, etc. Stu has a nice voice in person, but on the recording he had an annoying Midwestern twang. I refused to record my voice because of my Brooklyn accent. A friend of ours suggested that we use Ellen's voice for the recording. One weekend, when she was visiting us from Nashville, we asked her to record the message for us. After her death I used to call my home number from work, so that I could hear her voice. Finally, our friends told us that it freaked them out, so Steven recorded his voice over Ellen's, and now our son's voice answers when we're not at home. I wish we had at least saved the tape with Ellen's voice.

All day on her birthday in 1995 I kept thinking about Ellen's birth and about her death. Both were violent. It was the fashion in the 1960s, when I was pregnant with Ellen, to induce labor. That way, the obstetrician said, you could check into the hospital at eight in the morning and not have to wake anyone up (particularly him, I now realize) in the middle of the night. "We induce labor so you can walk into the hospital standing up straight, not doubled over in pain," he told me. I can't believe women at that time fell for that shit, but most women of my generation usually did what they were told, whether it was good for them or not.

My final checkup before I would go into the hospital to induce my labor was with my doctor's young assistant. He was a pompous ass who talked on the phone for ten minutes while I sat waiting at his desk. One of the things he said to whoever was on the other end of the line was, "The baby came face, and almost thirty minutes later she was dead."

When they brought me into the delivery room after having dripped something into my arm to induce the labor, and after giving me a spinal to eliminate any pain, I heard the doctor say, "The baby's coming face." What does "coming face" mean, I thought? Remembering the words of the assistant doctor, I became frightened that I might lose my baby.

Most babies are born head first with the chin down, tucked on the chest, so that the first part you see is the top of the head. In a face presentation the baby is looking overhead, and the first part that's seen is the face. The reason this is important is that it makes for a more difficult and sometimes hazardous delivery.

When Steven was born—after an easy birth—Stuart was home sleeping, because they told him the delivery would take a long time. For Ellen's birth Stu sat in the waiting room, because they told him it would take only a short time. He waited while I lay on the delivery table for three hours, while my doctor and his assistant sent Ellen back up the birth canal and did push-ups on my rib cage to turn her in the right position to be born. They couldn't do a cesarean section, as my labor had been induced and Ellen's home of the past nine months was contracting like crazy.

When Ellen finally was delivered, she weighed less than six pounds. I was so happy to have a girl that I quickly forgot how hard it had been to bring her into the world; we had a son, and I wanted a little girl, too. Stuart was one of four boys, and his father was one of eight boys and a girl. (The girl, Stu's Aunt Mary, weighed about three hundred pounds and shaved her face every day when she got old, so I don't think she counted.) I had a brother. Ellen was the first girl in the family in a long time. I was feeling pretty good, and they stitched me up and waited for the afterbirth, which refused to leave my body. My doctor told me they would have to give me ether to put me to sleep. I didn't want to go to sleep and told them to just go up and get it. I said that obviously I was able to bear pain—hadn't they been doing push-ups on my ribs for three hours? Had I yelled even once? I was terrified of being unconscious. But my doctor said they had no choice, as they had to relax my muscles. It took four nurses to hold me down, and I tried not to breath when they put the mask over my face. But you can't stop medical science, and although it took twice as much ether as usually would be necessary, against my will I went to sleep. I heard the young assistant's voice echoing in my head the whole time: "The baby came face, and almost thirty minutes later she was dead." I heard it over and over, and by the time I woke up, alone and freezing in the empty delivery room, I was weeping. I don't know why I was left there. A maintenance man came in and put a blanket over me.

On the day that should have been Ellen's thirty-second birthday, it occurred to me that she was just not ready to be born when they forced her into this world. She was coming face, and almost thirty years later she was dead.

MY MOTHER PICKED FLOWERS
AT 2 A.M.

My mother went out on the dark streets of Brooklyn at two in the morning and stole other people's flowers. She took them from gardens blocks away, in a better neighborhood. Daddy warned her, "You're going to die from buckshot in your pretty ass." She began the practice of going out in the middle of the night with a basket and scissors in 1943, when I was six years old. It was after we had moved to East Twenty-fourth Street from our house on East Seventh Street, where we'd had a garden that Mother missed greatly. She never took a lot of flowers from any one garden, but one from many. "E pluribus unum," she quipped in one of her rare attempts at humor. (My daddy was the funny one in our family.) Mother said no one would ever miss one flower. She never got caught.

1540 East Twenty-fourth Street was part of a four-family attached brick house. All the houses and the apartments were exactly the same outside and inside, except for the furniture and the color of the paint on the walls. Each apartment had three small bedrooms, a living room, a dining room, a tiny kitchen, and one bathroom. My parents slept in the largest bedroom. My brother Peter and I slept in a single bed in the smallest one. Carol, my mother's youngest sister, and her baby son, Seth, slept in the third bedroom. Carol's husband, Bernard Nussbaum, was fighting in Europe, and Aunt Carol was afraid to live alone. My grandmother, Rose Heller, was a widow and also lived with us. She had always had her own bedroom, but because Carol was now staying with us, Grandma slept on a daybed in the dining room.

A coal furnace heated the house, but because of the war, even coal was rationed, and the house was always cold. Before going to school I ate breakfast in the bathroom, after Mother had filled the tub with hot water to warm up the room. There was no backyard, only a strip of concrete driveway that led to the empty garage (we had no car to put in it) and a small plot of weeds in front—nothing to provide us with the fresh bouquet that used to greet us when we got up for breakfast at our house on East Seventh Street. My mother, an artist and poet, had a need for beauty. She once wrote in a poem

> No artist's canvas touched by human brush
> Can match forsythias in a blue bowl.

Though we no longer had a garden, Mother still wanted her family to wake up to the sight of her blue bowl filled with flowers. Sometimes she gave the neighbors' gardens a rest and picked weeds from the empty lot down the street. She respected weeds that were beautiful, goldenrod and Queen Anne's lace. Once, in late fall, there was an arrangement of beautiful gold leaves in the blue bowl. They looked lovely but turned out to be poison ivy. Mother itched for weeks, but I think she thought it was worth it. She didn't throw the leaves away. She told us not to touch them, just look at them because they were so pretty.

Mother had a slender figure and small, perfect breasts. She stopped wearing a bra decades before the feminists gave it their approval. Daddy said, "A man only needs a nice little handful," when he reached around and cupped Mother's breast as she washed the supper dishes and smiled her sardonic half-smile.

Mother's hands, unlike the rest of her, were not pretty. They were square and large and strong. Her nails were chipped, and she never polished them. She sucked her thumb until the day she died, plugging it into her mouth and wrapping her index finger around her nose as she contentedly sucked away with no embarrassment. She did this only during quiet times with our family, listening to music or watching television—never in front of company.

Whenever I got sick, Mother cut an apple in half, scooped out the inside by scraping it with a butter knife so that the flesh of the apple turned to mush, and fed me from the end of the knife, pushing the raw applesauce into my mouth with her thumb. I remember her hand smelled, not unpleasantly, of onions, which she was always mincing for something she was cooking. I love the smell of onions, but until this moment I never realized why.

My father, who, thanks to his hernia, never did *any* work around the house, had nicely shaped and dainty hands. His hands never touched the earth, in fact, and neither have mine (I was always Daddy's girl). Mother, however, loved plunging her hands into the earth to plant a bulb. She played the piano, which she insisted I start learning to play when I was five. She sat with me while I practiced, correcting my mistakes.

Mother always listened to WQXR, the New York station that played the classical music she loved. The radio sat on top of the refrigerator so she could listen while she cooked. She was a wonderful cook. She wept when her favorite symphonies were played. Her very favorite was Tchaikovsky's Sixth Symphony, the *Symphonie Pathétique.*

Because of her blond hair and blue eyes, my mother could pass for a Christian, which she told me she had to do sometimes during the depression, when prejudice often made it impossible for a Jew to get a job. She loved my daddy. He loved her. My friends told me that they'd seen my parents necking at the movies.

Before they were married, Daddy wrote a poem to Mother, which he recited often. I remembered it word for word and whispered it in his ear as he lay dying. I hope he heard me.

> If I should win the sweepstakes, dear,
> oh, wouldn't we have fun?
> We'd go to all the shows in town
> retire at rise of sun.
> We'd hop aboard a liner grand
> bedecked in regal tog;
> face each new day a different way
> and not stop short of Prague.
> Then we'd come home and have some kids
> two tots, one of each sex.
> You'd ne'er have need to use your hands
> except for signing checks.
> And then I wish we'd lose it all,
> for rich I still would be:
> for you are worth your weight in gold,
> and you belong to me.

In 1948 we moved to 1920 East Twenty-fourth Street, four blocks away. It was the first house my parents owned, and it had small gardens in the front and back. In the backyard was a trellis with a large honeysuckle vine climbing it, which Mother tended as if it were a prize rose bush. My mother loved honeysuckle and taught Peter and me to carefully bite off the end of the flower, gently pull out the stamen, and touch our tongues to the drop of sweet nectar that shimmered on the tip. She told us the stamen is the male organ of the flower, and I had a vague sense that what we were doing had a sexual tinge, which I would not understand until years later. Recently, when I told this story to a friend who is a professor of botany at the University of Tennessee, he told me my mother was mistaken about which part of the flower is the stamen. He said the part we pulled out to touch our tongues to was actually the female organ, which was surrounded by many small stamens. I told him he had just spoiled my childhood sexual illusion.

Mother often did paintings of her garden, not in the sweet style of many women, but in bold strokes, like Vincent van Gogh, her favorite artist. Her paintings were slashes of color, sometimes bright but often brooding, as she was. Maybe they were the early warning signs of the depression that was to come. We never noticed Ellen's early warning signs either.

What people called a "nervous breakdown" began for my mother in 1959. The year Stuart and I graduated from college and moved out of my parents' basement. She seemed to grow smaller, to curl into her body as a snail into its protective shell. Her blue eyes looked empty. She didn't seem to notice or care about her surroundings. Mother suffered from serious depression for ten years. Few people understood depression back then. I didn't understand it at all. I said to her, "You have a husband and two children who love you. You have a house and a car and a TV. What else do you want?" She answered, "None of it matters." She stopped playing the piano. She continued to write poetry, but no longer wanted anyone to read it. Her poems were her private sorrows.

In 1964 Mother and Daddy moved to an apartment building close to the beach. They lived on the sixth floor, so once again she had no garden to tend. She refused to leave the apartment by herself and would sit at the window for hours, staring at the ocean. Throughout those ten years Daddy took her to psychiatrists. She said to me, "If I have to talk to one more doctor, I'm going to kill myself." She called me on the telephone and didn't speak, only moaned. Because her therapy wasn't working, her psychiatrist suggested she be put in a hospital where she was given electroshock therapy in an attempt to cure her profound depression. They didn't seem to help her, though, and after she got them she was never able to cry again. When we visited her at the hospital Mother didn't seem happy to see us. Her large hands were clasped in her lap, and she sat so quietly in the nicely furnished visiting room that someone had tried to create to look like a living room (but failed), with comfortable couches and chairs and flowers in vases. Mother showed no interest in what any of us were doing, although I chattered away, trying fruitlessly to get some response from her. She couldn't remember the names of my children.

So I became her mother. Daddy brought her to my apartment every morning before he went to work, because we were afraid she would commit suicide if left alone. I was always still in bed when Daddy let Mother in with the key I had given him. She would climb into bed with me, and I would pretend to be sleeping, even though I was wide-awake. She would wrap her arms around me and cling to me like a lover or a child. I couldn't admit, even to myself, that being held in bed by my mother revolted me.

Daddy came to my apartment after work, and we all would eat dinner together. Then he took her home. Stu, coming home after work, was amazingly tolerant of this change in our normal routine, considering he never understood or had any tolerance for mental illness. He would have no understanding of Ellen's depression, or forgiveness for her suicide years later either. Stu couldn't even understand a headache, because he'd never had one. I often thought Stu could feel sympathy only if he saw someone bleeding. I was twenty-six years old at that time and had two small children of my own whose Grandma took little interest in them. I hate to confess that I resented it, but I did. I still wanted a mother, not another child.

Mother recovered in 1969, when she was fifty-nine years old. Her depression had probably been caused by a chemical imbalance. She was one of the first people to be given the antidepressant lithium, and three weeks after she started taking it, she was well again. (Why had no doctor suggested lithium for Ellen? Why hadn't I? Would it have helped Ellen as it had helped my mother? I'll never know.) My parents had recently moved to Huntington Station, on Long Island, to a house where Mother once again had a garden. It was the last house my parents lived in.

I think Mother was happy there. She read Rachel Carson's *Silent Spring,* the first book to warn of the danger of DDT and chemical sprays, and she never again sprayed insecticide on any living thing. When an infestation of gypsy moths was devouring leaves all over Long Island, Mother wrapped sticky tape around all of her trees, so that when the caterpillars tried to climb from the earth to the leaves they got stuck on the tape. Mother carefully picked them off and drowned them in a pail of water. Albert Schweitzer she wasn't. It was disgusting to see dozens of caterpillars writhing around in the bucket, taking their last breaths before drowning, but mother was doing what she felt had to be done to save the earth.

Mother's garden was her metaphor for the world. I think she saw both her life and her death as she saw her flowers. She wrote:

> I never dreamed that I would dread
> My garden growing up. Each bed
> Now showing brightest buds must fade
> With time, and blooms become decayed.
> Is drooping stalk and dying leaf
> The garden's symbol of my grief?
> A calendar to chalk off years,
> And what its sign when spring appears?
> Will purple iris be in flower
> When you await your final hour,
> Or sweet alyssum grace the sod
> You loved, when you must face your God?

I didn't know until I was in my thirties, shortly before she died, that my mother believed in God. She was shocked when I told her that I didn't. I don't remember how or why the subject came up.

"You don't believe in God?" she exclaimed.

I had to answer, "Why would I believe in God? The subject was never mentioned in our house.

I don't think I really knew or understood much about my mother until I started writing down my memories of her. There are many things about her I will never know. There are many things about my daughter that I will never know either. I don't remember missing Mother very much after her death. Do I miss Ellen? Does a person miss pain?

After writing that last sentence I took a break and turned on the opening performance of the 1995 season at Carnegie Hall, which was being broadcast on public television. The Boston Symphony has just started playing Tchaikovsky's Sixth Symphony, the *Pathétique.* I remembered the tears streaming down Mother's face when I was a child and this, her favorite symphony, was playing on WQXR. I realized, weeping, that it is my favorite symphony too.

MY DADDY'S HERNIA

My father had a hernia operation when he was twenty-nine years old and never lifted anything heavy (or light, either) for the rest of his life. The operation was done at the French Hospital in Manhattan. Daddy said he came out of the anesthesia singing "La Marseillaise," and I heard him sing it many times after that. He had a very good voice and loved to sing. At my wedding he was a bit drunk and sang another song he liked, "You're the Kind of Girl That Men Forget." Daddy sang it beautifully. I would rather he had sung "La Marseillaise."

How or why he learned every word of the French national anthem I'll never know. He graduated at fifteen from Commerce High, a trade school, and certainly never learned French. I wish I'd asked him when I had the chance. He died in 1990, at the age of eighty, from the complications of a bypass surgery.

My father won a gold medal at Commerce High for being the fastest typist in the class and the best in shorthand. He later had the medal put on a chain and gave it to me, and I wore it around my neck for years. I eventually gave the medal to Ellen, and it was in the music box that Steven sent home after her death. Daddy never learned algebra but could figure out the answers to algebra problems when I was in high school by the process of elimination. I was good at math, and he once suggested I become an engineer. My father said I would "break new ground" and probably be the only girl in my class. I didn't like math; I loved to draw. "I'm going to be an artist," I told him. "You can be whatever you want to be," he said.

My father read the *New York Times* cover to cover every day and always knew the answers to my questions. After dinner, our family sat at the table and discussed the events of the day; not just what happened in school, at work, or at home, but also what was going on in the world. Daddy always asked me what I thought and never made fun of my opinion. He carefully explained the various sides of issues to see if I understood them. He would have been a good teacher. The pity was that his family, immigrants from Riga, Latvia, who owned a candy store on East Eighty-sixth Street in Manhattan, didn't have the money to send him to college. He began working for the post office in 1930. He was twenty-one. He worked there for thirty-seven years until he retired in 1967.

The name on his birth certificate was John. The kids he grew up with said, "What kind of a name is John for a Jewish boy?" so everyone called him Max. He always thought of himself as John, though, and after he married Mother, that was the name he went by. His mother, his brother Moe, and his sister Helen, continued to call him Max. I guess his father was the one who named him John, and he died before I was born, so I could never ask him where Daddy's name came from.

John Friedman was always a good athlete and said the worst thing about graduating from high school so young was that he was too small to get on any of the teams. He told me that he was the stickball champ of

East Eighty-sixth Street, that he could hit the ball past three sewer gratings, and that as a result, his nickname was "Three Sewer Max."

My father had the gift of gab. He told me that there wasn't anyone who didn't have something to teach you; you could even learn something from a dope. He often charmed audiences after he was promoted to superintendent of his building for the post office. He was only thirty-two years old and was the youngest superintendent in the city. Even though there was a sign on his desk that said "John M. Friedman—Building Superintendent," when people came to his office they thought he was the superintendent's secretary and would ask to see his boss. He got a big kick out of that. My father loved *being* the boss. He gave speeches when people got promoted, at their retirement parties, and funerals where he usually cried.

The address of the building he managed was 90 Church Street, New York, 3 N.Y. There weren't zip codes yet; there were zones, which had only one or two numbers and were placed before the state abbreviation. A first-class stamp cost three cents. It was green and had a picture of George Washington on it. Mailing a postcard cost a penny; that stamp was purple and had a picture of Abraham Lincoln on it. I think those were the only choices. During the Second World War navy headquarters were located at 90 Church Street, and Daddy got to meet a lot of important people—admirals and people like that.

Daddy said he wasn't drafted because his job was considered "essential to the national interest." I don't know if having a wife and two children had anything to do with his exemption from service during the war.

Maybe because of his hernia he was considered too fragile to be in the army. He was not classified 4-F, and maybe he really *was* essential to the national interest; I can't even *imagine* my father as a soldier. I can still laugh (or cry) when I think of my daddy saying, "Hedda, my hernia." He used this when he wanted to get out of doing work around the house—from clearing the table to taking out the garbage.

My brother was born on February 2, 1941. Before he was a year old, the Japanese had attacked Pearl Harbor and the United States had declared war on Japan and Germany. Daddy, who saved every scrap of paper in boxes (Ellen did too) saved a newspaper, *PM Daily* that came out on February 2, 1942, Peter's first birthday. (I brought it back to Knoxville after my father died. The paper had turned yellow-brown and crumbled in my hand when I touched it.) The headlines declared "U.S. Hits Japs in Equator," and "Go Get 'Em, Navy!" Under *Battle News* the headlines read "Jap Fleet Destroyed Off Corregidor" and "Red Army Smashes Into Ukraine." There is a story about New York's mayor La Guardia saying he "would resign as director of the Office of Civilian Defense, but he didn't say when." Everything was rationed; coal, butter, sugar, gasoline. For many years after the war, Mother and Daddy never even *mentioned* the holocaust. It seemed Jews in Brooklyn didn't want to talk about it or, if they did, it wasn't in front of the children. I finally understood why they remained silent after I had Steven and Ellen. Parents don't want little children to think people could be killed merely for being Jewish.

. . .

Once a year, in the month of March, my parents got dressed up in formal clothes to attend the Supervisors' Ball. I don't know why it was called a ball because it was a dinner and there wasn't an orchestra that people could dance to. It was held at the Waldorf-Astoria hotel in Manhattan.

Daddy rented a tuxedo. Mother wore a long black skirt and a white silk blouse that had about a hundred tiny buttons running down the back. (She wore the same outfit for the first fifteen years of going to the ball.) To me they looked like a prince and princess. Mother sometimes piled her long blond hair high on top of her head. It was the only time during the year that my mother smoked a cigarette. She didn't inhale. Daddy put her cigarette in a long holder and she waltzed around our living room with it, laughing and looking glamorous. Now that I am the age that my grandmother was then, I think they were playing the children's game of dress-up, but it's hard to think of your parents as children when you're still a child yourself.

All the postal superintendents in the city of New York were invited with their wives to the ball to honor their contribution to the city by helping to keep the mail moving in rain or snow or sleet or gloom of night, etc. The postmaster of New York would be there. Everyone got to listen to him make a speech and tell them what a fine job they were doing.

Since we didn't have a car, my parents took the subway and then walked from the station to the ball. I always imagined everyone on the subway staring at them in awe, as my brother and I did, because they looked so dashing. The ball was the highlight of their year.

My father always had a job, even during the Great Depression, but he never made much money. We always had enough to eat, but we never bought anything that was considered frivolous. (To my dismay, piano lessons were not considered frivolous.) He read *Consumer Reports* faithfully, even though we almost never bought anything. When we did, it took a lot of research. When we bought a forty-five RPM record player, it took almost a year to decide which one was the best buy. It cost $14.95.

When Daddy finally bought a car, in 1953, it was a beat-up 1937 Chevrolet. It cost $150. He said it was a great buy. It was the ugliest green color I had ever seen, and it had running boards. My father was proud of it and it got us to places we had never been able to go before, such as a park way out on Long Island (that was considered a trip to the country to the people of Brooklyn). I was sixteen that year, and my parents told Peter and me we could go to the Supervisors' Ball with them. It was an event that I will never forget, and now, more than forty years later, I can still laugh (or cry) when I think of it.

We were not going to take the subway to the ball. We were going to drive in our new car. Peter and I would get to see the postmaster himself. As always, Daddy was in his rented tuxedo and Mother was wearing her long black skirt and white silk blouse. Peter and I were dressed in our best clothes. As soon as Daddy sat down on the driver's seat, the seat fell into the back of the car. To allow our father to drive from Brooklyn to Manhattan, Peter and I sat in the back and held the driver's seat up with our feet. I took off my new high heels for the journey so as not to punch holes in the upholstery.

When we got to the Waldorf-Astoria, the doorman, in his beautiful uniform, opened the car door for my mother. It fell off its hinges, barely missing the man's feet. He was gracious, despite the mishap, and never once even cracked a smile, sort of like the palace guards in London. If he had noticed that the front seat had fallen into the back of the car when Daddy stepped out, he gave no sign of it. He simply said, "We'll get that fixed for you, sir. It will be fine by the time you're ready to leave." We went into the Waldorf-Astoria and tried not to think about the car. Peter and I were goggle-eyed in the beautiful ballroom. We had never seen such elegance before, or been served a fancy dinner by such courteous waiters. When we left the ball our car was fixed. I don't know whom the doorman called or how he got it done, but he didn't charge us anything. Driving back to Brooklyn, Daddy just shook his head and said, "I don't believe it. That guy didn't charge me one red cent."

I believe my father could have been a great trial lawyer, I think that was his secret desire. He looked at an issue from all angles and could think on his feet. Daddy once had a chance to play a trial lawyer when he was twenty-eight and he told the story for years.

Grandma bought an expensive English baby carriage to wheel me around in when I was born. It was way beyond my parents' means. It was painted shiny white and my initials, G.F., were monogrammed in silver on the side. It was supposed to have a *genuine* leather hood. She bought it from Samuel Cohen, owner of the Atlantic Baby Carriage Stores.

After six months, the so-called genuine leather hood began to crack. Mr. Cohen denied that the hood was imitation leather. Daddy decided to go to small claims court and sue the Atlantic Baby Carriage Stores for selling a carriage with a phony leather hood. He removed the hood from the carriage and brought it to show to an expert in leather at City College of New York. The professor said, "That material never came off any cow's back." My father asked him if he would testify to that fact in court, which the professor was glad to do. In December 1937, my daddy won his first (and last) case. Grandma was awarded $22.40, and they got to keep the carriage. When his grandson Steven graduated from Columbia Law School in 1985 Daddy couldn't go to the graduation because he was recovering from his second heart attack. He cried.

Daddy loved the Irish and I think he would have liked to have been Irish instead of Jewish, or at least an Irish Jew. Whenever he had a close call that went well for him, he snapped his fingers and said, "The luck of the Irish!" He loved whiskey and went to every Irish wake that the men in the post office had. He said they were philosophical about death; so was he.

The surgery that killed him was the only other operation he ever had after his hernia. He was never sick a day in his life before he was seventy, when he had his first heart attack. He did not have surgery for either his first or his second heart attack. My father played tennis just about every day until he had the first one, when his doctor told him, "John, you're going to drop dead on the tennis court if you don't stop." Daddy used to say, "If you don't do the things you like, you won't live long. Your life will just *seem* long." But he stopped playing tennis. The rest of his life the only things he played were the stock market, the slot machines in Atlantic City, and the TV. Then the doctor said, "If you don't have bypass surgery you'll be dead in three months." He had the surgery and was dead in less than three months. I wish my daddy had died on the tennis court.

Ellen flew from Nashville to visit her grandpa and his second wife, Billie, when Daddy was in the hospital. It was the last time Ellen saw him. I found her impressions among the papers that Steven sent home:

> Shock, fear, compassion, monitors, pumps, IV bottles, white sheets, thick white blanket, metal trays and counters, green vinyl chair, serious, but friendly nurses, doctors holding Grandpa's file, Grandpa sitting in chair—shaking, shrunken dry tongue, cracked white lips, red gel on teeth I thought was blood, desperation in his sad eyes, gray stubble beard, skinny legs, Teddy Bear from my brother, no flowers or other forms of life, room 1503, snow, warm sun, skin was translucent, scar from heart surgery, tiny pupils, non-productive coughs, gasping for breath, paging doctors, quiet, trying to speak, but nothing we could understand, fighting for every breath, Billie telling him, "Ellen is here, you know Ellen?" He never said my name, but he would stare at me, man on other side of curtain watching Wheel of Fortune, Billie describing the clothes she bought me, medicine, no Old Spice, which was his trademark, Billie holding his head to her breast prying fingernails away from his palms. Fuzzy warm forehead, I'm stroking his forehead from his eyebrows to the back of his head, tight fists, he kissed my hand after I said, "you know I love you."

Daddy died on March 28, 1990. Ellen killed herself on March 29, three years later.

Because of Daddy's hernia, my mother shoveled the coal and hauled out the ashes in heavy metal barrels from the basement to the street. She mowed the lawn. She chopped wood and did the gardening. She cooked, cleaned the house and, before we got a washing machine, did the laundry on a scrub board. But she never wrote a check or drove a car. She never *seemed* to mind until a book of her poetry was published. She was sixty-two at the time. "From now on I'm going to do whatever the hell I please, and I don't give a shit who likes it," she told me. I jumped up and down and hugged her. I'd never heard her curse before, although she used to say "tough tittie" sometimes.

When Mother was sixty-four and dying of cancer of the pancreas, I came to New York from Knoxville to help Daddy take care of her. I couldn't do much except try to feed her or try to get her to talk. She wouldn't eat or speak. She spoke to me only once in the three weeks I was there. I was rubbing her back, shocked at how emaciated she had become, and she said, "It's so hard." "I know," I replied. She answered, "No, you don't know." Now, after Ellen's death, I think my mother's last words were the truest she ever said to me.

Daddy and I took turns helping Mother to the bathroom. One day I was unable to lift her. She couldn't have weighed more than eighty-five pounds, but she felt heavier than lead; she felt like dead weight, which I never knew the meaning of until that moment.

I called, "Daddy come help me. I can't lift Mommy." "Hedda, remember my hernia!" he said to her, and although she was almost in a coma, she got up and walked to the bathroom by herself and walked back afterward and got into bed. If I hadn't seen it with my own eyes, I wouldn't have believed it. She died the next day.

FROM CROOKE AVENUE
TO EASY STREET

Honesty was never the best policy in our house. I always thought it was both funny and perfect that the apartment my parents lived in at the time of my birth was on a street called Crooke Avenue. Everyone in my family possessed a semi-criminal streak. We all made a practice of getting away with whatever we could. Before my parents met, Daddy worked for Mr. Pardo, a crooked Realtor, who eventually went to jail. Mother worked as a shill for Joseph Brummer, a famous art dealer. She went to art auctions and bid on works that Mr. Brummer wanted to buy. If the savvy people bidding on art at the auction got wind of this dealer's interest, the price would go up, but no one knew my innocent-looking mother.

Peter and I were taught very early how to sneak onto the subway and the bus without paying the fare. We were both small for our ages, hardly having to stoop down to duck under the turnstile for the subway. For sneaking onto a bus, Daddy charmed the driver while Peter and I boarded it and walked straight to the back, without pausing to pay the fare.

If anyone in my family found something of value that someone else had dropped on the street, we never

looked for the rightful owner, we put it in our pocket
and kept it. When one of us got too much change for
something we'd purchased, we never told the sales clerk.
Daddy would return something he had bought the year
before and get his money back after having used it.
(That always drove his second wife, Billie, crazy.)

Crooke Avenue is near Prospect Park, a beautiful
oasis in the heart of Brooklyn, where my father met my
mother, Hedda Heller, in 1933. He said he picked her up
at an outdoor concert and that she was the most
beautiful woman he had ever seen. Mother was five feet,
seven inches tall, had light-blue eyes, long blond hair,
and high cheekbones on a lovely face. My daddy, John
Friedman, was a tall, dark-haired man, as thin as a
reed, with long, skinny legs. We called him "Daddy long
legs." He was almost six feet tall and weighed only 120
pounds. Mother fell in love with his "soulful brown eyes"
and his gentle manner. I inherited Daddy's skinny body
and for years suffered the jeers of other children. I used
to wish on the evening star:

> Star light star bright,
> first star I see tonight,
> I wish I may, I wish I might,
> get the wish I wish tonight:
> *Let me be fat*.

Crooke Avenue is also near the Brooklyn Botanical
Gardens, where Uncle Karl, my pseudo uncle, worked.
Karl was a friend of Mother and Daddy's and I knew
him all my life. I discovered only recently that he had
been in love with my mother for more than forty years,
and she with him. Karl and Mother remained in love
until her death, four months before my parents' fortieth
wedding anniversary.

I have Mother and Daddy's marriage certificate, dated June 2, 1934, where Uncle Karl's name is signed as a witness, along with Uncle Max's. Max Heller, a real uncle, was the husband of my mother's younger sister, Lydia (coincidentally, his surname was the same as Lydia's maiden name). There are no pictures of my parents' wedding. No picture of my twenty-four-year-old mother in a white gown and a veil. No picture of my twenty-five-year-old father in a tuxedo. No picture of my mother holding a wedding bouquet. When I asked him why, Daddy said, "We couldn't afford a fancy wedding on my twenty dollars a week from the post office." There are pictures that were taken on their honeymoon, though, three days on a farm in Connecticut. That was the first time Daddy saw a cow. He had spent his whole life in New York City.

There are lots of photos of my parents' first apartment at 89 Crooke Avenue, all neatly placed in an album. Daddy took a picture of the view from their bedroom window after a snowstorm. Even the snow couldn't hide the dreary tenements that surrounded them or the subway tracks that passed close by. My parents kept an album of my entire childhood beginning with my first month of life. They called it "Stepping Stones with Greta," which Daddy wrote in white ink in large print on the first page. In smaller print at the bottom he wrote, "Arrived 5:17 A.M. Thursday, May 20, 1937—Smiling." I think that was wishful thinking. In many of the pictures of me, even as a baby, I have a wise, worried look on my face, as if I already understood the world into which I had entered.

I was born with the umbilical cord wrapped tightly around my neck. I don't know if my birth was a difficult one. The only thing Mother told me was that it was a miracle I didn't die of strangulation in the process. If she had a hard time bringing me into the world, she wouldn't have told me anyway. She came to America at the age of ten as an immigrant from Czechoslovakia, survived a childhood of poverty, and almost never complained. Daddy, however, said my birth was very hard on *him*. He lived life by a highly organized routine and suffered if his plans for the day were upset. Daddy was miserable if he didn't get eight hours of sleep every night, followed by a breakfast of orange juice, three strips of bacon, two eggs, one piece of toast, a bowl of oatmeal, and two cups of coffee. Sitting in a hospital waiting room all night awaiting my early-morning arrival surely put a crimp in his schedule.

I was named after Mother's favorite movie star, Greta Garbo. (My brother was named after Mother's favorite composer, Peter Tchaikovsky.) It was hard being called Greta when all the other kids were Susan or Linda or Barbara or Carol. I hated my name when I was little, because Greta is not a child's name. Especially if your name is Greta Friedman. Maybe if our last name had been Hansen or something, it would have been OK. As I got older, I grew into it.

Their apartment was decorated in the art deco style of the 1930s; couches low to the floor with wide, fake leather arms and big, soft cushions. (Those couches would move with my parents four times. I loved them and it made me sad when my parents gave the couches to Goodwill when I was in my early twenties. They replaced them with hideous, black leather Spanish-modern couches that looked like they belonged in a doctor's waiting room.) There was a fake-fur rug on the wooden floor, a black-glass and chromium table, and a black-and-white piano. A fake black-and-white fireplace completed the decor. It had transparent coals, a red light inside, and a fan to make it look as if there was a real fire burning. There was no chimney for Santa to come down, even though I thought he did.

Throughout our childhood Peter and I hung our Christmas stockings from the mantel. Mother put a tiny white tree on it, decorated with blue lights and silver tinsel. We celebrated Christmas as the American holiday it had become for many Jewish children in Brooklyn. I believed in Santa Claus until a more sophisticated six-year-old, my best friend Dorothy, told me there was no such thing as Santa Claus; that he was really my daddy. When I was given this unbelievable news I ran into my house crying and asked Mother if Dorothy was right. Sadly, Mother told me the truth and I felt betrayed. It was the beginning of my life as a nonbeliever.

When I was eleven years old we moved to 1920 East Twenty-fourth Street, the first house my parents ever owned. Daddy told me that when we finished paying off Uncle Max the $1,200 dollars he had loaned us for the down payment, we would be on Easy Street. The house cost $12,500. My father was paying Uncle Max ten dollars a month on the down payment. The remaining $11,300 was being paid to the bank on a thirty-year mortgage. Easy Street was a long way off. (I thought about this the other day, when I paid ten dollars for a mediocre lunch.)

Max Heller was *born* on Easy Street. He graduated from Harvard Business School and moved straight up the corporate ladder of Allied Department Stores until he became their vice president. Lydia, who grew up in poverty with my mother and their younger sister Carol, adapted quickly to country clubs, golf, and full-time help. (She told me she'd hated growing up poor and had always been ashamed of it.) Max was a cold fish. He never showed any affection for Peter or me, even though he allowed us to spend a month each summer in Pennsylvania with him, Aunt Lydia, and our younger cousins, Linda and Howie. To Peter and me, a couple of Brooklyn street kids, this was going to the country. We loved our cousins and we loved Lydia, despite her regal manner; so different from our mother's. Lydia was nice to us, inventing games and sometimes setting up a stand on the street for Linda, Howie, Peter, and me to sell lemonade from. We made three cents a glass. During dinner, though, Peter and I laughed silently when Lydia rang a little bell for their maid, Audrey, who had difficulty breathing, to come huffing and puffing from the kitchen to bring something or other to the table. When we went home to Brooklyn at the end of the summer, Peter and I pretended we were ringing a little bell during dinner, and called to our mother in the kitchen. "Ooohhhhh Auuudreeey," we squealed in Lydia's lilting voice. Daddy always laughed.

Mother and Daddy were lifelong Democrats; Max Heller was a Republican—a dirty word in our house. Mother, Daddy, and especially Grandma worshipped President Franklin D. Roosevelt. Uncle Max hated him. When I was born he wrote my parents the following letter:

> *I believe the Friedmans are to be congratulated upon the addition to their family; one named Greta #12-3456-789, who on May 20, 2002, will draw a pension of X by the grace of His Majesty, King Roosevelt.*
>
> *Max*

(After Daddy died, Peter and I found it in one of those many boxes containing papers our father had saved.)

I was seven when Franklin Roosevelt died on April 12, 1945. Witnessing my family, especially Grandma, weeping uncontrollably was the first time in my life that I saw an open display of grief. It frightened me. Grandma put her arms around me and wept into my thin chest, saying that the world would never be the same. Daddy held Mother in his arms, while they both cried. Peter, then three, sucked his thumb in a corner.

Daddy talked about his dream of Easy Street on Sunday mornings as he walked me to the Kings Highway subway station, where I waited for the train to take me to the Prospect Park stop for my piano lesson with Mrs. Vogel. Piano lessons cost three dollars each, but were considered a necessity. One Sunday morning when I was twelve, I was standing on the Kings Highway station platform. I was the only person waiting for the subway. I saw a wallet on the station floor and, without pausing, swept it up and put it in my pocket. I fingered it until I got to Prospect Park. I was afraid to open it to see what might be inside. I could hardly concentrate on my lesson because I was so excited about the wallet in my pocket. When I got home, I proudly showed it to my parents. When Daddy opened it, he found two crisp twenty-dollar bills inside. I thought, *Four months closer to Easy Street.* We burned the wallet. I am ashamed of doing that now, but felt only joy at the time.

When he was a young boy, Daddy and his friends used to sneak into the movies. The admission price was four cents. Each boy would chip in a penny and one of them would buy a ticket. Then the legitimate ticket-holder would enter the theater and open the exit door at the back for the rest of them. The manager caught on to what they were doing and one day waited for them at the window above the exit. Before they could sneak in, he dumped buckets of cold water on them. Daddy told his mother he had been pushed into the lake at Central Park.

My grandparents sold illegal fireworks from their candy store below the tenement apartment where they lived. They would hide them whenever word came that the police were on their way. Daddy said proudly that the police never thought to look in the oven.

Daddy dreamed of someday striking it rich. Once a year he bought a ticket for the Irish Sweepstakes. He loved to gamble. The only chance he got to do so was once a year when the Catholic Church held a carnival to raise money. Bingo and roulette wheels were popular lures. Daddy entered contests. To win you had to write twenty-five words or less saying something brilliant about a product—a bar of soap, a candy bar, a laundry detergent. He loved the idea of getting something for nothing. We never won a thing.

Suddenly, one day, there was hope of big money. Hope went by the name "Uncle Doctor." I didn't even know Alexander Friedman, my great-uncle, existed until I was fifteen and he was eighty-nine. He was the brother of Daddy's father, Samuel. Alexander Friedman was a medical doctor, and although my mother and father called him Uncle Sasha, Peter and I were instructed to call him Uncle Doctor.

Alexander Friedman was born in Riga, Latvia, in 1863. It was the year of Lincoln's Emancipation Proclamation, Daddy was fond of telling me. That was either to give me a concept of how old his uncle was or to put his birth in some sort of historical perspective. Surely Abraham Lincoln meant nothing to the people of Riga.

It is a Jewish tradition when someone dies that the next of kin has an article of his or her own clothing cut in two by the rabbi who conducts the funeral, signifying that a loved one has been wrenched from you. Alexander Friedman refused to allow the rabbi to cut his necktie at his brother's funeral and no one in the family had spoken to him for almost twenty years.

The only reason Daddy's family had a change of heart and desire for a reconciliation was that Alexander Friedman was a doctor and had made a lot of money. In 1952, when Alexander was almost ninety, my father's family decided it would be nice to be left in his will as he had never married and had no children. I guess sometimes old people will forgive the earlier slights of their families in exchange for companionship and dinner invitations.

Uncle Doctor was a self-centered, nasty old man. He rarely bathed and smelled awful. He said Americans bathed too often and washed all the healthy oils off their bodies. He had a huge hernia that hung halfway down his leg but would never allow it to be operated on. He didn't believe in unnecessary surgery. Daddy picked Uncle Doctor up at his house in Harlem and drove him to our house in Brooklyn the first Saturday of each month for dinner. Each Saturday he shit his pants in Daddy's car. On these days Daddy offered Peter fifty cents if he could sneak the Air-Wick under Uncle Doctor's chair when he wasn't looking. Sometimes Uncle Doctor would call relatives up in the middle of the night and ask them to bring him a glass of orange juice. They would get dressed and do it. Greed supplied powerful motivation. He probably enjoyed playing with them, seeing how far he could get them to go for his money.

By 1952 Uncle Doctor was one of the last white men still living in Harlem in an old three-story brownstone. He used it as both an office and a residence. He was a general practitioner, not an obstetrician, but said he had delivered more than ten thousand babies. In the early 1900s Harlem was an affluent neighborhood. I suppose that was when Alexander Friedman made most of his money. He invested in the stock market and later lived off the dividends.

Unlike many older people, he did not want to talk about himself. Instead he quizzed us children on what we knew and he liked to hear me play the piano. Although I played classical music, his favorite song was the popular "Unchained Melody." Mother said Uncle Doctor thought it was called "Unchanged Melody," an appealing concept to a ninety-year-old man. He once asked Peter, then about fourteen, whom he thought was the most famous Italian painter. Peter answered Gino Cimoli. Uncle Doctor seemed satisfied with the answer. Gino played outfield for the Brooklyn Dodgers.

Alexander Friedman was a Mason, and when he died, in 1958, the Masons paid for his funeral. The funeral was a bizarre affair because Uncle Doctor's friend, Mr. Bandelo, a spry fellow of eighty-eight with a long white beard and a startling resemblance to Rip Van Winkle, wanted everyone in the family to gather around the open casket so he could take our picture with the corpse. He kept hopping around on the chairs to get the best view and his antics started to make us giggle. I don't think a single tear was shed.

I wish I had asked my great-uncle some questions about his life, of which I know virtually nothing. He must have had stories to share. He may have been lonely. Now I think how sad it was that no one in his family really cared about him at all. He was ninety-five when he died. He left Peter and me five thousand dollars each. He left Daddy ten thousand.

My daddy was born in 1909 and came of age during the Great Depression. I don't think he ever got over it. He was frugal to the point of obsession until his death. During my childhood, when money was tight, everything we bought was debated with great care. We rarely ate in a restaurant, and when we did, it was always Chinese food and always chicken chow mein, the least expensive item on the menu. We *never* went on a vacation. Mother never had a dryer for the laundry, even after my parents had moved to a nice house in Huntington Station. Until her death, she hung the wet laundry on lines strung in the tiny room that housed the furnace. My parents never had air-conditioning either.

In 1975, a year after Mother died, my father married Billie DePaul. Billie and her mother, Mae, moved into Daddy's house. They got clothes dryer but never air-conditioned the house. (They compromised and bought a window unit for the bedroom—a major concession on Daddy's part.) He said he was monetarily cautious, but Daddy could also be very stubborn. Years before their marriage Billie had been my father's secretary at the post office. After they got married she still treated him as if he were the boss, even though Daddy never went to college and Billie had a master's degree.

Billie once told me that termites swarmed every spring in their house, but my father wouldn't even consider getting it treated. She told me he thought he would be dead before the termites finished their dinner and she didn't know what to do about it. So I asked

Daddy if he planned to leave Peter and me his house
when he died. He said he did. I asked him to please take
me out of his will, because I didn't want to try to sell a
house that had been eaten up by termites. He saw the
logic of the situation and Orkin got a new client.

Billie's mother lived with them until she had to go to
a nursing home, where she died four years later at the
age of ninety-one. Both of my daddy's mothers-in-law
had lived with him. Some people said it showed his kind
heart, but Daddy genuinely liked Mae. So did I. She told
dirty jokes and it amused me to hear a ninety-year-old
woman say "fuck."

The old-fashioned house in Huntington Station had
only one bathroom. When I came to visit and had to use
the bathroom in the middle of the night, the worst thing
I could see was the back legs of Mae's walker
disappearing behind the closing door. When I finally
would get to use the bathroom I was always startled by
the sight of three sets of false teeth smiling at me.

Daddy bought a ticket for New York State lottery
every day when he went to pick up the *New York Times.*
If he won two dollars on the dollar bet it made his day.
Daddy and Billie went to Atlantic City once a month,
leaving early in the morning for the four-hour bus ride.
They spent six hours playing the slot machines and that
was my father's only extravagance; he continued to
pinch pennies until his death. I thought my air-
conditioner-less and dryer-less mother would turn over
in her grave if she could see her husband feeding dollar
tokens into the slots. Billie played the nickel slots. I
think she didn't really enjoy it and was just humoring
Daddy. Second wives will do that, it seems. (I told Stu,
"If I die first, your second wife will pretend to like
boxing and be interested in your exact running times.
Don't kid yourself.") Daddy always wanted me to go to

Atlantic City with him and Billie on my annual visits to New York, but I told him that I felt no compelling need to support organized crime.

When Daddy died and we read his will, we were all amazed. We had thought that the man who would argue for a 10 percent senior citizen discount on a fifty-cent cup of coffee was probably watching every penny because he hadn't accumulated anything. After Daddy retired he lived on his government pension, which kept getting cost-of-living increases, and he was actually making more money than he did when he was working. He joked that he was one of the people who was driving the U.S. government to bankruptcy. He also had invested the $10,000 that Uncle Doctor had left to him in 1958 in the stock market. When Daddy died, he left his family more than half a million dollars. Apparently he had found Easy Street, but had never learned how to take a walk on it.

THE SECRET PANEL

The worst thing I ever did as a child exploited both my learned sneakiness and the knowledge that Daddy dreamed of striking it rich. In 1948, when I was eleven, we moved out of our ugly four-family brick house to a small white wooden house with green shutters, called a Cape Cod cottage. I loved that house and lived there until I was twenty-two.

1920 East Twenty-fourth Street, in the East Flatbush section of Brooklyn, was built by a Swedish carpenter and had all sorts of nooks and crannies and places where a child could hide, secret places. In the dining room there was a false bottom to the china cabinet, which was built into the wall—sort of a poor man's safety deposit box, in which Daddy kept "important papers." The cabinet displayed the royal blue glasses with pencil-thin stems flaring out to wide tops with real gold (so I believed) in three lines around the rims, which Grandma brought to America from Europe. There were three different sizes. Whenever we had company Daddy served wine in the smallest glasses, Mother filled the large ones with fruit cocktail before dinner and the middle-sized ones with rice pudding for dessert.

Our house had a complicated pantry, with dozens of drawers and shelves in different sizes, and a finished basement that Mother and Daddy rented out. The wonderful attic stored all kinds of things that I loved to look at. There was a book of Mother's drawings from when she was a young girl, drawn with colored pencils on cheap newsprint paper that was so fragile I was almost afraid to turn the pages for fear they would turn to dust in my hand. (Mother was offered an art scholarship to Cooper Union in New York, but had to go to work instead.) Mother talked very little about her childhood. She remembered that during the First World War, when the bombs were falling, she and her sisters stood on a balcony while Grandma pointed to the sky and said, "Look! The Germans are shitting on us." When my mother developed breasts she was ashamed of them and bound them with tape. Her classmates taunted her about her name, calling her "Hedda lettuce." During her first (only) year of high school a boy, snarling "Dirty Jew," pushed her down a flight of marble steps and she broke her knee in the fall; that explained the twenty-inch scar on her leg.

In the attic, there were love letters that Daddy had written to Mother, which I liked to read. There was a book of the play *Lysistrata*, which had drawings of naked people in it. That was no shock to me, because sometimes my parents walked around the house stark naked. They were proud of their bodies. Grandma, when she saw them, looked away and left the room. Ellen was proud of *her* body, too.

With the exception of sixth grade, I was always the teacher's pet. Sometimes my teachers gave *me* presents for Christmas. My fourth-grade teacher, Mrs. Friedman (no relation), wrote on the left side of my report card an additional quality besides the things that were usually marked for satisfactory behavior, like "shows respect for others" and "finishes homework on time." Mrs. Friedman wrote "Poise and charm." Daddy, who always knew I was never as good as I pretended to be, said she really meant "Poison charm."

I loved the attic. To get to it you had to go through Mother and Daddy's bedroom, past the screen that separated their bed from Peter's, through a door and up a narrow, spooky flight of stairs. Once you reached the attic you stepped into musty air, with dust motes that floated in front of the semi-circular window when the sun shone just right. The window was nailed shut and couldn't be opened to let in some fresh air in the summer, when it was stifling hot in the attic. There was a sixty-watt bulb that hung down from a cord. I always brought a flashlight with me. There were shelves filled with books and cartons of letters.

There was one place in the attic where Peter and I were told never to go. We were *never* to step on the wooden joists that the second floor's ceiling panels were nailed to. Between the joists there was nothing but a thin layer of ceiling material and insulation. Horrible pictures were planted in our minds; we'd break our bones and crush our skulls if we lost our balance and crashed to the room below. I never stepped on the joists until the day I heard Peter calling me and didn't want to be found. I had started to read *Lysistrata* and was fascinated by the story of the women of Athens and Sparta refusing to sleep with their husbands until the two warring cities made peace. World War II had ended four years before, and I wondered if that would have worked with the Germans.

I was always an agile child and carefully balanced myself until I reached the farthest part of the attic. I shined my flashlight, which I also used to read under the covers when it was past my bedtime, into the dark space. My brother could not have found me without stepping on the forbidden joists. I heard Mother calling me after Peter had given up. I actually stayed there for a couple of hours, missing lunch. I hated to eat anyway. I probably weighed about seventy pounds at the time and might not have crashed through even if I *had* lost my balance.

When I finally came down from my hiding place, Mother was furious. "Where have you been?" she shouted at me. "I thought you had been kidnapped." (Mother's greatest fears were that Peter and I would get kidnapped and murdered like the Lindbergh baby or we would get polio from swimming in the ocean for too long and catching a chill. Mother thought that a person didn't get sick from germs, but from standing in a draft or from getting chilled. Maybe that's a Jewish thing.) "I was getting ready to call the police," Mother practically screamed at me, her cheeks turning a brighter pink than usual. *Uh, oh*, I thought, *I've gone too far.* And then a wonderful story popped into my mind. I told Mother that the most amazing thing had happened. I had leaned on a wall and a secret panel had opened. Behind it was a tiny room that contained nothing but a red velvet chair and a small, locked chest. I told Mother I had tried to open the chest but couldn't. I said there were papers lying around, and some letters, which I had read, making it all up as I went along. I refused to tell where it was, saying it was my secret.

When Daddy came home that evening Mother was all aflutter. She told him of my finding the secret panel and refusing to disclose its whereabouts. During the afternoon, to make my story more credible, I found an old red velvet glove and cut it up with scissors. I rubbed a piece of it on the bottom of my shoe to make it look old and dirty. Then I produced it as proof. Daddy, thinking we had struck it rich—the luck of the Irish—pleaded with me to tell him how to find my secret place. There is an expression: "He who rides a tiger dare not dismount." I was digging myself deeper and deeper into this lie. I didn't know how to get out of it, so I just refused to tell how to find this wonderful place that didn't exist. Also, I thought I would undoubtedly be spanked with Mother's hairbrush for stepping on the joists.

Daddy thought he could figure out where the hidden place was by measuring the walls and seeing where there was space that wasn't accounted for. He thought he could solve the mystery by the process of elimination, the same way he would later solve my algebra problems without ever having learned algebra. He walked around the house with a measuring tape and jotted down figures. He started tap-tap-tapping on the walls.

I told Daddy I *might* tell him where it was the next day. That night I wrote ten couplets, providing directions to the treasure. I sent Mother and Daddy to the attic and to the pantry and out to the garage. I wrote clues to every room in the house, except the basement, of course, which was being rented to a nice married couple, the McCauleys. Seeing my parents scurrying around, playing a children's game, I didn't know whether to laugh or to cry. I was beginning to feel really awful. My last couplet said: "It's all a joke, we're still broke." Daddy, for some strange reason, started laughing. Then he hugged me and said, "Poison charm."

• • •

Daddy never hit me until I was seventeen years old and dating Jon Arista, a Greek dancer nine years older than me. Mother called him a chorus boy, which was probably closer to the truth. I'd met Jon during my seventeenth summer, at Tamiment Resort in the Pocono Mountains, where I had worked from July to September as a "mother's helper" since the age of fourteen. Jon was part of Tamiment's summer stock theater group. He was unbelievably handsome, with coal-black hair, tawny skin, startling blue eyes, a beautiful, sharp-featured Greek face, and a perfect muscular dancer's body. People stared at us on the street. They were probably wondering what a man like that saw in me, who still looked pretty much like a child. I wondered too, but he told me I was adorable and that he adored me. I was in love.

Jon was an orphan, grew up in foster homes, and had been in the Merchant Marines. He had traveled the world, and I'd never been anywhere. He was the most romantic person I had ever known—exotic and so different from the Jewish boys I'd always gone out with. After coming home from the movies or wherever we had been, we would go into the kitchen, where I always made hot cocoa for him and served him a slice of Mother's homemade cake while we sat talking before going into the living room to make out. Part of the thrill, of course, was all my friends wondering what was going on and my parents suspecting what was. It was my secret, and I never told anyone.

Once Jon went upstairs to go to the bathroom and didn't come back downstairs for a long time. I waited on the couch for what seemed like hours before I finally went upstairs to see if he was alive. I found that my brother had tied a rope around the bathroom doorknob and had tied it to *his* bedroom doorknob, my doorknob, and Mother and Daddy's. Peter was a Sea Scout and had a merit badge in knot tying. Jon looked angry, but distinctly relieved when I untied the rope and set him free. I was very quiet, because I didn't want to wake my parents. Jon didn't want them to wake up, either. But I also thought if I strangled Peter with the rope and he made a loud gurgling noise and woke up our parents before choking to death, it would be worth it.

Jon Arista was, of course, too old for me, not Jewish, and my parents thought I would run off and marry him, not go to college, and ruin my life. After a shouting match with my mother, who told me I was *never* to see "that Greek" again, and after I said I had no intention of *not* seeing him, my gentle daddy, in desperation, started hitting me hard as I was running up the stairs to lock myself in the bathroom—the only room in the house to escape to because there was a lock on the door. Peter screamed at Daddy, "Don't hit her again!" I thought my brother would be more likely to scream, "Hit her again," because he was always getting smacked by both Mother and Daddy, and Daddy had never hit me before.

I think my daddy knew what he was doing, though. Jon Arista's penis was the first one I had ever touched—first in a rowboat drifting on the lake at Tamiment after midnight, and then lying on a blanket on the golf course on my last night before going back to Brooklyn, and afterward on my parents' art deco couch, my last year of high school. I was amazed by its wonderful smoothness and hardness. I had seen Daddy's penis many times, but, of course, had never touched it or seen it erect. In 1954, good Jewish girls didn't touch the penises of Greek chorus boys nine years their senior. Daddy won and so did I. I never went out with Jon again after my parents forced me to write him a "Dear John" letter. I had four or five different boyfriends after I broke off with Jon and before I met Stuart. They weren't all Jewish, but I never again *seriously* dated anyone who wasn't.

After graduating from James Madison High School I went to my senior prom with my boyfriend, Howard Director. We dated for about six months. Howard was six-foot-two and weighed 250 pounds. I had reached my full height of five-feet-four, but I still had not reached the 100-pound mark on the scale that was my goal; I weighed ninety-three. Howard had light blond hair and looked like a Nazi storm trooper, but he was Jewish and very gentle.

That summer, my eighteenth, I had left Brooklyn as usual to work at Tamiment as a mother's helper—a nice term for a kid who is really a maid. I baby-sat for the three children, cooked a little, cleaned the cottage, washed and dried the dishes, scrubbed the floors, and was paid ten dollars a week, plus room and board, of course. I probably would have done it for nothing to get out of Brooklyn where the heat was intense during the summer. Tamiment was in the mountains, cool, with a lake to row a boat or to swim in, so different from the ocean where I had spent my childhood. It was also a great place to meet boys (and sometimes men like Jon Arista) and get away from Mother's watchful eyes. I started working there when I was fourteen. I lied about my age. I pretended to be fifteen, but I looked about twelve. I wondered why nobody ever asked me to dance that year.

In my eighteenth summer, I met Marvin Klotz at Tamiment, and even though he was not much taller than I was, I thought that I loved him. At the end of that summer I broke up with Howard. Afterward, Mother told me she used to have terrible nightmares that Howard was on top of my skinny body and had crushed me to death or just snapped me in half. I don't think Mother liked Marvin either. She thought he was too short—or too poor. I can't really remember Mother liking *any* of my boyfriends, or my *girlfriends*, either. My oldest friend Barbara recently told me she never felt welcome in my house and that my mother was always yelling at me. I guess I've blocked it. It took me a long time to understand that Mother was mentally ill.

The only other time I saw Jon Arista was on December 27, 1966, my tenth wedding anniversary. To celebrate it, Stu and I went to the off-Broadway production of *Man of La Mancha*. Jon was one of the muleteers raping Aldonza the whore. Not a lot of career advancement in twelve years. Touching Jon Arista's penis and watching him ejaculate into a Kleenex was the best-kept secret of my young life. But my touching him was as far as it went, because my second best-kept secret was that I didn't have any breasts worth mentioning.

It was actually not *my* choice, but Peter Pan kept me a virgin. No, not the terminally cute little boy who could fly, wouldn't grow up, and exploited Wendy for the rest of her stupid life. I am talking about a preshaped bra called Peter Pan that flat-chested girls like me wore to give the illusion that we had breasts. The nicely shaped cups were hollow inside.

• • •

My best friend in sixth grade was a girl named Joyce Patterson. We were friends until the first year of high school, when her family moved to Florida. Throughout elementary school I always befriended the one or two Christian children in my class. From a very young age, I was concerned about the welfare of the underdog. Growing up Jewish in Brooklyn, I thought I was part of the majority, and I felt sorry for the Christian kids in my school. All the Jewish kids were given the day off on Jewish holidays, of which there were quite a few. Most of us had no idea what they were about, and all we did was play outside in the street. The Christians had to sit in school doing busywork all day.

My friend Joyce "developed" when she was about nine years old. By the time I met her, when we were eleven and I was the new kid at P.S. 206, Joyce had the body of a woman. Sixth grade was the year in my life that I hated the most. I pretended to be sick all the time, and stayed home from school a lot. (Mother said she should have named me Camille instead of Greta, and it wasn't until years later, when I saw the movie with Greta Garbo playing Camille, a woman dying of TB, that I understood what Mother had meant.) I covered my bed and the floor with *The Book of Knowledge* encyclopedias and paper and crayons, and spent the day drawing pictures and reading fairy tales or trying to find the hidden item that would answer the question "What is wrong with this picture?" Mother, one day when she was particularly exasperated with me, looked at the mess in my room, picked up one of the encyclopedias, hit me over the head with it, and walked out of the room without saying a word. This struck me as funny and I laughed out loud. Remembering it still makes me laugh.

I hated my teacher, Mrs. Friedless, and she didn't like me either; I messed up her perfect attendance record all the time. I failed spelling that year, the first class I'd ever failed. In eighth grade I would fail sewing, the last class in my life that I would ever fail. I missed my old friends at P.S. 197, where the kids were too young to care about breasts. Joyce and I were together all the time. The boys, in the brutal brilliance of the young, called us ReJoyce and ReGret.

I wonder if we are destined to relive the pain of our own childhood through our children. Stu, Ellen, and I went to the opening receptions of three art shows. Ellen was almost fourteen. Each of the three art galleries in Knoxville had receptions on the same night. (Steven and Ellen, when they were kids, liked to go for the cookies. When they got older they actually liked to see the art. I think it made them feel like grown-ups. It was always a gala evening, with people getting all dressed up.) Ellen was at the age where she still didn't mind being seen with her parents. She had not yet started going out with boys. She was wearing a new sweater, and for the first time had put on lipstick. Ellen still had braces on her teeth and had not yet developed breasts, but she was starting to feel grown up and looked very pretty. Her long, curly hair framed her face. I could tell she felt good about herself that evening. She was starting to bloom.

We were at the Crossroads Gallery when a woman we all knew, a psychologist, came up to Ellen and me as we were eating our cookies. She said to Ellen, "You look very pretty but I see you still don't need a bra." I watched Ellen's face turn from joy to sorrow in a matter of seconds. How could any psychologist say such a stupid thing to a young girl? I thought maybe she was trying to drum-up future business. I gave her a scathing look, which I don't think she noticed, and thought *If looks could kill, you stupid bitch, you'd be dead.*

We went to the next art show but Ellen now seemed deflated. While we were looking at the art a stranger came up to Ellen and said, "You should smile more. You're a beautiful girl." I wanted to throw my arms around him and hug him, but Ellen didn't answer. The evening had already been ruined. I wondered if she thought I had told him to say that. (Ellen once asked me how old I was when I got breasts. I told her that I was about thirty.)

Once, soon after I discovered the miracle of illusion with the Peter Pan bra, I was riding my bike, wearing a new sweater, and the garbage man whistled. They were tough guys, and when I heard that whistle it was the happiest day of my life. I was still skinny, but now they thought I had breasts. It wasn't until years later that I realized the garbage men whistled when they wanted the truck to move on to the next house.

By the time I got to high school the Peter Pan bra was a must. The problem with wearing it was that if you danced too close to a boy, your breasts pushed in, but did not pop out again. It made a girl cautious. I began to think of myself as another sort of Brooklyn Dodger. I was a tomboy, and many of my friends were boys. I would listen to them talk as if I weren't even there: Kissing a girl was getting to first base. Touching her breast was second base. Getting into her pants was third base. Going "all the way," as we called fucking forty-five years ago, was a home run (still referred to today as "scoring"). I was very fond of first base but could never allow my date to get to third, because to do that you had to pass second. (Birth control pills were far in the future, but there *were* condoms. I don't think my generation was any less interested in sex than the kids after the sexual revolution. Nonetheless, we were careful not to get pregnant and always remembered the name of the one girl in high school that did.)

Anyway, because of my Peter Pan collapsible bra, neither Jon Arista nor any of my other boyfriends ever got near second base, and I remained a virgin until I started college and met Stuart. I weighed ninety-three pounds when I met him and was still wearing a Peter Pan bra. There was no way I could continue the deception at that point. Eventually, you have to take your clothes off. Stu loved me in spite of my flat chest, and we flew by second and third bases on our third date. It was worth the wait. Now, more than forty years later, I weigh 120 pounds, have genuine breasts, and Stuart still loves me.

There are so many secrets in my family besides my innocent secret panel and my not-so-innocent-touching of Jon Arista's penis. Most of them had to do with my uncles, both real and pretend.

UNCLE KARL WAS MORE THAN A FRIEND OF THE FAMILY

I never knew until the day in 1995, when I finally read what was in the envelope that I'd received twenty-five years before, that the man I called Uncle Karl had been my mother's lover (of the spirit, if not the body) for more than forty years. Their love for each other ended only with Mother's death in 1974, when she was almost sixty-four.

I had put the large envelope in the back of a closet. In it was some of Mother's poetry and a letter dated March 4, 1970, from Uncle Karl to me. After reading the letter I decided that the remaining contents of the envelope were a Pandora's box that I didn't want to open . . . yet. My parents were still alive, and I thought if I read the remainder of what was in the envelope, it would somehow be a betrayal of my daddy.

My first memory of Uncle Karl dates to when I was about four years old. He had climbed high up in the peach tree that was in the backyard of our house on East Seventh Street, and he was shaking the tree so that the ripe peaches would fall into the blanket that was held at its four corners by Mother, Daddy, Grandma, and me. Daddy would never climb a tree. It wasn't until more than fifty years later that I would learn that Karl and my mother felt such passion for each other, and that they were destined to spend the rest of their lives hiding from everyone but each other their deep romantic longing.

Karl wasn't my real uncle but a friend of the family. He, and his wife, whom I called Aunt Sara, and their three sons, visited us often throughout my childhood and for the many years that we lived in New York. Mother told me she met Uncle Karl when he was a gardener at the Brooklyn Botanical Gardens. He was already married to Aunt Sara. I have a photo of my mother, her sister Lydia, and Karl taken at the Botanical Gardens in 1933. They are all smiling. Karl is wearing a tie, so the picture must have been taken on his day off.

Mother and Daddy met in 1933 and were married in 1934. Uncle Karl's name is signed on their marriage certificate as a witness. I have a photo of Uncle Karl and my daddy, when they were both young. Karl's arm is around Daddy's shoulder. Daddy's look is skeptical; Karl's is sheepish. Now that I know, am I reading into their expressions things that were not there?

Daddy was tall and skinny. Karl was on the short side—shorter than my mother, compact and sort of stocky. Daddy had straight, black hair. Karl's hair was light and very curly. Daddy was not interested in flowers. Karl was a gardener. Mother always admired men who worked with their hands. Daddy didn't like to get his hands dirty.

Mother was tall, slender, and beautiful. Aunt Sara was short, rather shapeless, and plain. Mother's hair was long and blond. Aunt Sara's was a close-cropped, mousy brown. Mother had high cheekbones and high coloring. The only makeup she wore was a little powder on her nose and cheeks and a light lipstick. Aunt Sara was sallow and didn't wear any makeup, though it would have made her look better. Mother looked supple, and Aunt Sara looked brittle. Mother had an easy laugh. I don't remember Aunt Sara laughing at all. Aunt Sara and my mother did have one thing in common, they both loved Karl. At least I know that my mother did. I liked Uncle Karl but never liked Aunt Sara. She seemed like such a cold fish. Now I wonder if she knew that her husband loved my mother. Karl and Sara always remained friends with my parents. After Mother's death Karl and Sara came to Daddy and Billie's wedding and were friends with them until Karl died.

I wouldn't know how profound the chemistry was between Karl and Hedda until the day when I finally read the packet of my mother's poems, which I received with the following letters:

March 4, 1970

Dear Greta,

The enclosed note from Hedda to me explains why I am sending the poems to you. I hope you enjoy them as much as I did—it is perhaps the poetry that keeps some people going—a great value in this mercenary world.

I guess I have, and always had, some "special feelings" for you, too, otherwise I couldn't send the poems or trust you to be discreet. Drop me a line some day, to the Garden.

All's well here, we hope to see John and Hedda soon again.

As ever,
Karl

Uncle Karl had attached a letter that he received from my mother, with this request from her:

> *Karl, I have given much thought to what you mentioned to me last summer about the packet of my poems which you couldn't bear to dispose of. My opinion on this matter would be for you to address them to Greta. She and I have a perfect understanding and I've been frank with her and she is aware of my special feelings for you, and if she were to some day receive these (she has never read any of them) it would give her much pleasure. If you agree with me on this matter, her address is . . .*

What followed was my address and, until Ellen's death, one of the greatest shocks of my life. I didn't have "a perfect understanding" with Mother about Uncle Karl being her lover. I knew she liked him a lot, but Daddy liked him a lot too, and so did I. Often, when I was little and came home from school, Uncle Karl and Mother would be sitting on the couch, laughing and talking about Mother's garden. At that time they were almost thirty years younger than I am now. I didn't know they were lovers. When I was in my twenties, Daddy discovered one of the poems that Mother had written to Karl. He didn't speak to her for a month. It was the only time my parents ever came close to getting divorced. I didn't understand it. I read the poem, but I thought my daddy was exaggerating its meaning. I was either very innocent or very stupid, or I really didn't want to know.

Here's what I did know. My mother loved Daddy, and she also loved flowers and her garden, but Daddy couldn't care less about gardens or flowers. He loved my mother, and I guess he thought he met all of her needs.

I know that Karl and Sara had come to America from Germany before the Second World War, but I don't know if they came here because they sensed the danger of the Nazis. Sara was Jewish, and Karl was not. He started out as a gardener in the Brooklyn Botanical Gardens. He eventually got a doctorate and, in the years to come, became a renowned paleobotanist. My mother and I visited him at the Gardens once when I was a child, after he had become the director. We went into one of the hothouses for tropical plants and then to Karl's office, where he had a parrot in a cage. He told me not to put my finger in the cage, or the parrot might bite it off. There was little chance of the parrot getting near my finger. I always hated birds and would never try to make friends with one.

Karl wrote books and articles for professional journals, which he sent to my mother. He and Sara traveled around the world. My parents never traveled anywhere. Mother wrote poetry, which she sent to him, typed on the thin rice paper on which she drew lovely pictures. When I finally read the ones Karl sent me I saw that they were laden with a passion unfulfilled, bursting with the longing that lasted for more than forty years. Mother wrote of her waiting for him to come back, when the tulips were blooming or the leaves were falling. She wrote to him:

I will give my songs
To the four winds of April
To carry to you.

They talked of the flowers that they planted together in my mother's garden. I believe those flowers were their children. She wrote a poem called "I Speak to You through My Garden."

I speak to you through my garden
Look about you there and see
The posies patiently planted
Can truly speak for me.

Understanding me is simple
Open your true blue eyes
See what my garden is saying
My garden never lies.

Mother wrote poems to Karl on his birthday, on Valentine's Day, on New Year's Eve. The poems were their secrets, and he kept them all. She wrote to him, "The river we cannot cross runs forever." She wrote of his boyish spirit, their kindred souls. Mother wrote about the "latent depths of a woman's love." There were poems about lips and hands that touch and his true blue eyes. (Daddy's eyes were brown.) She also wrote of restraint. Of not spoiling what they had by the physical intimacy that they obviously both craved. She wrote:

There's a special place in my life for you,
Not Number One, One-and-one-half must do.
Forget-me-nots planted in our prime
Unsullied and eternal to the edge of time.

Mother had died of cancer twenty-one years before I read the letters. She died in the month of February, before her flowers bloomed. After her death, Daddy sent me the many volumes of poetry that she had written. I put them in the garage, knowing someday I would find the time to read them again. When the children were grown. When I had retired.

Steven is grown, Ellen is dead, and I have retired, but the books of poetry are lost. I've searched for them. They may be somewhere in the back of a closet. For now, all I have of my mother's poetry is the slim volume *The Sound The Heart Makes*, which was published in

1972, and the love poems she wrote to Karl. When he sent them to me, he asked me to drop him a line at the Garden. I never did. I couldn't because Daddy was still alive. Now I wish that I had. Karl died years ago of leukemia. His request to me that I be discreet no longer seems to matter. When my mother asked him to send her poems to me and said that someday, if he did, they would give me much pleasure, she was right. Thank you Karl. Thank you Mother.

Steven gave me a loose-leaf notebook in which my mother typed his poems when he was a child. Ellen's poems, however, are lost. They were not among the things that Steven sent home from Seattle. I have not been able to find them in our house. I've searched for them. They may be somewhere in the back of a closet. The only poems that I have of Ellen's are a get-well card and *The Bad Day*.

I DIDN'T TELL ON UNCLE BERNIE

When Johnny came marching home at the end of the Second World War, my Uncle Bernie was with him. Unfortunately, the home he came marching back to was ours. Aunt Carol and her baby were still living with us at 1540 East Twenty-fourth Street.

Bernard Nussbaum was heavy and blond and intimidating. He was an M.P. in the army, and when he came to live with us he still thought of himself as a member of the military police. He started bossing everyone around. Daddy couldn't stand him, and the only one who seemed happy to see him was Aunt Carol. His son, Seth, who was about two years old, had never seen his father and was frightened by him. He cried when Bernie picked him up and bounced him around roughly.

My mother's youngest sister was born Aurelia Heller, but by the time she met her husband she had changed her name to Carol because she wanted it to sound American. She was a delicate flower, and he was a brute. The name Nussbaum never suited her, and I don't think the man who came with it did either. Something about him must have suited her just fine, though, because she was soon pregnant with my cousin Susan, and they all moved to their own place.

It was a relief to see them go. I loved Aunt Carol and my baby cousin, but Uncle Bernie took up too much space at the table, and when he came back from work, his booming voice filled the house. The good news for Grandma was that she was able to give up the daybed in the dining room and have her bedroom back.

Even after Aunt Carol and Uncle Bernie moved out, they still came to visit us every Sunday. Mother made lunch, and she and Carol talked while Daddy, who never had anything to say to Bernie, played Casino with him. I can still see Daddy wincing every time Bernie turned over a card, slammed it down on the table, and shouted, "Take that, John!" Daddy took it because he knew how much my mother loved Carol.

Sometimes, when I was alone in a room, Uncle Bernie would whisper things in my ear. When I was about ten years old he told me he got a hard-on when he looked at me. I had no idea what a hard-on was, but I knew by the way he whispered it that it was not something he should have been telling me. When I was eleven Uncle Bernie told me about having oral sex with Aunt Carol and informed me that a woman couldn't tell if her husband *really* loved her unless he was willing to do that, and then told me what "that" was. When I was thirteen he called me on the phone from his office and said, "Greta, I bought a beautiful white bathing suit for you, and I want you to come over to my office and try it on." I was never frightened of Bernie when he was at my house, because my parents were always there. But he disgusted me. I wasn't stupid; I declined the offer of the bathing suit. I never told my parents what Uncle Bernie was saying to me because I loved Aunt Carol and didn't want her to have to stop visiting. Uncle Bernie never touched me. He never asked me to come to his office again, but he never stopped making lewd remarks.

Aunt Carol, although the younger of my mother's two sisters, was always the most fragile and, in 1970, was the first to die. She was in her early fifties when she succumbed to cancer. After Carol's death, no one in my family ever had anything to do with Bernie, and only then did I even tell Stuart what Bernie was like when I was growing up.

One day, more than fifteen years after Aunt Carol's death, the phone rang just as I got home from work. The almost familiar voice at the other end of the line said, "Is this the home of Stuart Eichel, the artist?" I replied that it was. The voice said, "Is this Greta?" I said I was Greta. He said, "You'll never guess who this is!" I asked if he was going to tell me. He said, "This is your Uncle Bernie," and I replied, "Holy shit!"

When I regained my composure, I asked him where he was. He told me that he and his new wife, Janet, were in Knoxville for a reunion of his old army buddies. I am not a person who bears grudges. Bernie had never *really* hurt me, I told myself, and I was curious to see how he had aged, and if his voice was still as booming as it used to be. I invited them to dinner, and he accepted. When he and Janet came to the door, I was startled to see that Bernie looked exactly the same, only older and a bit thinner. He was still loud. Janet was a pleasant-looking woman in her sixties. I liked her.

Stu and I took them to a restaurant for dinner, and then we all came back to our house for a visit. Bernie said that no one in our family had ever called him after Carol died. I couldn't think of anything to say, but Stuart can be a great diplomat when he's needed. He said to Bernie, very gently, that people have different ways of dealing with their grief. Bernie seemed satisfied with that answer and asked us if we wanted to join them at the reunion the following night. It was to be held at the Howard Johnson motel. We said we would love to go. After Bernie and Janet left that night, I called Daddy and said, "You'll never guess who Stu and I just had dinner with!" When I told him, Daddy said, "Just don't give the son-of-a-bitch my phone number."

About a hundred men were at the Howard Johnson with their wives. These men had all landed at Normandy on D-Day. They were in the second wave. For Bernie, and I'm sure many of the other men, that was the highlight of their lives; the first wave of men to land on the beach had been almost totally wiped out. The men who were meeting in Knoxville that weekend gathered in a different city, where one of their group resided, every year. They kept in touch through a newsletter written and mailed to all of them by my Uncle Bernie. He showed me the newsletter, and it was almost illiterate. Bernie had had virtually no education. When he got out of the army, he worked in his parents' ribbon business, which always seemed like a strange occupation for such a big, gruff man. When his parents died, he quickly ran the business into the ground. My daddy helped Bernie get a job at the post office sorting mail. I learned many years later that Bernie had almost been fired for "annoying" some of the women who worked with him. Daddy said with disgust, "I was able to save the dumb bastard's ass this time, but I won't be able to do it again."

Many of the men at the reunion were highly educated. We sat at a table with a doctor, a lawyer and an entrepreneur. They made emotional speeches. They had all been a part of one of the greatest achievements in modern warfare—the beginning of the defeat of Nazi Germany. My Uncle Bernie was the leader of the group and the last to speak. He said it was great to see all the guys again, but this reunion had a special meaning for him personally, because he got to see his niece, Greta, whose parents he had lived with when he came home from the war, and whom he hadn't seen in almost twenty years.

Stuart and I were so moved by what Bernie said that we cried. We realized he *was* more than anybody in my family had ever given him credit for. He had troubles of his own, which we were to learn about only when, a few years later, we met his daughter again.

In 1991 Stuart and I went to New Jersey for a wedding. My cousin Susan, the younger of Bernie and Carol's children, lived nearby, so we called her and took her to dinner. She told us that her father had recently died, one week after he had graduated from college, at the age of seventy-eight. We talked of our parents and our childhood. She didn't know that my mother suffered from depression; I didn't know that my Aunt Carol suffered from depression. Susan's mother never got help. Susan told me that she thought her mother was a monster and hated her until the day she died. She thought her father was a really good guy. I guess perception is everything.

About a year after Ellen's death Susan called me:

"Do you mind if I ask you a very upsetting question?" she said.

"I couldn't be upset more than I already am," I told her.

"Was Ellen ever diagnosed as manic depressive?" she asked.

"No, she wasn't, but I believe that's what she   *might* have been. She certainly suffered from depression. Why do you ask?" I said.

"Because my son Andrew was just diagnosed as manic depressive and said he planned on killing himself no matter what I did to stop him, even if he had to jump off a roof. I wonder, since the last time we met you told me your mother suffered from depression and I told you that my mother did, too, do you think it runs in our family?"

"I'm sure that it does. Lithium saved my mother's life. It's too bad Stu and I didn't put it together before Ellen killed herself. Did you try to get Andrew put on lithium? If we had, Ellen might still be alive."

"Yes, but it didn't work for him," Susan said.

Andrew was sixteen when this was happening. Maybe perception *isn't* everything.

UNCLE MOE WAS A LIAR

Uncle Moe was fat and jolly, but his small black eyes were dull, reflecting no light. Moe was Daddy's older brother, and the two looked alike, except Daddy was thin and had gentle brown eyes. Moe worked as a night watchman.

He came to our house in Brooklyn twice a month for Sunday dinner and always brought a cake from an Italian bakery in the Bronx, where he lived with his mother, my Grandma Friedman. Their apartment was dark and gloomy, and Mother said it must have looked like Grandma Friedman's house in Latvia; she detested her mother-in-law. Mother said Daddy took after his father.

Mother, Peter, and I dreaded the two times a year when we had to go to visit Grandma Friedman. Getting to the Bronx took almost two hours on the subway, and we couldn't stand to eat the food she cooked. She spoke only broken English and seemed ancient. Her body was shrunken, her hair a thin, dull gray, and her face deeply wrinkled. I never had a conversation with her or felt any affection either for her, or from her, during the sixteen years that I knew her. I didn't feel any sadness when she died.

When Uncle Moe came to visit us he liked to hear me play the piano, and he and Daddy would sing along.

Although Moe played the violin, he never played it for us, and I never asked him why; it was a time when the children didn't question the grown-ups. Once I overheard my parents having an argument about Uncle Moe. Mother said something about Moe's bimbo, but it was before I knew what a bimbo was, and I didn't ask.

Uncle Moe always smoked a big, fat cigar and stunk up the house, but he was such a nice man and didn't have a wife or children. We felt sorry for him, so we never asked him not to smoke his cigar. Daddy said that during the depression Uncle Moe had been rich. He played the violin in Paul Whiteman's orchestra and was paid one hundred dollars a week (my daddy earned twenty), but he lived very high and squandered all his money. It was at that time of his life that he married "the bimbo."

I first met the daughter of Moe and the bimbo, my cousin Jacqui, when I was seventeen. Jacqui, who was twenty, just showed up in New York. She wanted to find her father and had tracked him down through the Department of Social Security. Although Jacqui was fat, like her father, and I was skinny, like mine, when I looked at her I saw my own face. She had been living in California all those years, having been deserted by her father before she was born.

Her visit to New York was miserable, Jacqui said later. Moe apparently was not happy to have been found by his daughter. He did, however, introduce her to his family. (Moe never remarried.) He didn't even take Jacqui to the airport for her return to California; she took a taxi to La Guardia Airport. But she refused to give up. When she was about to get married she contacted her father once again. She wanted him to walk down the aisle with her and give her away to her husband, Ralph Heiland—and he did. After Jacqui and

Ralph had children, Moe was happy, in his old age, to visit them in California and play with his grandchildren. She writes me a letter and sends me a card every Christmas, and, when they were young, her cards always had a picture of her children on them; that was the way I watched them grow up. She once sent a picture of her house. It was elegant and modern.

In 1985, one year after Uncle Moe died, Stuart and I went to California. I called Jacqui and asked her if we could take her, Ralph, and their children to dinner. She met us with her daughter, Carla. Her son, David, was away at college. Her husband was dying of cancer.

At that dinner I learned for the first time that her mother had been committed to a mental institution when Jacqui was still a young child, and that is where she died. She and Moe also had a son, Jacqui's brother, who died at home while she was in the hospital giving birth to Jacqui; he was two. (Jacqui has tried for years to find her brother's grave, but so far has never been able to get any information on where he was buried.) Jacqui grew up in foster homes and told me she had been in therapy for years. I wonder how Moe felt when his son died, or even if he knew about it. He didn't see his daughter until twenty years later.

Jacqui is a schoolteacher. She is funny and smart, and that evening was the only time we ever talked about those things in our family that were never spoken of in front of the children. There were so many secrets, and Moe's daughter was one of the best-kept secrets of all. It solved for me the mystery of why Moe had never married, because I learned that, at the time, a person couldn't divorce a spouse who was in a mental institution. I told Jacqui about Uncle Doctor, whom her father had never mentioned, and why people in the family who lived in New York had never heard of him. Moe was also left $10,000. I wish I had known Jacqui when we were children, and that we had played together, as I did with my other cousins.

When I wrote to Jacqui in 1993 about Ellen's suicide, this is what she wrote back to me:

> *Dear Greta and Stu,*
>
> *I was overwhelmed by your letter, not only by the awful news but by the strength with which you are dealing with it. I was deeply touched by the thoughtfulness and warmth of your letter. I suppose as the years pass, one accepts life's disasters.*
>
> *Love, Jacqui*

When I was seventeen and discovered that my "bachelor" Uncle Moe had a daughter and a wife, I was surprised, but didn't give it a lot of thought. He was my favorite uncle and I didn't know or care about Jacqui. After meeting her as an adult, however, I liked my cousin a lot and saw the damage Moe had wrought on her life—growing up in foster homes because she had been deserted by her father, having her mother die in a mental institution, not knowing where her brother was buried, and spending years in therapy trying to come to terms with these burdens. I now despise my uncle. I feel betrayed by his awful lie. Surely not as much as his betrayal of Jacqui, but because he had lived his life hiding from a daughter who needed him.

When I sent Jacqui this chapter she said the only thing that surprised her was that my parents thought of her mother as "a bimbo." She said her mother was educated and worked as a secretary.

In spite of knowing that Uncle Moe's life was a disaster, I now wish that I had told him to put out his smelly cigar. I wish I had never played the piano for him. I wish Moe were still alive so that I could spit in his face. Unlike my cousin Jacqui, I have not learned to accept life's disasters. I wonder if I will ever learn to accept the disaster of my own daughter.

FINDING LIFE IN A CIGAR BOX

My grandmother, Rose Heller, was thirty-three in 1919, when she arrived in America. She was a widow when she left Czechoslovakia with her three small daughters, my mother the eldest. Grandma spoke no English and earned her living scrubbing floors and sewing people's clothes. She also created beautiful embroidery, which she sold out of her house to people who appreciated her careful needlework and original designs.

Grandma loved Peter and me without reservation, the way grandmas do. She was the only baby-sitter Peter and I ever had when Mother and Daddy went out to visit friends or go to the movies. But it seemed as if she had no life of her own. She had only one friend that I remember—Bella Gerstein, an eccentric woman only slightly younger than Grandma, who lived nearby and used to introduce Grandma as her "friend's mother." Peter used to baby-sit *her*, because Bella was often afraid to be alone. In all the years she lived with us, Grandma rarely left our neighborhood, except to visit Lydia in Pennsylvania or Carol ten blocks away. Sometimes she took Peter and me to a movie in the afternoon. Grandma would, however, get dressed up every day and go for a walk. She always wore a hat and white gloves, but she never went to visit anyone except crazy Bella. After her husband died, Grandma never went out with a man.

Forty years after Grandma's death in 1954, I found an old Dutch Masters cigar box. Daddy had given it to me after Mother had died and he had married Billie. He told me there were family papers in it. This box sat in my house unopened for twenty years. After Mother's death I found it too painful to look at, so I put it away. Then I forgot about it.

When I finally found it again and opened it, I saw it was filled with pictures that I had never seen of Grandma, her parents, and her brother. Until I looked in the box, I realized I had never even known Grandma's maiden name, which was Goldenberg. There was her American certificate of naturalization, which she received when she was thirty-seven, and there was a page from a newspaper dated October 9, 1914, which had a drawing of her on it. I discovered the picture had been drawn from a photograph of my grandmother and grandfather that I also found in the box. At the time the photo was taken, my grandfather was an officer in the Austrian army and was stationed in Prague, where my mother was born.

Heinrich Heller, my grandfather, had given his wife a gold locket for their fifth anniversary, and she was wearing it in the picture. I realized it was the locket Mother gave me after Grandma died. I'd worn it many times, but until I saw the photo and read the story, I had never known its meaning. Grandma was also wearing the earrings that Mother wore every day of her life.

In the photo, Heinrich is seated and wearing civilian clothes, not his army uniform—a dark jacket, a tie with a large knot, a vest, light trousers, and two rings on his left hand, which rests on his thigh. He is looking straight at the camera with a slight smile on his lips underneath his handlebar mustache. He has light, wavy hair. Rose is standing behind him, not smiling and also looking straight at the camera. Their gaze is so direct that I feel they are looking at me. Grandma's hair is piled high on her head, elaborately arranged. Her cheekbones are high, like my mother's. Her lips are full and her eyes set wide apart. Her waist is slim. Her dress is elegant, with a white-fringed collar up to her chin and those Victorian gloves that cover only the hand and the thumb. Seeing her dressed that way, I realized that she came from a well-to-do family. At that moment in time, could they have had any idea that their fifth anniversary photo was the last they would ever have taken together?

I thought when I first saw the newspaper page that it might have been Grandma's wedding or engagement announcement. It wasn't. It was written in German, and I had it translated. This is what it said:

MISSING PERSON:

Lieutenant Heinrich Heller of the 28th Infantry Regiment seeks his wife, Rose, and their three children Hedwig, Lydia, and Aurelia, who were last known to be visiting Lemberg. Any information should be sent to the "Bio-Kanbilt" in Prague.

In the box I also found the story of why Grandma came to America. Though she eventually was able to speak English, she could never write it, so she told the story to Mother, who wrote it down. I read it and wept. It is called "A Soldier's Heart." I wish I had known Grandma's story before she died, but she never talked about it. At the end of the story is a poem written by my mother.

80

A SOLDIER'S HEART

BY ROSE HELLER
(as told to her daughter, Hedda Friedman)

The tenth of January 1914 has blown in on a chill, gray wind. It is our fifth wedding anniversary. Heinrich takes out of his uniform pocket a small blue velvet box. In it is a heart-shaped locket on a gold chain; a scroll in the box reads:

To Rose, A Soldier's Heart

We sit in this twilight hour and bask in our love. We go into our little girls' nursery, and Heinrich and I peek at their ruddy sleeping faces. Blond, blue-eyed Hedy is four, Lydia of the Mona Lisa smile is three, and Aurelia, chubby and chestnut-haired, is one. We must venture on our long-delayed visit to my parents in Lemberg as soon as my husband has his leave. We recall the five happy years since Heinrich brought me here as a bride; his spiraling military career, first to Second Lieutenant of the Twenty-eighth Infantry Regiment of Austria to his present post as Quartermaster. After his transfer to Prague, we found our lovely home, with its quiet, walled garden, and a warm circle of dear friends.

It is July 15, 1914, and we wait in the stark, slate-colored waiting room of the railroad station ready to embark for Lemberg. What joy lies ahead of us all on this visit with my parents and my brothers, postponed until our little girls were old enough to make the trip. How handsome my Heinrich looks in his officer's uniform, with the decorations for distinguished service to his regiment. As our train puffs into the station, an unexpected deluge of tears from Hedy, begging us not to go. I dry her tears, assuring her Grandma and Grandpa in Lemberg will be so happy to see her and her two little sisters. When we arrive at our destination, a carriage drawn by two prancing black horses takes us to the home where my parents live and where I was born. What a wonderful reunion after our long separation!

July 25th, our first night here, and Heinrich is awakened from sleep by a military messenger, requesting his immediate return to Prague and to his regiment. As we embrace I assure him I will live up to the courage expected of an officer's wife. Little did we realize we would be separated for four long years.

Mobilization placards everywhere as July 28th dawned. Austria has declared war on Serbia. Throngs of people milling around everywhere. Long lines of men marching away. The girls and women and children stand at their open windows, cheering them on and some are throwing fresh flowers to the soldier's reaching hands.

Notices to evacuate our town are posted everywhere. All those who can get away have already left, and a terrifying stillness fills the air. I have decided to leave with the children for Tarnapol, where Heinrich's parents live, hoping to find there a peaceful retreat until Heinrich and I are reunited. I implore my parents to flee with me. Thinking of their sons, who only yesterday marched away to the conflict, they decide to stay. We bid them a tearful good-bye.

Tarnapol looks tranquil as we approach it on this dusty August day. Heinrich's parents welcome us into their fold. But there is no escape from this war. Soon along the outskirts of town trenches appear. The nunnery is turned into an army hospital, where the wounded are brought daily. We are cut off from the outside world.

I help Heinrich's father with the dairy products which he trades in. We deliver the butter and eggs as far out as the hospital for the officers' tables. My work helps to assuage the ache of loneliness and fear which lies like a stone in my heart. Hedy asks where all the wounded soldiers are coming from and what they have done. How can one explain war to a five- year-old?

The boom of cannon echoes constantly. My little girls are standing out on our balcony chanting, "The enemy is throwing eggs." Deception is one way of preserving their sanity. Many children have gone mad from fear of the bombs. It is hard to believe this war has been raging for more than two years. Yet never a morsel of news from Heinrich. Is he still alive? How the worry for us must weigh him down!

The falling leaves of September blow in the courtyard. I go to the well for water, Hedy at my side. Suddenly a crash demolishes our well, and a huge crater where the cannonball fell marks the spot where my bucket lay.

Spume of sleet and whirling snow are harbingers of the typhoid epidemic of 1916. Coffins large and small are carted out of the shuttered houses. When my little ones are stricken, days and nights of silent vigil while their fever rages and their lives hang in the balance. I find the strength to endure the sleepless nights, and at last they're out of danger. The work-filled days and lonely nights keep pace with the calendar, which keeps turning, turning.

It is now the winter of 1917. Christmas is not far away. Almost eight months since America entered the war. Rumors of peace spread. They say that fighting at the front is slackening. An open sleigh stops outside my window. The peasant driver salutes the passenger in the back seat and throws back his blankets. The officer alights and soon his boot marks are hidden by the swiftly falling snow. The driver paces back and forth, blowing on his frozen hands to keep them warm. I open my window and ask him to come in out of the cold. Over a steaming cup of coffee he talks. In response to my anxious query, he says it would be possible to cross our border if one had the proper authorizing papers. I take my little girls and we go to see the governor, who remembers Heinrich as a boy before he left to enter the Austrian Military Academy. If I am willing to take the risk, he will give me the passport to cross our frontier. I assure him that to be reunited with my husband I would take any risk.

The peasant driver returns with his sleigh, and, after poignant farewells with Heinrich's family, we are ready to leave. Our belongings are tied on the back of the open sleigh, and our driver covers us with warm blankets. We are on our way back to Lemberg, where we left my parents three years ago. Deep ice covers the river, and our faces are lashed by the cutting December winds.

As we approach the desolate frontier area, black crows circle overhead. The ground is pockmarked with devastation. Our driver finds it difficult steering the sleigh over the torn earth. How merciful when darkness settles, so that our eyes are spared the rubble of battle. We keep going forward, and tonight the horizon reveals a light, then another. A voice out of the night calls, "Halt!" How shocked the young sentry is to see an open sleigh with a woman and three small children in it.

It is Christmas Eve. From the trenches ahead we hear soldiers' voices singing Christmas carols. In the barracks to which we are escorted, the officer in charge gives up his bed for my daughters. He asks me if I would care to join in the Christmas festivities. I thank him, but my heart is too heavy. I put the back of my chair close to the children's cot and drowse.

A pale dawn ushers in this Christmas Day. An army vehicle is prepared for us, and the young soldier escorts us over the border, where a farmer and his wagon are waiting. He takes us on to Lemberg, where my parents and I parted. A strange woman comes to the door. "Your parents are dead," says the woman; her grief-etched eyes show sympathy for our loss. I dare not think of that other door I must yet enter when I reach Prague. I have no time for grieving. We must go on.

Our journey back to Prague ends. Heinrich kept our home intact through the four long years of our separation. From my friends I learn the shocking news that he has been hospitalized for three months with a brain tumor. The past week he has been in a deep coma. By some unexplained miracle, on the day of our return Heinrich wakes out of his deep sleep. He is informed of our safe return by his doctors. His wish to be allowed to go home to his wife and children is granted.

I am fully aware of the seriousness of Heinrich's illness, and I steel myself for our reunion. Can I rally my willpower to hide my fear? When I see my beloved all I can do is whisper his name.

Two weeks of happiness, and on February 24, 1918, death stole him away from us. Heinrich's last request from me is a promise to take our little girls to America, where a brother and sister live. I give him my solemn word. The long walnut casket is lowered into the wet February earth amid the firing of guns of a military burial and the accolades of fellow officers for a departed brother. Silently three little wreaths are dropped on the casket.

Peace spreads over Europe again. Czechoslovakia becomes a republic. Tomás Masaryk, the Czech patriot and war hero, becomes its first president. Austria is partitioned, and many new countries are born. On November 11, 1918, an armistice ending the war is signed.

Sons and fathers, brothers and husbands have now returned to their homeland, their banners folded, their battles done. Out of the ashes of yesterday, of which I will forever be a part, the new green hope of our tomorrow is born.

A SOLDIER'S HEART

An empty rocker on our patio sways, where
We can still see you, Mother, sitting there,
Deep in quiet thought, your mind oceans away
Roaming Prague's poppied fields where he
    left for the fray,
Shiny bayonet on his strong shoulders slung
Handsome, proud, and so pitifully young.
Yet, yours were the shoulders the true burden bore,
Three tiny tots, you sought a strange, new shore.
In our fatherless house with so many problems fraught,
Watching your struggle, this lesson you taught,
When the burden is heavy, learn how to be brave,
God's helping hand reaches—even past the grave

—Hedy

CREMATING GRANDMA

When I found out that Grandma had left instructions that her body be cremated, I almost went crazy. I was seventeen years old and very emotional. The very thought of burning Grandma made me sick. I cried and for weeks threw up the dinner I was forced to eat every night. My weight dropped from ninety-three pounds to eighty-nine. I got so hysterical that Daddy, the gentlest of men, finally lost patience with me and said, "Do you think it's better to lie in the ground and have the worms piss on your head?" Actually I did. I was not afraid of worms but was terrified of fire.

Our house at 1920 East Twenty-fourth Street had an upstairs and a downstairs. There was no room for a sick person downstairs and Grandma was dying of cancer. It was too hard for Mother to keep running up and down the stairs to take care of her, so Grandma went to stay with her middle daughter, my Aunt Lydia, who was rich and had a big house in Reading, Pennsylvania. I went there to visit Grandma once when she was dying, but she didn't know who I was. I didn't go again. The next time I saw her she was in her coffin.

Grandma was not very old when she died, only sixty-seven, and, after they removed one of her breasts the year before, we thought she would get better. She showed me her naked chest after the surgery. She always had a beautiful body, and her breasts were something I envied, because at seventeen I didn't have any. I was surprised that her chest didn't look as awful as I had imagined. The remaining breast still looked very nice.

Grandma thought I was beautiful; She told everyone that I looked just like Margaret O'Brien, the famous child movie star. I didn't look at all like her. Grandma was at all of my birthday parties, though sometimes I wished she wasn't. I remember one birthday party, my eleventh, when I was wearing a hideous blue taffeta dress. I weighed about seventy pounds. Grandma went up to every boy in the room and said, "Isn't my Greta the prettiest girl at the party?" I wished the earth could have opened up and swallowed me. Sometimes it's hard for a girl to be skinny and funny looking and have a grandmother who thinks she's beautiful.

Grandma, whose room was right next to mine, brought me warm milk in the middle of the night if I was coughing. I hated warm milk, so she always brought a candy that I could suck on to help the milk go down. If I wanted something special to eat, she would cook it for me, sometimes to Mother's great annoyance. I always felt that I had two mothers; if one of them wouldn't do something I wanted, I could ask the other one.

I guess it was hard for Mother to share her house and her children with her own mother. She would never let Grandma help with the cleaning, and I always thought that was because she didn't want to exploit her. Now that I am older, I see it as a territorial thing, although I myself never had those feelings. Anyone who ever wanted to clean my house or cook my dinner was welcome to do it. I despise housework and have never liked to cook. Mother, who loved to cook, never seemed to care about cleaning the house, instead she would much rather work in her garden. After I had moved to Knoxville, I visited Mother and Daddy in Huntington Station about once a year. Although no great housekeeper myself, I noticed that there was a thick coating of dust on all the knickknacks that Mother had recently bought at Saint Vincent de Paul's charity outlet. They were cluttering up her house. I said, "Mom, give me a rag and I'll dust all this stuff." She said, "Good. When you come back next year you can do it again." I thought my mother was finally not only developing a sense of humor, but was now doing only the things she wanted to do, and I laughed when she said that.

Once, while Aunt Carol and her baby were still living with us, we thought Grandma was ill, because she slept on her daybed in the dining room well into the late morning. We tiptoed around her, until, not seeing any movement at all, we began to worry that she was dead. Mother called her name; no response. Mother finally drew back the covers to find that Grandma had built a dummy of herself with pillows and was down in the basement scrubbing the floor.

Grandma had brought a wonderful feather blanket with her from Europe. It sat very high on her bed, and it was cozy and warm beneath it. When Peter and I were little she would let us crawl under it with her, or sometimes she would let us take a flying leap and jump on it. It was so fluffy we never got hurt. For some reason, although there were the blue glasses and some other things in the house that must have belonged to her, I always thought of Grandma's feather blanket as her only possession.

When I was in my teens and discovering the joys of male companionship, I once asked Grandma why she never went out with a man. When she told me she wanted to go back to Heinrich in heaven as a virgin, it didn't make a lot of sense to me. I didn't believe in heaven, and I couldn't understand how a woman with three children could consider herself a virgin. She did watch wrestling on television, though. I guess looking at semi-nude male bodies didn't count as a strike against her loyalty to Heinrich. (My cousin Linda recently told me that her mother, my Aunt Lydia, had said that Heinrich, when he was on his deathbed, had made our Grandma promise never to marry again. When I heard this it made me want to cry or scream and wish that my grandfather had died in action—instead of from a brain tumor.)

Grandma was the first person I loved who died, and I was not prepared to deal with it. In 1993, when I was fifty-six years old, Aunt Lydia died and I became the oldest person in my family. There was no one left to answer any questions I might want to ask about the family. My cousin Jacqui, although three years older than I, didn't count, because she grew up in foster homes on the other side of the country and didn't know anything about our family. Both my grandmothers and grandfathers, both of my parents, all of my aunts and uncles, and now my daughter are dead. I now realize that you are never prepared for the death of someone you love. It doesn't matter how old they are, or, for that matter, how old or young you are.

Grandma's funeral was in Pennsylvania. I remember wanting the service to never end, because I had lost my battle to keep her from being cremated. Eventually we found ourselves at the crematorium and I watched in horror as her casket was rolled into the oven. There weren't any flames, just a dark space. I don't think Mother or Daddy had any idea of what to expect. We all went through the experience as if in a trance.

I insisted that Grandma's ashes be buried at the cemetery in Clifton, New Jersey, where my parents had reserved plots for her and for themselves. The day after the cremation we picked up the cardboard box with Grandma's ashes and brought it back in the car with us. I kept picturing a little, tiny Grandma in the box. I couldn't imagine her turning into ashes.

My parents buried the ashes to humor me. Daddy did not want to pay for a rabbi because it was just Mother, Daddy, Peter, and I who would be there, so Daddy conducted the service himself. He didn't really have his heart in it, though, and it was very brief. In the car on the way back to Brooklyn Daddy exclaimed, "Oh my God! I said 'May God have mercy on her soul.' That's what they say at executions!"

The next time I went back to the cemetery in New Jersey was a snowy day in February when, as I stood shivering, we buried Mother. It was almost twenty years after Grandma's death. The last time I went back was when we buried Daddy, on another freezing day, in March, seventeen years after Mother died. I will never go back again. Stuart and I both wish to be cremated. We had Ellen's body cremated. I no longer feel the need to bury ashes or bodies.

I have Grandma's locket and am looking at it as I write this. It is a gold heart on a chain, with three vivid green stones in the center—too green to be real. (Grandma's eyes were almost too green to be real too.) I first saw the locket when I was a child and it held a lock of Mother's blond hair inside it that I loved to touch.

Somehow the lock of hair disappeared and I don't know what became of it. When Ellen was two I cut a lock of her silky, reddish-blond hair and put it in a tiny cardboard box. I wondered if I should take Ellen's curl and put it in Grandma's locket so that it wouldn't be empty, but thinking that Ellen's hair was probably the first part of *her* to become ashes, I decided against it.

Twenty years after Grandma's death I dreamed about her. The doorbell rang late one night and when I went to the door, Grandma was just standing there. I was so happy to see her, but when I touched her face she turned into ashes. I dreamed about Mother years after *her* death. She also rang the doorbell late one night and when I opened the door she was shaking her shame-on-you-finger at me, saying, "Greta, you promised me you'd never eat doughnuts again and you lied." Will Ellen ring the doorbell late some night and tell me why she killed herself.

THE BUS STOP

In 1956 I had just completed the first half of my freshman year as an art student at Pratt Institute. The school was in a dangerous section of downtown Brooklyn called Bedford Stuyvesant. Bed-Stuy, as the muggers and muggees affectionately knew it, was at that time the murder capital of the United States. Pratt, founded in 1887, was considered the best art school in the country. When it was built, it had probably been in a good neighborhood.

When the English captured Manhattan from the Dutch in 1664, the Dutch director general, Peter Stuyvesant, surrendered it peacefully, and the city of New Amsterdam became the city of New York. The Dutch recaptured it in 1673, and then gave it back to Britain in 1674. The territory was still being disputed almost three hundred years later when I went to school there, but this time it was by the newest settlers in the area, who battled over who sold which drugs, and where. The students who lived in the dorms were advised not to go out late at night. Peter Stuyvesant may have been the last person to surrender anything peacefully in Bed-Stuy.

Daddy drove me to school every day, parked his car nearby, and took the subway to work. I was still recovering from a bad case of mononucleosis that I had caught while working at Tamiment that summer. I got out of bed the day before I started college, although I still felt weak; I couldn't stand the thought of missing a whole year of school. (Mono is called "the kissing disease" and I hadn't a clue who gave it to me. It had been a good summer in terms of boys.) Daddy also drove me because I would have had to take two different buses and the subway to get to school from my parents' house at the other end of Brooklyn, and we could barely pay the tuition, much less the cost of transportation. Daddy and I always liked to talk to each other anyway, and the drive to Pratt, which took almost an hour, gave us plenty of time. I also think that going to Bed-Stuy by myself frightened Daddy. He felt it would be safer to drop me off in front of the school and then, after work, pick me up and drive me back to the safety of East Flatbush.

Safety, however, is relative. When I was fourteen years old, I was molested on the street on my way home from a movie with my friend Barbara Tobias. I had just gotten off the Ocean Avenue bus at Avenue S and had four short blocks to walk to my house on East Twenty-fourth Street. Barbara stayed on for two more stops to get to her apartment. It was only 4:30 in the afternoon, but in Brooklyn it gets dark very early in the winter. Before I had reached East Twenty-first Street I heard footsteps behind me and for some reason knew I was in danger.

A man's hand began rubbing my bottom. He said, "Nice cheeks you've got there, girlie." I became almost paralyzed with fear, but not knowing what else to do, kept walking. I wanted to scream, but no sound came out of my mouth. He touched me all over my body, pulling down the zipper on the front of my heavy winter jacket. He told me my breasts were very small. I didn't *have* any breasts. I hadn't even started to menstruate. He kept up a constant stream of talk, saying the filthiest things I'd ever heard. Although I remember them very well today, almost fifty years later, I've never said them aloud or written them down. In the same way, I don't want to talk about the details of what Uncle Bernie told me about oral sex with Aunt Carol.

I saw a light in a house and, going up the steps to the porch, told the man that I lived there. I hoped he would go away. But he followed me up the steps and began pushing me against the wall and kissing me. I weighed only about eighty-five pounds and don't know where I got the courage or the strength, but I made a fist and punched him in the face as hard as I could. The years of practice I'd had fighting with Peter had finally come in handy. The man looked me straight in the eye and said in the coldest voice, "You hurt me. You shouldn't have done that." I thought, *I'm dead,* but he turned and ran away. I zipped up my jacket, walked the two remaining blocks to my house and rang the bell. (Children never needed a key; mothers were always at home.) I felt numb. I was just starting to cry and trying not to so I would be able to calmly tell my mother what had happened. When Mother opened the door though and heard me sniffling, she said, "Greta, I told you to take a scarf. If you've got a cold, I'm going to break every bone in your body." Just an expression of course, but not the words I wanted to hear at the moment.

I became hysterical at dinner and threw my food on the floor, behavior my parents had never seen from the good girl that I usually was. Mother called Barbara, but I had already left her on the bus, so she had no idea what could have upset me. The next day I told Barbara what had happened, but I never told my parents. I didn't go out by myself again for the next four years. My friends, if they wanted me to join them, always had to pick me up and bring me back home.

Now I know that, somehow, nothing ever gets left behind that was left unresolved in the past. One month before Ellen killed herself she phoned me and asked if she could tell me something that might really upset me. After all that had happened to her I foolishly said that I didn't see that it was possible. After her attempt at suicide when she was fifteen, after years of drugs, drunkenness, and sexual promiscuity what more could she tell us that we hadn't lived through with her? But then she dropped a bombshell and told me she had been raped in our house by the exterminator when she was sixteen. He came to spray the house once a month to keep our dog Stella's fleas from taking over the house. Ellen said she could still feel the man's mustache all over her body. I asked her why she had never said anything, and she said, "I was wearing a short pink nightie when I answered the door, and we smoked a joint together"—some of the things that I later read in a letter she had never mailed, written five months before her death:

> I keep feeling the compulsion to tell you I was raped by the exterminator when I was 16, but I don't think I would be taken seriously because I was wearing a nightie in front of a man and I smoked a joint with him before, and I didn't want you to know I smoked pot. I was afraid if I told on him, he'd tell on me. I never really thought about it for years. I keep wondering why I get repulsed when a man with a mustache kisses me, but it could go back to that.

Who knows, maybe mustaches could just be disgusting. I just want to let go of the baggage that the moving company packed with my furniture bound for Seattle.

The memory of the terror I'd felt when I was molested on the street flashed back to me and I realized I had never told *my* parents either. I didn't feel it was my fault that I was assaulted and I didn't blame myself—and I wasn't actually *raped*. And I realized that Ellen *did* think it was her fault and had been carrying that awful conviction around with her for the past thirteen years.

After I got off the phone with Ellen I was so upset and angry that I could hardly speak. I remembered perfectly well who the man was; he had been coming to our house long before I had started going to work and leaving the children at home. I wanted to go and get him. I really wanted to kill him, or at least get him fired. I think the person I was really angry with was myself though, because my daughter felt she couldn't tell me about something so terrible that had happened to her. Stu didn't want to do anything about it. He said, "Who would believe Ellen's word against the exterminator's anyway, even if we could find him after thirteen years?" Stu said Ellen's reputation in Knoxville would negate anything she alleged. I told him he sounded like a lawyer not a father and that a grown man had raped our child in our house—weren't we going to do something about it? Stu said Ellen had tried to ruin the first half of our lives, did we want to let her try to ruin the last half? I said that it seemed to be true that some men didn't understand rape in the way women did.

Ellen *had* been provocative, but that didn't give a grown man permission to rape a young woman who tried to stop him—in her house or anywhere else. (We still argue about Mike Tyson raping the beauty contestant.) Did Stu think men were animals who couldn't stop after they'd been told "no?" Deadlock. I realized that even after all these years, Stu and I could still have a screaming fight about Ellen and we would never agree about what to do about it. Stu said Ellen was now almost thirty years old and that it would be her word against the exterminator's, how could anything be proven anyway? I guessed he was right, so I backed down. I realized that my daughter felt she couldn't tell me what had happened to her in the same way I didn't tell my own mother though. The difference was I wasn't ashamed of being molested.

Instead of doing anything to confront this bastard, even if it were still possible, I wrote Ellen a letter. I found it in the same box with her unsent letter to us. I told her it didn't matter if she had opened the door stark naked. She was a child and the man was an adult who was sent to work in our house. I suggested she speak to someone at a rape crisis center in Seattle and get some help, that even if she thought she could deal with the trauma of a rape, she probably was still suffering from it. Eileen Kogan, a friend who works at the Sexual Assault Crisis Center in Knoxville, told me that most of the women that seek help there are older women who have just begun to deal with the issue of having been raped years before. Eileen told me the oldest woman she had talked to, who was raped as a child, was ninety-one before she was able to talk about it.

• • •

When I started college, in 1955, I was eighteen. I came straight out of high school. The class was filled with veterans of the Korean War going to school on the G.I. Bill. Everyone was very serious, and I had never worked harder in my life. It was difficult to get into Pratt and the competition to stay there was fierce. At the first meeting in the auditorium, I met another girl from Brooklyn, Margie Glazier, and we became instant friends. We are friends to this day. The dean made a speech. He said to the entire freshman class, "Look to your left, and look to your right. In four years one of you won't be here." He was right. By the time I graduated there were only five women left in my class and a number of the men had flunked out, dropped out, or been drafted. When we had a reunion nineteen years later, I was the only one of the five women who had graduated from our class who was working as an artist. Margie became a teacher.

I fell in love with Stuart the first time I saw him. Four new students had transferred from other schools for the second half of our freshman year. My future husband, a Korean War vet, was one of them. I didn't know his name yet, or anything else about him, but I knew instantly that he was the man I was going to marry; chemistry, I guess. I didn't believe in "love at first sight" until that moment. Before I saw him I had decided never to date a man in the same class as me. There were no elective courses at Pratt, so after choosing our major (both of us chose advertising design), we would be in the same class, with the same people, until graduation. I thought it would be awful for two people to go out together and possibly grow to hate each other, and then have to see each other every day for the next three years.

Every day in class I studied this man with whom I had fallen in love, but we hardly ever spoke. One day he was walking back to his dorm in the tight jeans he still loves to wear. I pointed him out to my daddy when he picked me up at school. I said, "That's him, Daddy. The man I'm going to marry!" Daddy asked me what his name was, and I said "Stuart." I didn't know his last name yet. I did know that he was from Detroit, though, which sounded very exotic to someone like me, who'd hardly ever been out of Brooklyn. Daddy said, "He's got a cute ass." He still does. That's why Stuart still wears tight jeans in his sixties.

At the time I started college, Marvin Klotz was my steady boyfriend. I had been going out with him every Saturday night since meeting him at Tamiment that summer. He was cute and probably the nicest and most pleasant man I had ever dated. He was poor and lived in the Bensonhurst section of Brooklyn. East Flatbush, the mostly poor neighborhood where I lived, looked classy compared to Bensonhurst. Marvin was easygoing and had no temper. (Stuart has a terrible temper and the last thing you can call him is easygoing.) I thought no name could be worse than Klotz. When I found out that Stuart's last name was Eichelbaum, I didn't think the change from my maiden name of Friedman, which I had never liked, was a lot to look forward to. When it comes to true love though, sacrifices must be made. Thirteen years after we got married, before we moved to Knoxville, we shortened our last name to Eichel. Enough sacrifice for one lifetime.

Wearing a fraternity pin was a sign of the attachment called "going steady." Marvin went to City College, which, like Brooklyn College, was free. Some people said that free colleges were one of the reasons that the city of New York was always verging on bankruptcy. I think they were among the things that made it a great city. They didn't have fraternities at City College, so Marvin gave me his insignia pin from when he was a Marine in Korea (his nickname in the Marines was "Blood"). I wore it proudly every day. "Fustest with the Mostest" was written on the red, white, and blue pin. It was really ugly. It must have meant a lot to Marvin, though, and I wish I'd given it back to him forty years ago, but Marvin Klotz, who loved me, told me to keep it. I finally threw it away about ten years ago. Stu sometimes reminds me that he saved me from being called Greta Klotz and possibly having children nicknamed Blood.

I was wearing Marvin's insignia pin when I decided that Stuart Eichelbaum was the man I really wanted. One day I was sitting in the student lounge, waiting for class to start. Stuart, who told me later that he had already fallen in love with me, asked me what the pin meant. I told him it didn't mean anything, took it off, and never wore it again. So much for an easygoing personality, which I had just kissed good-bye forever.

Pratt didn't have a football team. It did, however, have a championship basketball team. I was never interested in either sport, but after making sure that the pin meant nothing, Stuart asked me, very casually, if I was going to the basketball game that night. He wasn't asking me for a date or offering to pick me up. I hadn't gone out by myself since being molested, but immediately I said I'd be there.

I called Margie to see if she wanted to go to the basketball game with me. She lived one express subway stop away from mine, on Newkirk Avenue. You could be friends with people if they took the same subway line. Lucky for me, she also took the BMT (the Brooklyn-

Manhattan Transit subway line). If she had been an IRT person (Interborough Rapid Transit subway line) Stu and I might never have gotten together that night, and who knows what might never have happened? Daddy was stunned that I wanted to go somewhere by myself. He said, "How will you get home?" I told him the guy with the cute ass was going to be there and that we would probably go out for pizza and he would probably take me home—I hoped. Daddy drove me to the Kings Highway subway station.

I remember nothing about the game, which I didn't care a whit about anyway. I was searching the crowd for Stuart, who suddenly materialized after the game was over. He said a bunch of people were going out for pizza, and would Margie and I like to join them? We would, said I, without even asking Margie if it was OK. After we ate the pizza, Stuart, thinking it was probably safer in Korea than in Bed-Stuy, asked Margie and me if we wanted him to take us home. Margie's subway stop came before mine, thank goodness, and we walked her home. Then Stuart and I went to wait at the nearby bus stop, instead of walking all the way back to the subway station. I asked him if he was Jewish and he told me he was Protestant—a lie. I thought, after Jon Arista, that this would not make Mother and Daddy happy, but I was determined not to be so easily intimidated this time. Even though my parents were not religious, they wanted me to marry someone who was Jewish. Mother later explained, having experienced and seen so much anti-Semitism in her lifetime, that she didn't want her daughter to have a fight with her husband and have him call her a "dirty Jew."

It was late at night, so there were fewer buses running, and Stuart and I waited a long time for the bus to come. When it did, we found out we were waiting on the wrong side of the street, and the bus would be going back toward Pratt. So we crossed the street and waited for another hour. It was a Tuesday and I'd been up since six in the morning, but I wasn't the least bit tired. We talked, among other things, about school and our hopes for finding great jobs after we graduated. I kept wishing Stuart would kiss me.

Stuart asked me where I had gotten the coat I was wearing. I had never really cared about what clothes I wore. As I glanced down at the rather ugly blue coat draped over me I replied, "It was my Grandma's." He said, "It looks it." When he saw my little house on the narrow street where I lived, he said in a very derogatory manner, "I can't believe you live here!" (When I got to see his house, which was twice the size of mine, on a beautiful, wide, street I almost understood his tactless remark, if not his odd, sometimes inappropriate, sense of humor.) I thought, *Who does that arrogant son-of-a-bitch think he is, anyway?* He didn't kiss me.

The next day, back in school, Stuart said to me, "I'd ask you out, but you live too far away." I told him I'd just have to move closer. He said he was only joking and asked me out for the following Saturday night, and the Saturday after that, and the Saturday after that. Now, more than forty years later, I still haven't forgiven Stuart Eichelbaum from Detroit for not kissing me at the bus stop. Maybe I never will.

On our third date, March 31, 1956, Stuart asked me to marry him. I don't know what took him so long. We both knew before we had even gone out together that *this was it!* We went to see a performance of a one-man traveling show called *"Theodore: In an Entertainment of Sinister and Disconcerting Humor."* The *Brooklyn Eagle* called it "Eerie . . . unearthly . . . nightmarish." Stuart and I discovered that not only were we madly in love with each other, we had the same sick sense of humor.

In some ways that is what has kept our love alive for more than forty years.

When I started college my parents gave me the basement apartment they had rented out to use as a studio. I had my paints, brushes, sketchpads, and books all over the place, and I stayed up very late at night doing my homework. My bedroom on the second floor was tiny, but down in the basement, where I spent almost all of my time when I came home from school, I had plenty of room and could work as late as I wanted without disturbing anyone. It was very private.

Stuart was just the right size for me—neither very tall, like Howard Director, nor short, like Marvin Klotz. Stuart's compact body is covered with thick blond hair that curls. He has strong arms and tree-trunk legs (he was once a boxer—he quit because he said his face was too cute to mess up). A handsome, well shaped head. Hazel eyes that change to green or blue in different lights. A straight nose and straight teeth (after four years of braces) and a full, sensual mouth. Square hands, that are exactly the same shape that Ellen's hands would be. A deep cleft in his chin (that would also be inherited by Ellen—they called themselves "the tushy chins.") Flat ears. A flat, hard stomach. I loved every part of him. And still do.

After coming home from my third date with Stuart, we went down to my basement hideaway. At four in the morning my mother came down the steps to the basement and called out to me, "Do you have any idea what time it is, young lady?" I said, "We just got engaged." My mother said, "Good night." I guess she knew when to give up. Or maybe she was just happy that her future son-in-law weighed only 150 pounds and was Jewish.

After we got engaged Stuart moved out of the dormitory at Pratt and into the basement apartment of the little house that he had turned his nose up at the first time he took me home. Technically, I still slept in my bedroom upstairs, but my parents, if they knew, pretended I didn't sneak down there every night. Stu was not only happy to be with me all of the time, he was happy not to have to take two buses and a subway to get back to school after a date. He was also glad to leave his roommate in the dorm. Fred was not only an incredible slob, piling his junk all over the place, even on Stu's side of the room, he was also a Nazi sympathizer who put swastikas up all over the room. Stu is very tidy and didn't have much love for a Nazi. I had not yet learned to be very neat, but I was a much better roommate. Fred flunked out at the end of freshman year.

Exactly one month after our third date, we flew to Detroit with Mother, Daddy, and Peter to meet Stuart's family and formalize our engagement. No one in my family had ever been on an airplane before. Stu had flown many times while in the army. He told me later that whenever he had to ride in an army plane, the first thing he did was take off his hat, so that he could throw up in it. I thought I might die from the excitement of flying. I spent most of the flight with my nose pressed against the glass. I had never looked down at the clouds and I thought it was the most beautiful sight I had ever beheld. Stu, to my amazement, refused to look out the window. He said if he did he would probably get sick. (Something I witnessed a number of times since that first flight together.) I realized I still had a lot to learn about this man.

DETROIT ART STUDENT TO WED NEW YORK MISS

Mother and Daddy were very romantic people and understood love at first sight. (It had happened to them.) Stuart's parents planned an engagement party for us for April 28th, after they realized they couldn't talk their son out of marrying a girl he barely knew. They put my picture in the *Detroit News,* and it ran under the headline "Detroit Art Student to Wed New York Miss." I thought that was very droll. New Yorkers like me, I thought to myself, were more sophisticated than Detroiters and would never have run such an announcement in the newspaper. Also, I was an art student—just like Stuart—not merely a "New York Miss." I was eighteen years old. Stuart was twenty-three.

I had never been anywhere outside of New York, New Jersey, and Pennsylvania. When the plane landed, I kept saying to myself in amazement, "I'm in Detroit, Michigan," as if it were Paris, France. Stu's parents owned a popular delicatessen in downtown Detroit called The Bagel. His father sold Stu's car so that his mother could use the money to buy me a beautiful engagement ring. It was strange to meet Stuart's identical twin brother Eddie for the first time—a double of the man I had fallen in love with. I wondered if I might have fallen in love with Eddie if I'd met *him* first. After getting to know Eddie, I realized that the only thing he and Stu had in common, besides being artists and boxers, was the way they looked. Their two other brothers didn't look anything like them.

The first time I hugged my mother-in-law to be, Elizabeth Eichelbaum, I felt her spine stiffen, and it shocked me, because I came from a family of huggers. When I was twenty, a year after Stu and I had married, Elizabeth tried to tell me about her childhood and began to cry. I was to hear her cry only twice again (so far), once when she talked about her sister Zeena's death, and when I told her that Ellen had killed herself. I did not see her cry at her husband's funeral.

I would learn about her only after she graduated from college, when she was sixty-nine. She was the oldest graduate at Wayne State, and her sister, Zeena, told their story to the *Detroit News*. Elizabeth had never gone to high school and when her husband died she decided to get her high school diploma. She got a GED and went to college, later getting a master's degree when she was eighty-one. Elizabeth now lives in Knoxville and is getting her doctorate. She is eighty-nine and has incredible energy. Stu is just like his mother. I have said to him that he takes after his mother and gets all the credit, and I take after my daddy and get all the blame, and it isn't fair.

Elizabeth was born in Odessa, Russia, in 1910. She and her two older sisters were left by their mother to live with their grandmother when Elizabeth was a year and a half. Their father had died and their mother went to America, hoping to send for her daughters when she was settled and had saved enough money. But the First World War started, and then the Russian Revolution, their grandmother died, and the girls were placed in an orphanage, huddling in the dark as German bombs fell and almost dying of starvation. It took ten years for their mother to find out where they were; she hired an agent to smuggle them out of the country.

When I hugged Stuart's father, Martin Eichelbaum, the day I met him, he put his arms around me and said, "I've waited twenty-three years for this day." I was very touched, although I didn't know if he was happy that I was marrying his son or glad to get rid of him. (Now, I think it was a toss-up.) He had never shown much affection for any of his four sons.

Stuart's parents also gave us a huge wedding eight months after our engagement. My parents couldn't afford a big wedding, and I didn't care at all about even having a wedding. I've never liked tradition. Mother took me shopping, and she bought me a beautiful wedding dress at Macy's. It cost ninety dollars, which was more than I'd spent on clothes in the previous ten years combined. For the first time ever, I had a dress that didn't come from the bargain basement of S. Klein's.

The only time Stu and I could get married was during our Christmas vacation from school. We still had to go back and finish our sophomore year at Pratt. There were 250 people at our wedding; six of them were from my side: Mother, Daddy, Peter, my Aunt Lydia and her daughter, my cousin Linda, and my best friend, Barbara Tobias, who was my maid of honor. Stu and I, my parents, and Peter, flew to Detroit. Mother and Daddy used the money it would have cost for a small wedding and paid for the flight. Aunt Lydia was the only member of our small family who had money and could actually afford to fly to Detroit. Barbara took the Greyhound bus. Before we went to pick my friend Barbara up at the bus station, Stu told his twin brother, "Greta's best friend is fat and ugly but *please* be nice to her." When slim, beautiful Barbara got off the bus, Eddie's jaw dropped open. Eddie, who was the best man, fell in love with Barbara and joined us on our brief honeymoon in Manhattan. They went out together two more times, but their relationship didn't last much longer than our honeymoon.

Our wedding was held on a Thursday night, December 27, 1956, during a huge snowstorm. Like the carriers of the mail however, neither rain, nor snow, nor sleet, etc., stops the people of Detroit. As I waited in a little room for them to play the "Wedding March," I heard a loud burst of laughter. I learned later that Stuart had raced down the aisle, not walked in the slow, measured steps of the rehearsal the night before.

I had no religious training. I had been inside a synagogue only once, for Peter's bar mitzvah. Stu and I were not married in a synagogue, but in a place called the Rainbow Terrace. Toward the end of the ceremony, while we stood under the chuppah, the traditional marriage canopy, the rabbi read our marriage certificate in Hebrew, but said "Brooklyn, New York" in English. (I guess there is no Hebrew translation for *Brooklyn, New York.*) It struck me as funny and I started to laugh. Laughter, being contagious on solemn occasions took over the ceremony, and soon, to the disgust of the rabbi, all of us under the chuppah had caught it. (Except Stuart's father. He, after all, was paying the bill.) We were laughing so hard, and trying to stop, and our shoulders were shaking. The audience, seeing only our backs, thought we were so moved that we were crying. When we walked back down the aisle, we realized that

Stu's cousin Ethel had taken movies of the ceremony. Luckily, she had forgotten to put any film in the camera, a genetic flaw.

After the ceremony there was a big dinner. Stu's brother Eddie made a speech. Daddy sang. There was a band. I danced with my daddy. I danced with Stuart's father. My new husband and I danced the waltz, which was always Stu's favorite. I had a wonderful time.

We spent our wedding night in Windsor, Ontario, across the river from Detroit. We stayed at the Prince Edward Hotel and it cost ten dollars and ninety-four cents, with tax. (I still have the bill. I used to put stuff like that in an album.) Stu forgot to bring the condoms—we sure weren't ready to have a baby—but, being a traditionalist, Stuart believed that it was mandatory that we make love on our wedding night, although we'd been doing it in my parents' basement since our third date. It was well after midnight during the continuing snowstorm, and Stu left me waiting in the hotel room wearing this ridiculous short red nightie he had bought for me. It looked like something a hooker would wear. He went back to Detroit to buy the rubbers, and by the time he returned to the hotel, I was sound asleep. It had been a very long day. Stu didn't wake me and we missed our chance to make love legally for the first time, in Windsor, Ontario.

The next day, as we were driving back to Detroit so that we could fly back to New York, Stu's mother's car broke down in the Windsor Tunnel (she had lent it to us for our wedding night). We had to be towed out, and while we waited for the tow truck, I watched my husband of one day beat the shit out of a car. It was the first of many more car beatings that I would witness. We arrived at the Detroit airport with only one minute to spare before our plane to New York departed. Stuart was still in a terrible mood. I wondered if I had made an awful mistake.

We honeymooned for four days at the Astor Hotel on Times Square in Manhattan. We ordered room service once, but it was too expensive, so we didn't do it again. We saw three plays and three movies. I couldn't stop crying after seeing the movie *La Strada*. Stu's brother Eddie and my friend Barbara saw *Inherit the Wind* with us. Paul Muni was the star, and it was the best play I had ever seen in my life. Our first New Year's Eve together was on our honeymoon. It was hard for us to believe that on December 31, 1955, we had both been on dates with other people. We saw the musical *The Most Happy Fella*. It cost ten dollars and fifty cents for an orchestra seat. (I saved the ticket stub in my album.) We couldn't get back to our room for a long time because the traditional huge crowd was in Times Square celebrating the coming of the New Year. The only other time I had been to Times Square on New Year's Eve was with my first boyfriend, when I was fifteen. (His name was also Stuart.) I swore, after the first time, I would never go back. It scared me to be part of a crowd that large, my body moving in whatever direction the crowd moved. The second Stuart and I never went out on New Year's Eve after that. Organized hilarity has never been to our liking.

In many of the years that followed, Stuart and I forgot our anniversary. It is two days after Christmas and there was always, until recently, a lot of company and confusion. Because we got engaged and married so quickly, I think our fellow students at Pratt thought I was pregnant and had to get married, but I didn't have a child until after we graduated. For years afterward, on December 27th, our son had to remind us that it was our anniversary. He used to be pretty traditional.

THE BATHTUB WAS IN
THE KITCHEN

During the first two and a half years of our marriage Stuart and I were together twenty-four hours a day—except during summer vacations from school, when we had jobs in different firms to earn our tuition. We met for lunch whenever we could.

One day Stu took me shopping to buy a new winter coat. He said he couldn't stand seeing me wearing my dead Grandma's ugly blue coat, even if it *was* practically new. We bought a beautiful gray fake-fur coat. I loved it. It cost forty dollars, but Mother said that was extravagant and told me to take it back. I threw a childish tantrum and refused. After all, I was now a married woman, even if I was still my mother's child living in her house. Daddy drove us to school every morning and picked us up every night. Stu and I couldn't afford two-way carfare for both of us. We lived on the $135 a month that Stu received from the G.I. Bill, plus the $75 his parents sent us every month. My parents let us live in their basement for free and Mother cooked all of our dinners. I did the dishes, and then Stuart and I went down to the basement and did our homework until the wee hours of the morning. It really wasn't like being married at all. It was like being given legal permission to sleep together.

The apartment was never really meant for people to live in, even though Mother and Daddy had rented it out for fifty dollars a month to people who couldn't afford anything better. It was what you might call a "finished basement." It was very small. The only place for the bathtub was in the kitchen; I didn't cook a single meal in that kitchen for the four years we lived there. The kitchen had a little pantry, but Stu and I turned it into a darkroom to develop pictures for our photography class. The door allowed light to leak in, so when one of us was developing a photo, the other had to lean against the door as hard as possible, to keep the light out. We had a single bed, because there was no way to get a double bed down the tiny, curving stairway. When we had an argument, Stu had to practically paste himself against the wall so we didn't have to touch each other. It kept us from having too many disagreements. Our drawing boards were side by side in what could have been a laundry room, but Mother did our laundry as well. Stuart and I weren't even *playing* house.

Shortly after we got married, someone gave us two Easter chicks. We named them Irving and Zelda, and they lived in the bathtub until they got so big and hostile that I was afraid to go into the kitchen for fear they would attack me. I guess I would have been hostile, too, if I were a chicken and didn't get to do anything but grow up in a bathtub located in the kitchen of a basement. There was too much light for developing photographs, but not enough light for developing chickens. We mercifully gave them to a farmer on Long Island, (not soon enough, I'm afraid, for Irving and Zelda) who probably cut off their heads that same day. I hated the stupid birds anyway.

Daddy told Stu he should buy a hat so that when he interviewed for a job he would look like a serious person. He bought one and it looked ridiculous on him. (This was not long before John Kennedy, by his example, made wearing a hat unnecessary for a man.) Stu started having some trouble with his eyes around the same time. He saw flashing lights one day while playing handball. The eye doctor told him he had an astigmatism and needed glasses, so he bought them as well.

One day I walked into the kitchen and found Stu taking a bath, wearing his hat and his glasses. The sight was only a little less frightening than the one of Irving and Zelda giving me the evil eye. He told me he thought he should wear his new hat and his new glasses at least once before he threw them both away. He never again wore a hat and didn't need glasses until about thirty years later.

In spite of being Jewish Stu and I always got something for each other for Easter. On the second Easter of our marriage Stuart bought me a chocolate bunny. It was holding a foil-wrapped chocolate egg, which we ate. Stu, anthropomorphizing as he usually did, said, "We ate the bunny's egg. Now we can't eat the bunny." Don't ask me to try to explain this. Stu once wouldn't let me return a damaged lamp because he said it liked living in our house.

You can just imagine what it was like years later, after moving to Huntington Station, when we bought a dog, a Chinese pug. We named her Stella, after the wife of Stanley Kowalski in *A Streetcar Named Desire*. We brought Stella home and the next day took her to the veterinarian for a checkup. The vet told us the dog was sick and to take it back to the pet store. Of course Stella had already spent a night in our house and liked it. Stu also wanted to go outside in a torn T-shirt and, like Stella's brutish husband, yell "*Stell-aaaahh*," and if we had traded her in for another dog Stuart would not have been able to do that. After all, Stella was *her* name. Thirteen years later, when we were living in Knoxville, we finally had to put Stella to sleep. Stu still cries when he thinks of it.

Although I was the one who wanted a dog and Stu didn't, I told him that every child ought to have a dog. I hadn't had a dog since the one I'd shared with Arthur Meyers when I was in third grade. Mother never wanted me to have any pet other than a canary, but I wanted something I could hold in my lap and pet or take for a walk. We *always* had a canary in a cage, but I hated birds. I still do and take no pleasure in their chirping or squawking outside my open window. Daddy used to tell a joke about a guy who buys a canary, and when he brings it home he notices that it has only one leg. He brings it back to the pet store to complain about his defective bird. The owner of the store says, "So what did you want, a singer or a dancer?" I didn't care if our canary could sing opera or dance the part of the prince in *Sleeping Beauty.* To me it was always a stupid bird that left disgusting droppings on the paper in its cage.

Miss Finnerty, my third-grade teacher at P.S. 197, announced to the class one day that her dog had given birth to puppies. She said if we each brought a note from our mothers saying it was OK for us to have a dog she would put our names in a box and give a puppy to the person whose name she drew out. I was ecstatic. I lied to Mother; my parents had taught me so well how to not tell the truth. I told her that everyone in the class was bringing a note from home to get one of Miss Finnerty's puppies. I said that if she wrote one for me I would practice the piano every day without her having to find where I was hiding. I would have promised almost anything. My mother thought the chances of my winning were slight; there were thirty-five kids in the class.

When I brought Mother's permission note to school the next day, only one other person had brought a note from their mother. He was a new kid named Arthur Meyers. He had just moved to Brooklyn from Alabama, where he later told me the Jewish kids and the Catholic kids got beaten up every day on their way home from school. He was the type of chubby, Jewish boy who got beaten up in almost every place but Brooklyn. In Brooklyn, if you could avoid the Catholic kids when they got out of parochial school, having spent the day trying not to get smacked by the nuns, you were pretty safe; Israel was not yet its own country, and the Jewish kids never beat up anybody.

Miss Finnerty did not know what to do. She got Arthur and me together to see if we could decide who would get the puppy. Arthur had lied to his mother too. He lived in an apartment house where dogs were not even allowed. Since I lived in a four-family house that had a basement, we decided to share the dog. It would live at my house and Arthur would take it for walks.

Mother, accepting that she was stuck with a dog, said I could keep it in the basement, which was OK with me. The basement was where the coal furnace was. It was the warmest place in the house. It had a little room that we fixed up with a table and chairs and a rug on the floor. Arthur came over twice a day to walk the dog, which we named Rusty, and Arthur became my best friend. We played a board game called Rich Uncle, in which the winner inherited *all* the uncle's money (this was years before I knew that I really had a rich uncle), and sometimes we played Monopoly. Eventually Rusty got so big that Mother said we could no longer keep him in the basement and she gave him to someone who had a farm on Long Island. I wonder if it was the same farmer who took Irving and Zelda. (I had always thought we had to give Rusty away because he had gotten too big. Fifty years later, Peter told me that Mother had given Rusty away because the dog had snapped at him. Peter, of course, had neglected to tell Mother that he had been trying to ride on Rusty's back.)

Arthur came over every day anyway, even after the dog was gone. I think he was the first boy I ever loved. By sixth grade my family had moved and I went to P.S. 206. I never saw Arthur again and never got another pet until I was married and had children of my own, who, I told Stuart, wanted a dog. Stella was probably the dumbest dog that ever lived, but we loved her. The only time she was ever frisky was in the pet shop that sold her to us; maybe they put her on speed. The first night we had her, she cried all night and Steven took his blanket down to the lower level of our house in Huntington Station and slept on the couch to keep her company. After that Stella just sat on her blanket and chewed her rawhide bone that looked like a cigar. Actually, Stella, with her pushed in face, looked a lot like Winston Churchill. Ellen said her stuffed frog was more fun than that dog. She said the chocolate bunny was more fun than that dog, too.

Anyway, because Stu said we couldn't eat the chocolate bunny, we put it in the refrigerator in its pretty decorated box, but without its egg, of course. When we moved to our next basement apartment two years later (1829 East Twenty-ninth Street had a shower in the kitchen), the bunny moved with us. Mother looked into the refrigerator one day and said, "That's not the same bunny that you had in the refrigerator in our house, is it?" I had to confess that it was.

The bunny moved with us two years after that to Lindenwood Village, our co-op apartment in Howard Beach. By this time, Mother was suffering from severe depression. Although she didn't even care about herself, when she looked into the refrigerator, she still said, "That's not the same bunny is it?"

When we moved to our house in Huntington Station, Long Island, Mother had not yet recovered from her illness and didn't bother to ask if it was the same bunny. She just said, "It's really disgusting to keep a chocolate bunny in a refrigerator for almost ten years." She also said she had just cleaned out my kitchen cabinet and found fourteen opened boxes of cookies. I never claimed to be the best housekeeper on earth. Or the best cook, for that matter. Or the best at baking homemade cakes or cookies.

My favorite cookies were those wonderful little spice drops covered with powdered sugar called pfeffernüsse. Steven and Ellen loved them too, but they were only sold at one time of year, beginning at Thanksgiving and ending at Christmas. I have loved them since childhood, when you could buy a whole bag of them at the A & P for thirty-five cents. One day when Steven was five years old and Ellen was two, I was reading one of those magazines that young mothers always used to read, such as *Women's Day* or *Ladies' Home Journal,* that told us everything we would ever need to know about how to keep our bodies desirable, our children healthy, and our husbands happy. In one of them I found a recipe for pfeffernüsse cookies. I filed it away thinking, now I could make my favorite cookies in the month of May, if the spirit moved me. I had, however, never baked a cookie in my life.

I am of that generation of women who came of age in the apathetic 1950s and, when we were young, were easily manipulated by the popular press and the arbiters of fashion who knew we didn't make major life decisions on our own and did what was expected of us. It never occurred to most of us not to get married or not to have children. We slavishly followed the styles of the day, which were dictated by designers who hated women. We actually had no choice. The shops sold only what was in style, and we felt ridiculous if our skirts were the wrong length. We crammed our square feet into pointy, high-heeled shoes that could do permanent damage to the wearer or her dancing partner. If we were small-breasted or (heaven forbid) flat-chested, we wore padded or Peter Pan bras. Regardless of whether or not we had shapely legs, we wore miniskirts. We went to the hairdresser, who teased our hair so high and used so much hair spray that we forgot what our scalps felt like. Once, after Stu, the kids, and I had moved to Knoxville, and teased hair had gone out of style, Ellen put her hands on my head and told me that was the first time she had ever felt my scalp and that it was a real thrill.

I, a woman who always thought of herself as an independent thinker, found it almost impossible to escape the mores and fashions of the day. After all, I had two children and a husband, all of whom I wanted to be healthy and happy. So I read the magazines and did what was expected of me. I cleaned the house, ironed the clothes, and cooked the meals. I displayed my skinny legs in the stylish miniskirts. All the time, though, I knew in my heart that I was really an artist and intellectually above it all. Don't get me wrong, I loved being a wife and mother. I was always able to do freelance artwork at home and can't remember ever being bored. The only things I refused to do were work in the garden, make cookies from scratch, and sew.

When I was in grade school the only classes I ever failed were spelling and sewing. I bet people growing up today, with coed de rigueur, can't believe that when I was in eighth grade, in 1951, the girls had to take classes in cooking and sewing and the boys had to take classes in "shop" (i.e., carpentry). The boys made birdhouses; the girls made applesauce. Why anyone would want to push cooked apples through a strainer when you could open a jar from the supermarket escaped me, but I managed to pass cooking class with the help of my friend Joyce Patterson. Sewing was quite another story. In the first half of eighth grade, our teacher, Mrs. Moftie, the sewing teacher from hell, taught each girl how to make a blouse. I think to this day I have a mental block against sewing because of Mrs. Moftie. My blouse was so inept, and so beyond saving, that I threw it away and told Mrs. Moftie it either was lost or someone had stolen it. She knew I was lying, of course, and she had me spend the rest of the term cleaning out the closet and searching for the blouse that I knew had gone down the incinerator. Then she flunked me.

For the second half of eighth grade we were required to make our own graduation dresses—ghastly, flouncy, white things. The day before graduation I brought the various separate pieces to Joyce Patterson's mother, and she quickly stitched them together on her sewing machine. I would have hated to miss my graduation from P.S. 206 because I was so glad to get the hell out of a school I detested.

At James Madison High the girls in the college-bound program neither had to cook nor sew, and I thought my days of fumbling with a needle and thread were over. After I got married and had children, however, I wished I had paid more attention in grade school. I have never been able to even sew on a button. When Steven and Ellen were little, my purchase of a device called a Buttoneer amused them greatly. We would read the instructions together, putting a button on an object of clothing using neither a needle nor thread but a plastic thing shaped like an H that you attached with the magic Buttoneer. They always waited eagerly for the last of the six steps, which said: "Your button is now firmly and attractively attached!" They would fall on the floor laughing while searching for the button that had flown off somewhere in the room.

I don't think we ever know what possesses us to do certain stupid and self-defeating things. One day in April I retrieved my recipe for pfeffernüsse cookies, which had been moldering for a year in a fairly empty file. I spent seven dollars on the ingredients for cookies you could still buy for thirty-five cents a bag. But they were only sold in November and December.

Steven and Ellen were upstairs, taking their afternoon naps. I had told them that I was going to bake our favorite cookies while they were sleeping. I lined up all the ingredients: sugar, eggs, flour, powdered sugar, honey, molasses, spices, and whatever else was called for. I preheated the oven. So far so good. The first step in the recipe said, "Stir the sugar in a pan until it spins a thread." Spins a thread? I had no idea what that meant. It might as well have said, "Stir the sugar until it knits an afghan." I stirred the sugar in the pan, but the thread failed to materialize. Mrs. Moftie, my old sewing nemesis, drifted before my eyes on her broom, screeching, "I always knew you threw your blouse in the garbage, you little shit. You'll never be able to spin a thread if you live to be a thousand years old, heh, heh, heh."

Well, not believing in witches—yet—I continued on my ill-fated mission. I poured all the other ingredients into a large aluminum bowl and added my threadless sugar. I stirred it all together with the wooden spoon I had bought especially for my first attempt at being a woman that *Ladies' Home Journal* would be proud of.

When I bake cookies, I don't fool around. I was going to make enough cookies to freeze for the entire summer. We would feast on pfeffernüsse cookies in July. I might even give some to the neighbors who had given homemade goodies to me.

The greased cookie sheet awaited the arrival of its first cookie. The recipe now said, "Roll the dough into small balls and place on the greased cookie sheet one inch apart." I plunged my hands into the mountain of batter but was not able to roll a small ball out of the dough and place it on the cookie sheet, because I was not able to remove my hands from the bowl. I was not able to turn on the hot water to run into the bowl in which my hands were now stuck, as if by quick-drying cement. I was not able to phone for help.

Five-year-old Steven was fast asleep. I didn't want to frighten him by screaming that I was being held captive by cookie batter in a large aluminum bowl. I called as softly as I could, "Steven, come and help Mommy. My hands are stuck." The sleepy little boy came down the steps rubbing his eyes. I said, "Do you see that bag that says 'flour' on it? F-L-O-U-R." Lucky for me, he had already learned the alphabet. "Take the bag and start pouring the flour into this bowl. Make sure your hands don't touch the stuff in the bowl." I had this terrible vision of both mother and son glued to the bowl, and two-year-old Ellen awakening from her nap and screaming to be released from the prison of her crib.

Steven poured about half the flour in. "Now try pulling the bowl until Mommy can get her hands out."

Nothing happened. My beautiful engagement ring was on my finger. It was the only piece of real jewelry I ever wore, and I hoped, if I ever got separated from the batter, it would still be there. This was happening before the days of 911, when little kids could call and save mothers trapped in bowls. I told Steven as calmly as I could to pour in the rest of the flour. As if by a miracle my hands came loose and I was able to wash the disgusting gunk off in very hot water. Steven asked, "Aren't you going to bake the cookies, Mommy?" I told him we'd just have to wait for Thanksgiving. I threw the rest of the batter in the garbage. If I'd poured it down the sink I would have had to call the plumber.

At the time of my first and last attempt at making cookies, the chocolate bunny was really disgusting. It had actually become a very interesting chemical experiment. It turned white in Howard Beach and turned brown again in Huntington Station. The white-to-brown changes began occurring more frequently. I put the bunny in a sealed plastic bag and put the bag at the top of the linen closet.

When Stu and I decided to move to Tennessee, our marriage was thirteen years old. Steven was nine, Ellen was six, and the bunny was twelve. I took it down from the closet in order to properly pack it for our move south; I was going to put it in a Styrofoam cooler with ice, so it wouldn't melt (our car was not air conditioned; I'm the one who melted), and I was amazed to find that the bunny had exploded. There was more chocolate dust in the bag than seemed possible from one little old bunny. We could not feel any loyalty or affection for chocolate dust, so we threw it away. The defective lamp and our defective dog, Stella, however, made the move to Knoxville, and both of them seemed to like living there very much.

WHEN THE FIRST RABBIT DIED MY MOTHER THREW UP

On June 8, 1959, three days after Stuart and I graduated from Pratt Institute, we took off for a summer in Europe. It was Stu's twenty-seventh birthday. We'd decided to spend the five thousand dollars that my great-uncle, Alexander Friedman, had left me in his will on a few months of carefree travel. Mother was appalled that I was taking the money that we had groveled for and, after Uncle Doctor had finally had the decency to die at the age of ninety-four, throwing it away on a trip to Europe, of all places. The punch line to a joke that I no longer remember is, "Why would I want to go to Europe? I was born there." Mother, however, said it with the utmost seriousness. She said that Europe was a terrible place. Her memories of Europe *were* terrible. Mother said we could use the money for a down payment on a house. It had taken my parents more than fifteen years to buy a house after they were married. Stuart and I felt that when we earned the money, and could afford it, we would buy a house. Six years later we did. But in 1959 we were young. We had no jobs. We had no children. We had no responsibilities at all, and we were going to Europe.

I wanted to go by boat. When I was a child I had gone to a movie called *Luxury Liner*. I thought it was the most glamorous thing I had ever seen, and I still remember it. I had never been anywhere in my life except New York, where I was born; Pennsylvania to visit Aunt Lydia, Uncle Max, and my cousins; New Jersey to bury my Grandma; and Michigan, where Stuart's family lived. I was ready for the luxury liner of my fantasies.

Stuart told me that when he was returning from the Korean War he had been sick on the boat all the way back from Japan to the United States. I, who grew up three miles from Coney Island, was never sick on anything that moved, or turned you upside down, or whipped you around in a circle. I could ride the Cyclone, the roughest roller coaster in the world, until my baby-sitting money ran out. Stu couldn't watch the merry-go-round without feeling nauseated. But I felt that I couldn't graduate from college one day and wake up in Europe three days later. I needed time to adjust. I assured him a luxury liner was different from a troop transport. After all, I'd seen the movie. Stu said we would compromise by taking the ship to Holland and flying home from Ireland. He took Dramamine. I didn't. I started throwing up before we passed the Statue of Liberty.

As soon as we left New York Harbor they served lunch in the magnificent dining room of my *Luxury Liner* dreams. I couldn't even look at, much less eat, the chicken à la king that the waiter placed in front of me. It bore a horrible resemblance to vomit. The ocean liner was nothing like the rides in Coney Island. The ship looked like a big hotel, but it rocked, very gently, and I couldn't get off it for nine fucking days, unless I threw myself into the Atlantic Ocean, which I was considering. Stu, justifiably getting even, sent postcards to everyone back home, with cartoons he drew of me puking over the rail. He wrote, "This is a picture of Greta, on our way to Europe, poisoning the fish." If we hadn't had airline reservations for the return trip, I might still be there. For months after getting off the boat I felt as if my bed were rocking. I was never so happy to put my feet on solid ground as when we got to Holland. We traveled around Europe for three months and came home exhilarated by the experience. "Greta from Brooklyn" was now a world traveler. We swore we would return, by air of course, every five years. It took us thirty, but we did return.

Someone once told me it was hard to conceive a baby, so when we got back from our trip, we stopped using birth control. I wanted to have a baby sometime in the future. I was twenty-two years old and I wanted to work for a while. I was offered a job as a designer for a creative printer, the John B. Watkins Co., after my first interview. Three weeks later I was pregnant.

When I got the news that my rabbit test was positive, I didn't feel sorry for the rabbit, which had given its life to prove that I was going to have a baby. I felt sorry for myself. In the '50s, if you suspected you were going to have a baby, you gave a urine sample to your doctor and he sent it to a lab. They injected it into a bunny. If the rabbit croaked, you needed to open a savings account immediately, for orthodontics and college.

Who told me it was hard to conceive a child? Why did I believe them? On the day I got the bad news, we had plans to go to a Broadway play and then to dinner with my parents. We were going to celebrate our safe return from the Europe of Mother's nightmares. We were still living in their basement. I don't recall the play, but I remember we went to Chinatown for dinner.

On the drive back to Brooklyn I told my parents that I was pregnant. Mother asked Daddy to stop the car. She got out and threw up. Her baby was having a baby. She said we could continue to live in their basement after I had the baby, and she would help me take care of it, but we decided to move to another basement five blocks away. The rent was eighty dollars a month, and I hoped we would be able to afford it.

I didn't tell the people who had hired me for my first job that I was pregnant until late in my fifth month. By then it could no longer be kept a secret. John Watkins and his younger brother, Scott, owned the company that I worked for. When I told them I would be leaving in three months, Scott was kind, but John Watkins never spoke to me again. I broke the news sadly to Audrey and Fran, the two other artists with whom I worked and who had helped me to break into the working world. Audrey was pleasant enough about it, but Fran, an older woman who had never married and still lived with her mother, was annoyed. She had worked for the company for twenty-five years. She said she had warned John Watkins not to hire me. She told him I was married, young, and would probably get pregnant. When I left at the beginning of my ninth month, Audrey and Fran chipped in and gave me a pretty yellow baby blanket for the carriage. In those days you couldn't know beforehand whether you were going to have a boy or a girl; yellow was the neutral color of choice. I used the blanket to keep both Steven and Ellen snug in the carriage.

I had two weeks of morning sickness and then I felt fine—never better. I'd always hated to eat, but now I was hungry all the time. I was so skinny that my doctor told me I could eat anything I wanted to. Stu and I went for a walk every night and stopped at four different candy stores. I bought an ice-cream cone at each one. I weighed ninety-six pounds before I became pregnant and gained forty-one along the way. I looked like a string bean that had swallowed a watermelon. I was so big that the doctor gave me an X-ray, because he thought I was having twins.

In the first few months I was warm all the time. Pregnancy does that. All those weird little hormones race around in your body, preparing you to be a Mommy. At John B. Watkins my drawing board was right next to the radiator that heated the whole room. I didn't want to tell anyone I was pregnant. I thought they might hire someone else if I did, and I liked my job, so I turned off the heat as soon as I got to work at nine o'clock. At around eleven the people in the office would start to get chilly. I told them it was too warm where I sat, but they wouldn't move my drawing board. Everyone at John B. Watkins got mad at me by eleven o'clock each day that winter. I think they were glad when I left, and by the time I did, so was I. One evening in my eight month, on my way home from work, I raced a guy for a seat on the subway. I beat him to the seat, sliding in just ahead of him. He sat his fat ass right on top of me, and I shoved him off. When he saw how pregnant I was he muttered, "Why don't you stay home where you belong?"

I did freelance work at home until the day before I went to the hospital. Stu said we might have to cut a big half-circle in my drawing board so I could get near my work. After becoming a mother I freelanced at home for the next thirteen years, until I got my second full-time job, working for the University of Tennessee, where I spent twenty-two years designing publications. I took early retirement at the beginning of 1995.

Steven weighed eight-and-a-half pounds when he was born, and I was on the delivery table for less than ten minutes. Stuart, who had taken me to the hospital at midnight, was home sleeping. They had told him it would take a long time. For the anesthetic I had a spinal block right before the delivery and felt no pain. I felt very self-congratulatory and afterward told my friends that I didn't know why women made such a big deal out of having a baby. There was nothing to it. The doctor looked down at me after the easy birth and said to the nurse, "Give me these long, skinny women any day."

The worst part of Steven's birth was when a rabbi called a moehl, who circumcises Jewish boys, came into my room three hours after my delivery smoking a big, fat, smelly cigar. Because I'd had a spinal block, I wasn't allowed to raise my head. I had to lie flat for five hours so that I wouldn't get a violent headache. The rabbi told me the briss (a ceremony in which a Jewish baby boy is welcomed into the faith by having a rabbi remove the foreskin from his penis) would be on Tuesday. I wanted a doctor, not a rabbi—especially not one who leaned over a mother of three hours, puffing cigar smoke in her face—to circumcise my baby. I told him to take his cigar and follow it out of the room. I heard from some other new mothers afterward that the rabbi was also a drunk, so I think I made a good decision.

Stuart designed a birth announcement for Steven. In huge letters it said, "WE'VE HAD IT!" In tiny print in the dot at the bottom of the exclamation point it said, "Steven Paul Eichelbaum. July 19, 1960. 8 1/2 pounds. 20 inches." Even though Steven was the product of an unplanned pregnancy and I was not happy when I found out the rabbit test was positive, I loved being his mother, staying home, and taking care of him. I was never bored. I could watch him for hours. He was a baby who had a sense of humor. He made funny faces to make us laugh. He toilet trained himself when he was a year old. I kept his playpen next to my drawing board and talked to him while I worked. I played classical music for him, thinking he would absorb it and grow into a cultured person (he loves rock music). I have never regretted having a child when I believed I was too young.

When I decided to have a second child I was twenty-five years old and no longer considered myself a child. This time it took me six months to conceive. My second pregnancy was not as easy as my first one was. I threw up every day for months. Two-year-old Steven once stood behind me while I was on my knees on the bathroom floor, throwing up into the toilet. He held my forehead, as I did for him when he was sick to his stomach, and he said, "It's OK Mommy." When I was in my fourth month Stu and I went to see a very upsetting movie called *A Child Is Waiting*. We didn't have any idea what it was about. It starred Judy Garland as the mother of a child with Down's syndrome. By the end of the movie, when they were pulling the child away from his mother to put him in an institution, I was weeping uncontrollably. Stuart almost had to carry me out of the theater. When I got home I was bleeding. I spent a week in bed, taking vitamin E so as not to lose my baby. This time I gained very little weight. Ellen's was a breech birth.

Steven seemed interested in his new sister, but not thrilled to share Mommy and Daddy with a stranger. When Ellen was about a month old I heard a howl from her room. I ran to see what was the matter. Her nose was bright red. Three-year-old Steven, who was standing by her crib, looked me straight in the eye and said, "I didn't pinch her nose."

Stuart designed Ellen's birth announcement also. It had a drawing of Steven saying:

I just got a baby sister.
Her name is Ellen Rae Eichelbaum.
She was born August 15th
and weighed 5 pounds 15 1/2 ounces.
I need her like a hole in the head.

Now, when I look at that announcement, I'm horrified, and I wonder if it was prophecy.

From birth, Ellen was a difficult child. Sometimes she refused to drink from her bottle or to eat anything at all; in the first few months she lost weight. She howled when Stu picked her up, upsetting him so much that he stopped trying. She was headstrong from the day she was born and always did exactly as she pleased. She resisted any attempt at toilet training. I hoped that she would become toilet trained by the time she entered kindergarten. I tried hard not to compare her to Steven, who potty trained himself when he was a year old. When she was three and soiled her diaper she gave me her "Gotcha!" look, narrowing her eyes and smiling a sly half-smile.

When she was three-and-a half, I lost patience. For the first time in the battle of the potty I tried punishment, knowing even as I did that it was a mistake. After her lunch I put Ellen in her crib and told her she could come out and play when she said she needed to use the potty. Not before. She stayed there for hours, clean and dry, playing with her toys. By early evening she was still in her crib.

After dinner we were going to a children's musical, "Camelia," that two friends, Alan Arnold and Burt Wolfe, had written. I wanted Ellen to see it. I had forgotten all about the performance when I confined her to her crib-prison. For many months, as they were writing it, we had all been listening to Alan and Burt perform the play in Alan's living room—we knew the words and music by heart. I told Ellen that we were going to see "Camelia" on a real stage, so I was going to take her out of the crib so she could see it with us. I dressed her in pretty clothes and, as an extra incentive, tried bribery. I promised to play ball with her all day the next day, if she would just tell me when she needed to use the potty. Ellen loved the play, and clapped wildly with the rest of the audience when it was over. As soon as we got home she shit in her diaper, gave me her "Gotcha!" look and said, "I don't want to play ball with you anyway." I didn't know at the time that it would become her motto.

For my 50th birthday Ellen sent me a card, wishing me a lovely day and saying she loved me. The printed card said: Mom, out of all the things you taught me, one of them sure comes in handy each and every day of my life. . . . Potty Training. (I can't thank you enough.) Happy Birthday. Ellen added: I didn't want to play ball with you anyway, and signed the card, "Your Little Monster."

Although she was such a strange child, I was delighted with her and her weirdness; it was so charming in a child. Ellen was imaginative, mischievous, and witty. She was pretty and petite, with curly, reddish-blond hair and enormous brown eyes that looked straight at you when she spoke—and she spoke quite candidly. Once, when she was three, she walked up to a homely woman on the street and said, "You look like a witch!" I almost died of embarrassment. I thought it would make it worse if I apologized to the woman, so I grabbed Ellen, continued walking, and had a long talk with her about being careful not to hurt people's feelings.

I enrolled Ellen in Dancer's Studio when she was seven. She loved it but when she started to get good as a dancer, five years later, she quit—a pattern that would last for the rest of her life. Her friend Nancy, from Mount Olive, also went to Dancer's Studio, and sometimes I drove Nancy to class with us when her mother was busy. I loved watching the children dance and I didn't ever ask Nancy's mother to take Ellen to class.

Nancy flashed me an adorable smile the first time I met her. Her front tooth was missing. Nancy told Ellen that the tooth fairy had come during the night and left her a quarter. Ellen said, "Do you know what the tooth fairy does with your tooth?" Nancy replied, "She saves it in her golden pocketbook." Ellen said, "No. First she takes a hammer and smashes it to smithereens. Then she flushes it down the toilet." Nancy started to cry and I told her that Ellen was only fooling—but it was time for another talk when we got home.

In dance class, when she was eight, the children were asked to make up a dance—to be something that was not human. The other kids were birds or turtles or cats. I thought surely Ellen would be a frog, but she chose to be a cigarette. At he end of her cigarette's life cycle she put herself out by rubbing her head on the floor. The whole class laughed and applauded.

In her first dance recital Ellen was a butterfly, dancing to the music of Eric Satie. After she died, the first time I heard that music on the radio, I broke down and wept and then wrote a poem:

ELLEN DANCING

I hear the song
soaring, floating
You are seven.
    A butterfly
yellow and green wings
dancing with other
small butterflies.

A white moth
drawn to the flame
Twenty-six.
    Topless
under harsh lights
dancing
alone.

I once scribbled down a sentence on a scrap of paper. I can't remember where I heard it, who said it, or where it's from, but it made me think of Ellen in Seattle: "Butterflies are hard to find in the rain."

Ellen wanted to wear the same dress every day when she was in first grade. It was green-and-blue plaid. I washed it every night and she put it on every morning. Her classmates must have thought she was the poorest child in school, but she didn't care. I called her "Hypothetical Ellen," because she always asked me the strangest hypothetical questions. She once asked, "What if the sky was green and the grass was blue? Would I have to walk on my hands?" I thought it was funny when, on our daily walks, she sang, "Step on a crack. Break your mother's back," and proceeded to step on all the cracks. Maybe she was trying to tell me something, but I didn't get it.

Ellen's best friend when we lived in Huntington Station was a boy named Drew Goodman. They met when they were both five and in the same car pool for nursery school. After Ellen committed suicide I wrote to Drew to tell him what had happened. He wrote me a letter and told me about the first time he met Ellen and how vivid his memory of her still is. He told me stories about her that I had never heard. One was of Ellen rubbing two sticks together near a pile of leaves in his backyard and his terror that she would start a fire. He said the more he objected, the more fun she had. He told his father, not to be a tattletale but because he was merely trying to save Huntington Station from devastation by fire. He wrote that when he read in my letter that Ellen had been performing as a stand-up comedian before she died, he immediately thought of that story and the pleasure she got from rubbing those two sticks together.

My friend in Huntington Station, Gloria Arnold, lived directly across the street from us. One day she told me that she had seen Ellen, who was four, crossing the street without looking first. I told Ellen *never* to do that *ever again*. I spanked her bottom. She never spoke another word to Gloria for our remaining time in Huntington Station.

When Ellen was in her twenties and living in Nashville, she came to Huntington Station to visit my father and Billie. She decided to call Gloria and try to see her. Gloria didn't recognize Ellen's Southern drawl, and sounding confused, asked who she was. Ellen said "You know, Ellen—the little girl that crossed the street without looking."

Ellen was a child born into an achieving and competitive family and perhaps she never made peace with that. Stu, Steven, and I entered our work in contests and won awards. Ellen once entered a contest that she found on the back of a cereal box. It was called the Something Green Contest. She drew a picture of a frog. She won an honorable mention and, although quite young, was still aware that everyone who entered the contest won an honorable mention. She once wrote a paper that stated: "My mother won blah, blah, blah. My father won blah, blah, blah. My brother won blah, blah, blah. But *I* won an honorable mention in the Something Green Contest."

Although Steven and Ellen were good friends when they were children, had their own secret language, and often played together after school, Ellen's sibling rivalry with Steven never abated. I never understood its intensity. I believe I treated both children the same way, but maybe that's an illusion. If anything, I felt I favored Ellen because she seemed so fragile.

Stuart, however, never learned to talk to children (perhaps because his father rarely talked to him, and when he did it was with an unhealthy dose of sarcasm). His mother told me she yelled at her children a lot. Times were hard and she had a difficult husband to contend with. Stuart needed to succeed in spite of his father, from whom he never received the slightest encouragement. He did succeed. He is the most competitive person I've ever known. Stu is the oldest of four boys (his twin brother arrived ten minutes after he did). I wish he'd had a younger sister. A boy can learn a lot from a sister. If nothing else, he learns how to talk to a girl. Stuart sometimes talked baby talk to the children when they were at an age to resent it. He loved Steven and Ellen, but never quite got the hang of how to talk to them when they were little.

Stuart once accused Ellen of cheating at Old Maid. She *was* cheating, but who cared? She was only six years old. But Stu just didn't like to lose. If it had been a question of morality, I might have gone along with it. Maybe not. Stuart makes Abraham Lincoln look dishonest and I still have my family's criminal streak. Ellen also cheated at Scrabble and frequently beat the grown-ups. (Ellen took after me.) She never got caught but confessed it to me years later.

Steven, who took after his father, never cheated at anything. From the time he was a baby he had an almost photographic memory. He learned the alphabet before he was two. He spoke in complete sentences when he was two and a half. He was also small for his age. When I got him on an airplane without paying for him by claiming he was younger than three (he was three and a half), he almost blew my cover by raising his hand and saying, "Oh stewardess, would you bring me a Coke?"

When Steven was three I taught him to play Concentration, a game that involved turning all the cards in a deck face down and then turning over two at a time. If you turned over two that matched, you kept them, and whoever wound up with the most cards won. You had to concentrate and memorize where the cards were. Steven beat me most of the time and always beat his father. As far as memory is concerned, Stuart is the exact opposite of his son. He can never think sequentially or remember where he put anything. I would be rich if I had a dollar for every time Stuart lost his car keys or his wallet or his comb or the book he was reading. If he is in a car and needs directions, he will concentrate on the first instruction and then pretend to listen to the rest. When he gets to the first point he has to stop and ask someone else for directions.

Once, by some insane fluke when Steven was four years old, Stu beat him at Concentration. Steven ran into his room and threw himself on his bed. When I went in to ask why he was crying he choked out, "Daddy beat me at Concentration." Playing my motherly role as the mediator and teacher I said, "Now Steven, you have to learn that sometimes you win and sometimes you lose. That's life." He stopped crying long enough to tell me that he already knew that, but said, "Daddy didn't have to say, 'Ha, ha, ha, I trounced the kid!' "

Steven was never a team player. He played tennis, not baseball, and he liked singles better than doubles. He liked to win by himself, like his daddy. When we moved from Lindenwood, the concrete village in Howard Beach, to the suburban town of Huntington Station, we finally had our own front and back yards. One day, after a huge snowfall, Stuart, Steven, and Ellen went outside to build a snowman. I watched them from the window while I made a hot lunch. Ellen, who was two, was helping her father create a snowman masterpiece—taller than Stuart, with black button eyes, a carrot nose, pebbles for teeth. Steven, who was five, was struggling mightily to build his own. After about an hour of intense effort, he came storming into the house, crying. I asked him what was the matter, and he said, "Daddy said that my snowman looks like his snowman's dog."

Stuart and Steven compete in sports to this day. When Steven started beating his father in tennis, Stu took up running. Stu was what is known as a tennis hacker. He won only one trophy and that was for losing in the first round. The trophy was a joke. The player on it didn't have a racquet and it sat on his dresser for years. Stu was very fast, he could always get to the ball, but when he did he would lose his concentration and hit it just about anywhere. Steven is an excellent player and he has received many trophies on which the player has a racquet.

As for running, however, Stu is a champion. From the day he started, he almost always has won in his age category. There are now hundreds of trophies and plaques cluttering up our house. Stu wanted to take paintings off the walls and replace them with running awards, but that's where I drew the line. Full-page stories about him in the newspaper have called him a legend. It is not easy to live with a legend.

Steven runs a lot faster than his father but never wins his age category. At least not now, when most of the best runners are his age. I once told Stu that the reason he wins his category all the time is that everyone else who would run at his age is already dead. But actually, he beats most of the younger guys, too.

Stuart, Steven, and Steven's wife, Belinda, who also runs, participated in Knoxville's biggest race, the EXPO 10,000, in May 1995. The EXPO 10K, a six-mile race, is a short distance for Stuart, who has run twenty marathons. (A marathon, for those of you lucky enough not to know, is twenty-six miles.) Stu, as always, won first place in his category, but Steven, who had a much faster time (even though he forgot to bring his racing shoes) didn't win anything. Belinda, a woman after my own heart, runs for the fun of it, a concept inconceivable to Stuart and Steven. When Steven and Belinda got back to Boston, Steven wrote us the following letter:

> *Thanks for a very nice weekend. Belinda and I had a lot of fun at the family functions, running in EXPO, etc. Although Dad's time was slower than my snowman's dog could run . . . uuuppps, dat's very cute dat you won your age category! I can see that once I wear my racing shoes, we'll have to go to the races in separate cars since I won't be able to stand around until you finish.... Okay, enough childish taunting! I realize that "he of few running trophies must tread lightly" (was that Confucius or Goethe?).*

Children *never* forget.

Steven and Ellen wrote poetry, like their grandmother. Steven, when he was ten, wrote a haiku called "Bark":

The bark of the tree
Is protecting the whole tree
From a tragedy!

I think he could have been writing about Ellen. Her bark was never thick enough to protect her from the tragedy that would become her life. When I congratulated her on graduating from the University of Tennessee with high honors, her reply was that Steven had graduated with highest honors. When they were children I once asked Steven not to brag to Ellen about his achievements. He said, "I can't pretend to be stupid to please Ellen," and of course, he couldn't. Ellen apparently decided that if Steven was going to be the good boy, she was going to be the bad girl. The only area where she was way ahead of him was in sexual experience. Ellen, when she was sixteen, wrote and illustrated a booklet, drawing stick figures in various sexual positions, which she presented to Steven called "How to Fuck.'"

• • •

At the end of October 1970, when she was seven, Ellen left me this note:

Dear Mom,
  I ran away but only for a week! You want me to go four weeks probably. I took an apple, five Hershey kisses, and three Oreo cookies. I left

141

*without my coat. (She had started to write Dont
worry, but crossed it out) I took my Frog with me.
I sneeked out the front door.*

Love, Ellen

I asked Steven if he knew where his sister had gone.
He said she was sitting by the side of the road at the top
of the hill at the end of our street and eating some Oreo
cookies. I asked him if he knew why Ellen had run
away, and he said she was angry that she had been
made to go to bed while the rest of us watched *The Six
Wives of Henry VIII* on TV.

An hour later Ellen came back without the
Hershey's kisses and the Oreo cookies and put the apple
back in the refrigerator. I couldn't help smiling. I told
her I was sorry she was upset, but she was too little to
watch *The Six Wives of Henry VIII* on TV. She wrote a
poem titled "I'm Too Little," but I've lost it.

The next time Ellen ran away she was seventeen
and there was nothing to smile about. It was a time
when we were barely speaking, although she was still
living at home. She was hostile, out of control, and we
all knew it. Steven was a junior at the University of
Tennessee, Ellen a senior at Doyle High. Steven's
roommates, Colin and Andy, were having their weekly
Sunday dinner at our house. The first time Steven
brought them home (along with his laundry) they
brought their guitars and sang for us. Stu barbecued
steaks. I made a huge salad, baked potatoes and a
chocolate cake, and they were wolfed down with such
gusto that I told Colin and Andy they were invited to
our house every Sunday, but they would have to sing for
their suppers. In the many months that followed, they
always brought their guitars and sang folk songs for us.
Steven always brought his laundry. I joked that, like

Pavlov's dog, we couldn't salivate without the sound of the washing machine going.

Colin and Andy were both handsome and smart. Dark-haired Colin wanted to be a doctor (he is), and blond Andy wanted to go into the Air Force (he did). I liked them both. I was no lover of having company for dinner every week, but I invited them because I wanted Ellen to see that there really were boys that were smart, cool, and good-looking who didn't take drugs and worked hard in school. Ellen fell in love with both of them and when Colin and Andy were at our house Ellen stopped being sullen and became a charming, bubbly girl—a part she played to perfection. She had left the awkward age behind. Everyone commented on how pretty she was. The braces were off her teeth and she had a winning, infectious smile. Her body was now the well-developed body of a woman. She was always so funny and quick, and I think both young men were quite taken with her. At the time, Colin wanted to be a psychiatrist and was probably also intrigued by what he knew about her deviant behavior (because Steven had told him). Among the papers that Steven sent home from Seattle was a folder titled "Things That I'm Proud Of." At the top of the very short list was "Getting Andy to sleep with me." Actually, I was to learn later, Ellen came on to many of Steven's friends and Andy wasn't the only one to have had sex with her.

On the Sunday night Ellen left with a girlfriend, they were both dressed in very short shorts and tight halter-tops. They looked like a couple of hookers. Stu, Steven, Colin, Andy, and I had decided not to even look at her, but of course I did out of the corner of my eye. Ellen had called earlier to say she was leaving and was coming home to get some things. She had reached the point where everyone who cared about her felt helpless and allowing her to create a self-serving scene with us begging her to stay was more than we were willing to do. She and her friend came into the house giggling, didn't look at any of us, and walked back to Ellen's bedroom, where she packed some clothes and stuff in a pillowcase and left in someone's car. We finished our dinners, but we all felt more than a little sick. I had never seen Ellen's friend before, didn't know her name, and didn't want to. They both looked unbearably smug, role-playing heroines in their own drama, as our daughter escaped the uncool parents and bookish brother.

I think now of a stanza from Ellen's poem "The Bad Day."

> I think I'll jump in the seven seas,
> but to do that I'd need six more me's
> I think I'll draw six more me's
> So I can jump in the seven seas.

I wonder now how she knew, all the way back then, that she would spend the rest of her life reinventing herself, changing roles, playing parts unsuited for her. As I write this it is hard to believe that we didn't try to stop her or call the police after she had left. Somehow, perhaps wrongly, I felt she wouldn't go far. I thought of her coming home with the apple when she was seven. We knew where she was. Friends had called to say she was wandering around on "the strip," the street in the college area that many of the bars and fast-food restaurants were on. She and her friend had moved in with a guy who tended bar at one of the joints that served liquor to minors. The three of them slept in the same bed, she told me later.

Ellen was gone for four days. At 11 P.M. the fourth night we got a call from a man who was the manager of Pizza Hut, where the girls were hanging out. He said our daughter and a friend were sitting in a booth and wanted to come home. They had told him no such thing. He had asked Ellen what her name was and had no trouble looking up our number, as we are the only Eichel in the Knoxville telephone directory. He was a nice person, Stu told me later, and thought he was helping two bereft waifs. Or maybe he just wanted the slutty-looking teenagers out of his Pizza Hut. Stu went to get them, but when he arrived they were acting like two tough little bitches, refusing to leave. Stu said that if Ellen didn't get in the car he would report her to the police, and if her friend wanted a ride he would drive her back to her house. Sullenly they got in the car, but then they told Stu they wanted to go back to the bartender whose room they were staying in. Stu drove straight to the police station and told Ellen and her friend that he was reporting them as runaways and to get out of the car. They refused and he drove Ellen's friend home (we never did learn her name) and then brought a furious Ellen back to the house.

The next day Stu found out where the bartender they were staying with worked and gave him fifty dollars.

"Why did you *do* that?" Ellen screamed when Stu told her.

"Because he didn't kill you," Stu said.

Twelve years later, on March 29, 1993, Ellen ran away for the last time.

Ellen thought she was ugly and no one could change her mind. She told us she had no friends, but she had many. The letters that Ellen saved were from both young men and women, and older men and women. The common thread uniting them was that they all loved her and told her so. She just never believed them.

Today Steven is still bringing us joy. Ellen is still causing us pain. Ellen was planned. Steven was not. *The best laid plans of mice and men often go astray.* Although the bitterness and rage I felt upon hearing of Ellen's death have abated, I will always feel such a terrible sadness for the child who had such a painful birth and such a painful life. We never understood her or the depth of her depression. I also feel pain for all the people who invested so much love in Ellen, who was never able to accept it.

I remember how elated I was the day I found out that my rabbit test was positive. I was grateful to the rabbit that had given its life to prove that I was pregnant with Ellen. When I reflect back on the day we got the news that Ellen had killed herself, I think, *if I had my life to live over again, the second rabbit would not have died.*

FROM THE BIG APPLE TO
THE BIG ORANGE

There was always a wind blowing where we lived in Howard Beach, in the inaptly named Lindenwood Village. There was not a single tree of any kind, much less a linden tree, and a bunch of six-story apartment buildings surrounded by concrete could not be called a village. We moved there in 1962. I don't think I ever hated where I lived until moving to that concrete village. Our address was 88-08 151st Avenue. It was a co-op apartment and to buy it we used the money my daddy had saved for my wedding gift. After Daddy finished paying off Uncle Max the ten dollars a month on his loan for the down payment on their house, he continued putting that money in the bank for me and gave me $1,100 when I got married.

Because Stuart and I had lived in basement apartments for six years, we thought it would be nice to look down from the window instead of up, so we chose an apartment, 6B, on the sixth floor. We were wrong. The view out the window of our top-floor apartment was of "Aqueduct Racetrack" and identical apartment buildings as ugly as our own. We were just a few miles from Idlewild Airport, later renamed Kennedy Airport, and sometimes I would clock the jets roaring overhead

147

at one every fifteen seconds. They were so close I could practically wave to the pilots. People said I would get used to the noise, but I never did. What's more, the building residents threw their garbage into incinerator chutes conveniently located on every floor and the windows to *that* "nonview" were always covered with a thin coating of soot. Perhaps we shouldn't have lived on the top floor.

Lindenwood Village was where we were living the day John Kennedy was killed. I had just taken Steven and Ellen down to the playground. A woman opened the window of her second-floor apartment and shouted down to the mothers and children below that the president had been shot. No one thought Kennedy would die, but we all rushed back to our apartments to turn on the TV and see what was happening.

The day was chilly. Steven, who was three years old at the time, had just been subjected to fifteen minutes of bundling to get into his snowsuit, hat, and gloves. He was looking forward to playing with the other children on the slide and being pushed on the swing, so he was not prepared to leave the playground so quickly. Although Steven was usually a cooperative child, he started kicking and screaming as I dragged him back to the apartment on the sixth floor. Ellen, who was three months old, was probably happy to get back to the warm apartment and out of the confining carriage, where she was tucked under a heavy woolen blanket.

Everyone left the playground and in our separate apartments we watched our TVs as the horrible events unfolded in Dallas. I wept while poor little Steven, mystified by my change of behavior, cuddled up in my arms. How could a mother explain to a three-year-old child what was happening? I remembered the day in 1945 when I was eight and the news came over the radio that Roosevelt had died and how frightened I felt seeing Mother, Daddy, and Grandma hysterically weeping in front of me. Ellen slept peacefully in her crib. When evening came I gave the children their dinners and put them to bed. I think Steven, who usually waited to see his daddy when he came home from work, was happy to go into the bedroom he shared with Ellen and escape the frightening grief of his mother.

When Stuart came home and saw me crying, he panicked. He thought something had happened to Steven or Ellen or that one of our parents had died. He had heard that the president had been shot earlier in the day, but never thinking it was a serious injury, had promptly forgotten about it.

Stuart and I, like almost everyone else in the country that night, sat transfixed before the glowing tube, watching replay after replay of the coffin being loaded onto *Air Force One* and of Jackie Kennedy in her blood-and-brain-spattered suit looking bewildered as Lyndon Johnson was being sworn in. I hadn't cooked dinner, and if I had, neither of us would have been able to eat it. Later we learned Jackie Kennedy had refused to take the pink suit off, saying, "Let them see what they have done." Somehow we all knew that nothing would ever be the same. Looking back on the years since that day, I realize nothing ever was.

Stu and I watched late into the night. I don't know if we went to sleep. The next day, Saturday, November 23rd, we turned on the television and saw the arrest of Lee Harvey Oswald and heard of the shooting of the forgotten man, Officer Tippet. The day after that we watched as Jack Ruby shot Oswald to death before the eyes of the nation. I fed the children, but we hardly ate anything ourselves. We were in shock along with the rest of the country. As they were moving Kennedy's furniture out of the White House, we wept even harder when they loaded his rocking chair onto the moving truck. We wondered why they had to show that. It was almost as awful as seeing his flag-draped coffin being loaded onto *Air Force One*.

November 24th was the first birthday of our friends Norm and Margie Kurtz's son, Stephen. They had invited a lot of people to his birthday party, set for three o'clock that afternoon. Margie called me up and asked if I thought they should cancel the party. Although it hardly seemed an appropriate time to celebrate anything, I suggested she go ahead with it. We could all use a break and turn off the television for a while. There was nothing any of us could do to make things turn out differently. Everyone she had invited came and brought their children. We celebrated birth and tried to forget about death, if just for a while.

I had dressed Steven in a red jacket, a red bow tie, and a white shirt that he always managed to stain with drool in the first five minutes. Steven, at three, was the oldest child there. He knew the words to a lot of songs and loved to entertain, so Margie asked him if he would sing a song for everyone.

We had no idea what he would sing. Throwing his arms out wide, he belted out in his surprisingly deep voice "Fly Me to the Moon." Tears filled everyone's eyes and several people started to weep. Were they all thinking, as I was, that President Kennedy had promised the country that we would beat the Russians and land a man on the moon during that decade, and now he would not live to see it? Now we're sharing the space station Mir with the Russians and a collector is auctioning off John Kennedy's things—even one of his rocking chairs.

I couldn't wait to get out of that Lindenwood apartment and move to a house. In 1965, after three years at Lindenwood Village, we moved to Huntington Station. It took us six months to find a buyer for our co-op and we lost all the money that my father had saved for my wedding present.

Huntington Station probably got its name because the Long Island Railroad station that served the affluent township of Huntington was there. It was the lower-priced part of the township, and the train ran right through it. We lived in a development called Foxwood. Why do they name low-income developments after English manors? I guess it could have been worse—they could have called it Foxwood Estates.

The neighborhood was pretty, with big yards (unlike Brooklyn) and lots of trees. After our apartment in Howard Beach, it was like we had moved to the country. When I look back on the four years we lived in Huntington Station, I realize they were some of the happiest years of my life. None of us had much money, but we were rich in many other ways. People entertained their friends for dinner—even I, who always hated to cook. We hardly ever ate out. There was no cable TV. We stayed up half the night talking, arguing, thinking we could solve the problems of the world. We were all so intense—still idealists in spite of the murders of President John Kennedy, Senator Robert Kennedy, and Dr. Martin Luther King, Jr. We all had a dream. We were young and hadn't a clue about the tragedies that awaited us.

Our house, on one-quarter acre, was white with black shutters, and there were two flowering cherry trees in the front yard. It was the first time I had ever lived in a "mixed" neighborhood. Most of the people weren't Jewish. Our house cost $18,500, and the payments were $140 a month. In the 1960s that was affordable for many working people, so Foxwood had teachers, artists, musicians, a dancer, an actor, truck drivers, and salesmen of various things. No doctors or lawyers or stockbrokers, though.

The day we moved in I heard an awfully loud noise while the man from Bell Telephone was installing our phone. "What the hell is that?" I asked. "Honey, that's the LIRR whistle," he answered. "Where is it, and why does it whistle?" He explained there was a railroad crossing nearby. When I looked out the bedroom window I could see that it was about 200 yards away. The real estate agent had failed to mention it, of course. I never got used to the sound of the whistle, especially when the last train of the night came through, at about 2 A.M. Stu's father, though, when he visited us, said he loved the sound of the train whistle. It reminded him of growing up in Dover, New Jersey, hearing a train, and wanting to be on it.

Later that day a precocious seven-year-old girl rang the bell and primly introduced herself. "My name is Pamela Arnold. Could I come in and look at your stuff?" We were just hanging the paintings. She got very excited and exclaimed, "Oh, you have paintings on the walls, just like my parents! Come over and meet them. We live right across the street." We are friends with the Arnolds to this day. Pamela's mother, Gloria, was a piano teacher. Her father, Alan, taught music in a local high school and is a violinist. He was teaching Pamela's brother, Paul, to play the violin.

Paul now plays the violin with the Philadelphia Symphony Orchestra, and Alan has written music that has been performed by them, as well as by the London Symphony. Alan eventually quit teaching high school and now arranges music for orchestras all over the world. In 1975 Gloria gave up teaching piano from her home and became a kindergarten teacher in a well-to-do school in Huntington. Many of her students, however, had fathers who were in the Mafia.

There was a black neighborhood about two streets away. The children who lived there came into the white area only on Halloween to trick or treat. One summer day, about five of the black children came over to play. Steven and Ellen had never played with black children before, because, despite all the liberal talk, the neighborhoods in the North were as segregated as any in the South. I thought the only way Steven and Ellen wouldn't be afraid was to become friends.

I invited the kids in for milk shakes and then asked them if they wanted to play in the small pool we had in the backyard. The friendship lasted for three days. On the fourth day a car pulled up in front of my house, and a black woman coldly asked me if her children were there. I said I didn't know who her children were, but there were some kids playing in the backyard. She asked a younger woman with her to go check. When the children came to the front of the house, she began slapping their faces, screaming, "I told you never to come here, didn't I?" Smack. "Didn't I?" Smack. Steven and Ellen were horrified and stayed in their rooms for the rest of the day. I explained to them that the woman was afraid for her children because some people in the neighborhood didn't like black people. One of the children, Jimmy, kept coming back anyway, at least for a while. He had a lot of courage.

I was furious at Jimmy's mother. I wanted to scream at her, "I asked them to play here. Your hating me because I'm white is no better than someone hating you because you're black." She gave me no chance to speak, however, but drove away with her crying children. This was at the end of the 1960s, when both the Black Panther Party and Black Nationalism were making their presence known. I had to keep reminding myself that Jimmy's mother was afraid for her children and I should try to understand her anger.

At around this same time, Stu was working at the last job he would have in New York before we left for Tennessee. One of his projects was to design an ad for a pharmaceutical company that produced medication to fight hypertension, a disorder prevalent among black people. The ad was to have a photo of a man coming home from work; his daughter would be jumping into his arms as he came through the door. Stu wanted to use our house for the interior and the Arnolds' house across the street in the background. The models, who were black, waited at our house until the photographer arrived. As soon as the photo shoot was finished and the models had left, our phone started ringing. People wanted to know if we were selling our house to blacks.

When Ellen started nursery school I met Marion Goodman, the mother of another child who would be in our car pool. She was a dancer—a bright and beautiful woman with flaming red hair. She said when she was in her twenties she had been the only Jewish chorus girl in the Catskills. Ellen and Drew, her son, became instant friends, and Marion and I became soul mates. Her husband, Arthur, was an actor who sold burglar alarms so the family could eat. We all became close friends, some of the closest I have ever had. Marion and Arthur were both political activists and got me to design posters for Senator Eugene McCarthy, who was running for president in 1968. Arthur was an alternate delegate at the infamous Democratic convention that year in Chicago. After we moved to Knoxville in 1969 Marion and I wrote letters to each other once a week. Her letters are a vivid history of the early seventies, when our country was at war in Vietnam and with itself.

In our tenth year in Knoxville, Marion and Arthur finally were able to make plans to come visit us. We always saw them on our annual trips to New York, but this year, 1979, they would visit us for Christmas. Marion was working in the Carter White House and Arthur was finishing law school.

In early December Arthur called and told us that Marion had been killed in an automobile accident the day after Thanksgiving. A sixteen-year-old on drugs had run a stop sign and smashed into Marion's side of the car, killing her. She was the first friend of mine to die. I loved her and miss her to this day. I still have all of her letters. I still have all of Ellen's too.

Ten years after Marion's death, when we had been living in Knoxville for almost twenty years, we got a phone call from Drew Goodman. He was living in Denver, worked as the sports announcer for Colorado State University, and was in Knoxville to broadcast the football game against the University of Tennessee. We asked him if he could have dinner with us. Although we hadn't seen him for many years, we recognized him at once. He looked exactly the same, only taller. I remembered how I used to fantasize that he would someday marry Ellen. Later, when I told Stu about this fantasy, he said, "Why would you want to do that to Drew? He's such a nice guy."

During the course of the evening Drew said he used to be jealous of me because his mother always seemed to be writing letters to me and wouldn't let him read them, although she did read certain portions aloud to him. He said his greatest sadness was that, because she died when he was sixteen, he never got to know his mother when he became an adult. I sent several of Marion's letters to Drew after his visit to Knoxville.

When I wrote to Drew about Ellen's death, he wrote me a letter telling me of his sorrow about it. He said when they were in high school he and Ellen wrote to each other, and Ellen sent him her picture. Drew said he thought, "Wow, how pretty she's become and how busty she looks." He remembered a letter I had written to his mother about Ellen's disappointment at being so flat-chested. He said the picture rekindled thoughts of marrying his nursery school sweetheart. He wished he had found the time to call her and rekindle their friendship. Somehow, though, they never managed to see each other again.

. . .

In early May of 1969, a classified ad changed our lives forever. Both Steven and Ellen were now in school, and for the first time in my life I had some time all to myself. I was relaxing on the chaise lounge on the patio—the concrete area outside the kitchen door where suburbanites keep lounges and barbecue grills. I was watching my two-month-old puppy, Stella, and thumbing through *Advertising Age,* a trade publication, when the ad caught my eye. It said:

> Wanted: Art Director. How would you like to live ten minutes from the office, half an hour from the Great Smoky Mountains, and work for one of the Southeast's best advertising agencies?

"Bingo!" I said to the puppy.

We had been living in Huntington Station for four years. Stuart had been working as an art director on Madison Avenue for ten years. He was commuting three hours a day. His life was an endless pattern: drive the car to the station; take the Long Island Railroad to Penn Station in Manhattan; take the subway to Fifty-seventh Street; walk the rest of the way to his office; work very hard; turn around; follow the same route in reverse. He had recently started a job that didn't even interest him, working for a company that advertised pharmaceutical products. At the time there were not many other choices. He had just been fired by the large advertising agency where he had worked for the previous five years. It was nothing personal. They fired his whole group. We'd finally had enough of the Big Apple. Stuart had the talent, but not the roll-over-anyone-who-gets-in-your-way-and-if-it's-your-grandmother-well-tough-luck-granny type of personality it took to survive as an adman in New York. If he did, I probably wouldn't have loved him. Stuart could never be another rat in the rat race. He was actually fired from three different jobs for laughing at the boss. Stu never liked living in New York, the city where I grew up and the city that I loved. When I would say to him, "Hurry up or we'll miss our train!" he would answer, "If it's our train, it will wait for us."

At first Stu had dreamed of going back to Detroit, where he grew up. He did get a job there, at the beginning of his career. It lasted for two days. When he went out there Stuart discovered he didn't even *like* Detroit. Before this quick episode we had thrown a big going-away party in our basement apartment on East Twenty-ninth Street and all of our friends brought us presents. We never did give them back, though we lived in New York for nine more years.

So when I saw the ad about living ten minutes from the office and near the Great Smoky Mountains (when we took a vacation, we often headed for mountains), I wrote a letter answering it. Just a short note with some brief information. When Stu got home from work, pissed off and exhausted as usual, I told him I had written a letter from him to an ad agency in Knoxville, and he should sign his name to it. I put a pen in his hand and pointed to the spot. He signed it without even looking at the letter.

A week later Stuart received a response from Arthur Lavidge, of Lavidge and Associates in Knoxville, asking for some more information about him. Where had he gone to school, where had he worked, what had he done, what did he read, where had he traveled, what were his strengths and weaknesses, and why did he want to leave New York? Stella, the pug, and I sat on the patio, and I answered the letter.

> *Dear Mr. Lavidge,*
>
> *Thank you for your letter, interest, and brief description of your company. You asked why I want to leave New York.*
>
> *I now live on the beautiful north shore of Long Island. I have a lovely home. Play tennis every weekend. Swim all summer. Ice-skate all winter. And commute three hours a day on the highly undependable Long Island Railroad. Did you really say no one lives more than ten minutes away from work?*

I answered all of the questions Mr. Lavidge's asked in his letter—except one. When Stu came home that night, I told him he had gotten a letter from Lavidge and Associates, the agency in Knoxville, and that I was writing them a reply. I said, "I wrote down your greatest strengths, but they wanted to know your greatest weakness, and I don't want to tell them you're crazy." He barely glanced up from reading the newspaper. He said to tell them his greatest weakness was strawberry shortcake. It was the best line in the letter, which he signed but didn't read. I ended Stu's letter:

> *I am looking for a company to grow with. One that can use to the fullest what I feel I have to offer. I am looking for a city that offers the pleasant living and congenial way of life we now have, but without the arduous commute. I would like to see my children before they are tucked away for the night.*
>
> > *Sincerely,*
> > *Stu Eichel*

Mr. Lavidge also asked for some samples of Stu's work so I asked him to put together some samples that I could send along with his résumé and the unread letter, which he did, reluctantly. I think he was humoring me, but I just knew he would get that job.

The next week we got a letter from Arthur Lavidge, president of the agency, thanking Stu "for his interest in them and sending samples of his excellent work," but telling him they had already hired another man. He invited Stu to drop by if he was ever in the area. Like we would just happen to be passing through Knoxville, Tennessee. I cried. I couldn't understand how they could give Stu's job to someone else.

One month later Stu received another letter from Art Lavidge saying that although he had originally applied for the job of art director, they had filled the position before they had a chance to talk to him. Art Lavidge said, "I was very favorably impressed with your summary, the samples of your work, and with your correspondence." He asked if Stu would be interested in being the creative director of the agency. I was jumping up and down when I read that letter. Being a creative director means that you are in charge of the entire creative department of an agency—both the art *and* the copy. It was the chance of a lifetime, one that could not have happened in New York for someone like Stu, who would never play the Madison Avenue game.

The next day Stu flew to Knoxville. When he got there he had to ask the stewardess as he left the plane which state he was in. He suspected he was somewhere in the South, because it was extremely hot. She told him he was in Tennessee. Driving his rented car to the hotel he saw a billboard that said, "Welcome to Big Orange Country," and wondered what it meant. "The Big Orange" was what everyone (except the faculty) called the University of Tennessee. The school's colors, worn by its athletic teams, are orange and white. College football, as we would find out, is a matter of life and death in Knoxville. We had been to one football game in our lives. Jim Nickel, Stu's ex-boss, the man whose entire group had been fired, had season tickets to the New York Jets, and he invited us to join him and his wife at Shea Stadium one Sunday. I was never so miserable in my life. Except for the North Pole, Shea Stadium in December is the coldest place on earth. Pratt didn't have a football team and I have no idea what the school's colors were. I am glad Pratt had a basketball team, though, and that I went to the game that was to start my relationship with Stuart.

Stu met with some of the people at the agency, got a tour of the facility and the city, and was offered the job. The next day, Sunday, he called me at Mother and Daddy's house, where I had gone with Steven and Ellen for dinner. Stu said, "The job is mine if we want it. The agency looks great, the people are very nice, the work is good but they can use my help, the city is in a beautiful area, the money is right, but I don't think I can take it." My hand went to my throat and I asked him, "Why not?" He said, "Because all they talk about is that fucking letter, and I didn't even *read* it." He said that Art Lavidge had taken him to the Cherokee Country Club for lunch, and when it was time for dessert, had poked him in the ribs and said, "How about some strawberry shortcake?" He thought Arthur Lavidge might be nuts, but I reminded him of the best line in the letter. I said, "Take the job. We just won't ever tell them who wrote the letter. It isn't dishonest. It was all about you and you did write the most memorable line." We never did tell. Until now.

Before we left the Big Apple for the Big Orange, we still had to contend with life in Huntington Station. As it turned out, we were getting out in the nick of time.

Until he set our car on fire and threatened to kill us, I thought of our new next-door neighbor, Rick, as a friendly person. He was a lowlife and criminally inclined, but I was nice to him, his wife, and their four-year-old daughter, Tammy. I certainly didn't want to get on his bad side. His wife, Ramona, had diabetes and was always collapsing into unconsciousness because she was too dim to remember to take her insulin shots. Little Tammy used to wander the streets in her underwear after her mother had passed out in the house. I used to feed her lunch and let her play in the backyard, near, if not with, Steven and Ellen, who thought she was a moron. Rick was one of those people who, if he liked you and had nothing against you, would do anything for you. But if you crossed him, he offered to blow off your head. He thought we had crossed him.

Rick worked for a flooring company and told us that if we ever needed new carpeting or linoleum, he would install it for us free of charge. Shortly after they moved in, Rick and Ramona invited us into their house. Their dining-room table was covered with drugstore items: razor blades, toothpaste, lotion, etc. Rick said, "Take whatever you want. Just leave a couple of bucks." Stu and I, innocent souls that we were, said, "Where'd you get this stuff?" He looked at us as if we were stupid. "It's hot," he said. His friends had hijacked a truck. (Probably the same friends who later set fire to our car.) He was just trying to be friendly. We declined to take anything, and he casually said, "Your loss." Another time he asked us if we wanted forty frozen chickens. His buddies had hijacked a chicken truck. None of this was unheard of on Long Island, a haven for the Mafia. Once, on the Long Island Railroad, a guy Stu knew only casually asked him if he wanted a color TV for $100. It was 1967, when a color TV cost five times that or more. The only catch was that Stu had to take ten of them.

Except for their criminal associations, our new neighbors seemed like nice people. Rick worried about his wife because she was sick so much and always thanked me for looking after his daughter. They both seemed to love animals and had a veritable zoo in their backyard: six cats, a bunch of rabbits, ducks, and two Doberman pinschers. Ramona came running to my house one day screaming that one of the cats was going crazy in her house, jumping from wall to wall, tearing the curtains, and hissing at her. She asked me what she should do. I had no idea, so I called the police. The officer listened politely and said to me, "Lady, the only thing I have for a crazy pussycat is a .44-caliber pistol." He kindly called the humane society, which sent someone out who tranquilized the cat and took it away.

One night Rick called us to see if Stu could come over to watch Tammy, as he once again had to rush

Ramona to the hospital. Stu called me about an hour later to let me know that both Dobermans were eating a loaf of bread in the living room and he didn't intend to interrupt their snack, lest he take its place.

Two enormous Great Danes later replaced the Dobermans. Rick came over to show me his new pets. They immediately dashed down to the lower level of the house, where my little pug, Stella, lived. I was looking down the stairway to make sure Stella had not become an hors d'oeuvre when one of the Great Danes came dashing back up the stairs, wagging his tail. Unfortunately for me, my mouth was in the exact spot where the tail was wagging, and when it smashed into my front teeth I thought it had knocked all of them out. My teeth were only loosened and did tighten up after several days of pain. But did I complain? No!

What I did complain about was the smell that wafted into my backyard from the addition to the menagerie of two horses, which lived in the newly constructed barn in the backyard. They deposited their manure all over the yard, frequently near my fence. Apparently another neighbor was also offended by the stench and reported the addition of the barn to the town property assessor. Rick's taxes went up, and he thought we were the ones who had ratted on him. Suddenly we had become *the enemy!* And in Rick's world the enemy gets punished.

Shortly after his taxes went up, our car went up in flames sometime during the night, while parked in our driveway. When we got up the next morning and saw our little white Plymouth Valiant had become a little black Plymouth Valiant, we called the police. Now the police often went to Rick's house to shoot pool (he had built several elaborate additions to his house, including a big rec room), and when we showed them the burned car they said a short might have started the fire when the wind rocked the car back and forth the night before. Rick quickly came out of his house and showed them (his police buddies?) the spot where the gasoline had been poured. He wanted us to know it was no accident.

Stu called Rick to tell him that we knew he, or one of his friends, was responsible for burning our car. Rick threatened to kill us. We were afraid he really would shoot us with the gun he had boasted about owning. So we called the police again and told them we had been threatened. A nice detective visited us and told us there was nothing they could do without a provable act of violence. They had no way of knowing—and we had no way of proving—how our car got burned. Now I was really frightened. Stu, who used to be a boxer and was not afraid to punch someone or be punched himself, called Rick and said, "Listen pal, we didn't report your shitting horses or your fucking barn to the tax people. If you want to fight come outside like a man and you can punch me, and I'll punch you. Let's get this over with. You're scaring my wife." Now, whether it was a reproach to his manhood or the fact that he was scaring the woman who had helped him so many times in the past, we'll never know. He said, "Aw, Stu, let's just forget it. Why don't you come over and we'll shoot some pool?" I didn't want Stu to go for fear Rick wanted to shoot more than pool, which Stu didn't play anyway. Stu didn't go to Rick's house and we had to buy a new car. But that, it seemed, was the end of it.

When Stu was offered the job in Tennessee, he accepted it right away and went down to Knoxville to start working. I stayed behind to sell our house. About a week after Stu left, while I was sleeping, Stella woke me up, barking madly. It was about 1 A.M. and I heard a knock on the front door, went downstairs, and asked, "Who is it?" "It's the police," answered the gruff voice behind the door. "Well, I don't know if you're really the police, my husband's not home (how stupid of me to tell), and I'm not opening this door for you or anyone else." I tried to sound firm. The man said more kindly, "Well, peek through the window, and I'll show you my badge." So I did, and he showed me a badge. He asked, "Have you seen any strange cars in your neighbor's driveway?" I said, "There are so many strange cars in my neighbor's driveway that I wouldn't know a strange car if I saw one." He thanked me and left.

My mind began to race. The officer wasn't wearing a uniform. What if the badge was a tin one from the five-and-dime? What if it was one of Rick's car-burning friends, checking to see if I had noticed the many cars in the driveway and if I would tell if I were questioned? I lay for three hours with my eyes wide open, my heart racing, and my senses attuned to the slightest noise. Steven, Ellen, and Stella were sleeping soundly.

At about 4 A.M. I didn't hear anything but sensed something. I got out of bed and looked out the window. Six police cars with their lights out were quietly approaching the cul-de-sac we lived on. All of them parked facing Rick's house. As I watched in astonishment, all the police cars' headlights went on at once and a bunch of police officers rushed into the house. I dashed downstairs and, even though it was the middle of the night, called the Arnolds. "Look out the window," I said. "You won't believe your eyes." I expected to hear gunfire, but apparently Rick had been taken by surprise. Alan Arnold went out in his pajamas to ask an officer who was standing around outside what was happening. He was told it looked like our neighbors were operating a chop shop. The next day the police found parts from forty stolen cars in Rick's garage. They had traced the cars to him by following a trail of oil from a car that had been stolen right up to Rick's driveway. He went to jail, but not for very long. Eventually he killed someone and was sent back to prison. But at least it wasn't us. We had already pulled out of Huntington Station.

Stu and I flew to Knoxville together for the first time in the middle of July. The airport was so tiny that we just walked onto the tarmac and picked up our luggage. We rented a car and drove to the Campus Inn, where Art Lavidge had reserved a room for us. School was out and the college area was almost deserted. Mr. Lavidge gave a pool party for us at his beautiful house in the Sequoia Hills development. All the principals in the agency were there and looked us over. I was fascinated by their accent. I had never heard anything that sounded remotely like East Tennessee before. They, in turn, seemed to be enjoying my Brooklyn accent, which was more pronounced when I first moved to Knoxville than it is now. Everyone seemed anxious to make sure we had a good time, and we did.

The next day Art Lavidge drove us all over the city. He pointed out the only tall building, the Andrew Johnson Hotel—fourteen stories high—built in 1927, and said with a smile, "There's the Knoxville skyline." The downtown area was deserted and depressed, but the residential areas were wonderful. Art told us we probably wouldn't be happy where he lived, because all the Jewish people lived in West Hills. We told him we had just come from a mixed neighborhood and that hardly mattered to us. But we could tell that he wanted us to look elsewhere. The next day he got John Carter, who owned the best real estate agency in town, to drive us all around Knoxville so we could find a place that we wanted to buy. Nothing was for rent except apartments, and after living in our house in Huntington Station, we could never be happy in an apartment again.

John Carter told us that West Hills was the best place for us to live (I guess Art had told him we were Jewish), but when we saw that area we didn't like it: too new, too few trees. We told him that West Hills looked just like Long Island and we were hoping for something a little more wooded—something that looked more like Tennessee. So he drove us over the Alcoa Highway Bridge into South Knoxville. He showed us a house in a beautiful, quiet, wooded area, and we liked it right away. I still had to sell our house in Huntington Station before we could commit ourselves, but we told him that was probably the house we would buy. He told us we were picking the wrong section of town, that the city was moving west and we would never make any money on that house. He also said, however, that we wouldn't lose any either. Stu and I couldn't get over that we would be able to afford such a nice house. It cost $31,000. In New York it would have cost five times as much, and we would have had to be millionaires to live in a neighborhood like that. We made an $8,000 profit when we sold our house in Huntington Station, after living there for only four years. We used that money to take over the mortgage of the house in Knoxville, which was only six years old. The monthly payments would be $186.

The house, in the foothills of the Great Smoky Mountains, was made of brick and had a big front lawn. There was a large living room with a lot of wall space to hang paintings on. We would have our first separate dining room, one that wasn't part of the kitchen or that was called a "dining area." One of the dining room walls had an ugly wallpaper mural of a southern plantation, and we quickly covered it with black burlap. (At our house in Huntington Station we had hidden a ghastly mural of a fountain that same way.) Our new house had a paneled den with a fireplace—our first. Each window had a marble windowsill. Talk about fancy! There were dense woods across the street and we had only one neighbor on our left and one diagonally across from us. There were woods on our right side that Steven and Ellen would use as a burying ground for the mice that the cat that was about to move in would kill.

When I went back to New York the next day I put our house up for sale and sold it to the first people who came to look at it. After getting stuck with our Lindenwood Village co-op four years before and losing almost all the money we had put into it, I was ecstatic. Stu immediately called John Carter and told him we wanted the house in South Knoxville.

One month later I gave a big party in Huntington Station for all of our friends and said good-bye. I would miss them all, more than I knew, but I was happy that Stu, after ten years on Madison Avenue, had finally found a job and a city that he liked. I decided that I would learn to love Knoxville, Tennessee, no matter what.

We drove down to Knoxville in the middle of August and settled in our wonderful house. Steven and Ellen started school at the end of the month. In November, when the leaves fell off the trees across the street, I shouted, "Holy shit! There's a lake across the street!" It was actually the Tennessee River. Until the leaves came down we had no idea it was there. A more pleasant surprise than hearing the Long Island Railroad whistle on my first day in Huntington Station, or the sound of the jets at Lindenwood Village. (Stu and I were never that observant when choosing a place to live.)

A black cat showed up the second week we were there. Stu hated cats and told me to get rid of it, or at least not to feed it. I had already given her all the leftover macaroni and cheese from our dinner and there was no way that cat was going to leave. I told Stu that it was now my cat. He said if I wanted to keep it outside I could, but there was no way that cat was ever coming in the house. In December I called Stu at work and told him the cat, whom we had named Midnight, was standing at the front door and she was sneezing. Stu said, "Well, don't leave her out there. Bring her in." It turned out he had been playing with Midnight every morning before he went to work and had decided he didn't detest cats after all. Stu once got mad at me when I hit Midnight after she had bitten me. During the next year more than the cat would bite me.

THE GROOVE THEORY OF EVOLUTION

I had never heard of the groove theory of evolution before moving to Knoxville. I had never been farther south than Pennsylvania (except for a short vacation driving the Skyline Drive in Virginia) and I had a lot to learn. On our honeymoon Stu and I had seen the play *Inherit the Wind*, about the famous Scopes Trial in Dayton, Tennessee. In 1925 Clarence Darrow defended high school teacher John Scopes, who was fired from his job, thrown in jail, and prosecuted by William Jennings Bryan for teaching the theory of evolution, which violated state law. Little did we know in 1956 that, in 1970, the famous "Monkey Trial" would come back to haunt us.

When we moved to Tennessee in 1969, Steven was in fourth grade and Ellen was in first. Now that I've lived here for almost thirty years, I have grown to love it. My first year, however, was quite an adjustment. I knew nothing about the area, the people, the accent, the schools or the climate. I almost gave away all of my winter clothes before we moved. Knoxville normally has mild winters compared with those in New York, but it does get some very cold days. The coldest we've had since I've been here, a definite aberration, was twenty-four degrees below zero. It was the coldest place in the country that day, including Alaska. Mount Olive Elementary, the school that Steven and Ellen started at, was as much of a shock as that day's weather.

Steven came home very upset after his first spelling test. Mrs. Hinchey, his fourth-grade teacher, had given the class three words to spell. Lucky for him she had used each word in a sentence, because if she hadn't, he would have had no idea what language she was speaking. All three words—*pin, pan,* and *pen*—sounded exactly the same. In her perfect East Tennessee accent, Mrs. Hinchey had given the examples: "I have a straight payin. I have a fryin' payin. I have a fountain payin."

I asked Steven to try to remember how much Daddy hated working in New York, how much he loves working in Knoxville, and how nice it is that it takes Daddy only ten minutes to get home from work, instead of an hour and a half. Our son tried.

Mrs. Hinchey realized Steven was far ahead of his fourth-grade class. They were just learning things he had learned in first grade, and he was bored out of his mind. I hate to sound like a New York snob, but facts are facts. I asked the teacher if she could give Steven some extra work to do. She assigned him to create bulletin boards for subjects being discussed in class, but that was not the intellectual stimulation I'd had in mind for him. At least she was kind.

The next year was worse. Though there was a small Jewish community in Knoxville, almost all lived in West Knoxville. We lived in South Knoxville, and Steven and Ellen were the only Jewish children in their school. There were two black students. There were three teachers for the fifth grade: a bigot, a sadist (she seemed to enjoy saying to one of the orphans who lived in a nearby home, when he was misbehaving, "If no one wanted *me* I don't think *I'd* be behaving that way"), and an illiterate (she couldn't spell, spoke incorrect English, and had never been certified as a teacher). Steven got the bigot. I would have chosen the illiterate but wasn't offered a choice. Throughout the year, when I reflected on our moving here, I thought, "What the fuck have we done?" I began to think maybe John Carter really did have our best interests at heart when he tried to get us to buy a house in West Hills.

One day Steven came home from school and, with a perfectly straight face, said, "Mrs. Morris explained why the black people are so much dumber than the white people." (On this day I was glad that the two black students in the school were not in Steven's class.) Mrs. Morris was about sixty, with a pinched-looking face and tight-curled gray hair. Knowing that Steven didn't believe a word she said, I asked him exactly what Mrs. Morris had told the class. Steven was always a great mimic, and repeated in Mrs. Morris's East Tennessee twang, "Have y'all ever seen pictures of a brain? You know how there's all those grooves in it? Well, it's them grooves that make you smart! Black people don't have them grooves. Their brains are completely smooth! It ain't their fault that they're not as smart as whites. It's evolution." Hardly what John Scopes had had in mind in 1925. The line about how much Daddy hated New York was wearing thin.

I felt like a real coward for not speaking out about that outrageous statement. But I had told my children to lie low, to try not to attract attention to the fact that they may seem different from the others. I felt we were truly strangers in a strange land. I was behaving in the exact opposite way I usually did. I was lying low, too.

Not that growing up in the North was any great shakes when it came to integration or understanding. The only difference was that segregation up north had never been the law. It was just an ugly fact.

When we moved to Knoxville I noticed an easy friendliness between blacks and whites that did not exist in the North. Before the Supreme Court decision on desegregation in 1954, black children did not attend *any* white schools in the South, but they often lived in adjacent neighborhoods with white children and often played with them. My neighborhood in Brooklyn had not been integrated. When I was a kid, the only black child in my elementary school was Ozzie James, the son of the janitor of the apartment building down the street. The only Asian child was Su Yim Goon, the son of the man who owned the local Chinese laundry. When I wanted to invite Ozzie to my sixth birthday party, my mother told me I couldn't. When I asked her why not, she said the other mothers wouldn't like us having a Negro child at the party. She told me she didn't care at all, but said if I wanted a party, I should forget about inviting Ozzie. I said I just wouldn't have a party, and I didn't. Bigotry, when I was a child, was subtle and largely unspoken. The people in the North didn't have a lot to brag about when it came to racial equality. But at least no one ever said anything as nutty as blacks have no grooves on their brains.

I told Steven that when he got to seventh grade we would send him to Webb, an excellent private school in Knoxville, but until then he would just have to let every idiotic thing his idiotic teacher said go in one ear and out the other. It was very drafty in my son's head that year.

Paddling children was a common occurrence at Mount Olive. I told Steven and Ellen that if a teacher ever tried to paddle them, they should run out of the classroom, go to the principal's office, and call me. I thought if we had to contend with things like that we would just have to move back to New York and Stuart could sit on the Long Island Railroad for the rest of his life.

By the worst possible luck, Ellen was assigned to Mrs. Morris's class when she entered fifth grade. One day she came home, threw her arms wide, and started dancing around the room singing, "I'm a person! I'm a person!" When I asked her how she had come to that conclusion, she said, "Mrs. Morris just got back from a trip to the Holy Land and she learned that Jews are people, just like blacks are people." Mrs. Morris had also shared with the class her new understanding of interacting with such people. She learned not to say "Jew them down," but to say "bargain with them." I gave Ellen the drafty ears advice and promised to get her out of there as soon as we were able. Webb was the only private school in Knoxville and it had just changed its policy; the following year it would start admitting students in fifth grade, instead of seventh grade (the year Steven had to wait for). Ellen would start as a student at Webb in sixth grade.

On another day Ellen came home and said that Mrs. Morris had asked the class how many of them went to church. All the children raised their hands, except Ellen. Then Mrs. Morris asked how many children didn't go to church. Ellen didn't raise her hand. She had been a student at Mount Olive for five years and had learned to lie low. She was trying to fade into the background, but her friend Dana said, "You don't go to church, Ellen. Raise your hand." Reluctantly, Ellen did. Mrs. Morris, who I would have liked to stick in the eye with a straight *payin* and hit over the head with a frying *payin,* then asked the class, "Who would like to take Ellen to church with them?" She knew perfectly well that we were Jewish. Steven had been in her class only three years before, and there was not a plethora of Eichels at Mount Olive. Many children volunteered to take Ellen to church. The "fade into the background" routine was not working.

The next day Ellen came home crying. She said a boy in the class had said to her, "I asked my mother, 'Who doesn't go to church?' and she said 'Jews.' That means you're a Jew, you dirty little Jew." That was our first personal experience with vocal anti-Semitism. Enough was enough.

Stuart had recently quit Lavidge and Associates. When we moved to Tennessee Stu started drawing again. Drawing was an old love, something there had been no time for when he was commuting for three hours a day. He was now doing beautiful pencil drawings of the rural areas close by. He was traveling around the U.S. selling prints of his drawings. Because he was now playing artist, not creative director, his costume had changed. No more of the suit and tie of the advertising executive; his hair was down to his shoulders, and he wore blue jeans and T-shirts. He was, after all, an advertising man who knew how to play his role.

After the church episode his role was to pay a visit to Mount Olive School and haul Mrs. Morris' ass on the carpet. He cut his hair. He put on a suit and a tie. He met with the principal and Mrs. Morris. She was pretending not to know what Stu's visit was about, but she must have had some idea. She was ignorant, but wily.

The first thing Stuart asked her was if she taught the "groove theory of evolution." She didn't ask him what he was talking about, or what "the groove theory" was. She simply denied teaching it. Stuart then told her that if she ever asked anyone to bring our daughter to church again, we would take her to court. He reminded her that public schools in the United States were not allowed to recruit for the church. He mentioned the Constitution, the separation of church and state, etc. He got the feeling he was spitting in the wind. Mrs. Morris just sat there, stone-faced. The principal said he would talk to Mrs. Morris privately. He *seemed* to understand the issue, but who could tell if he would do anything about it?

Our solution at that point was to take action. Other parents, as disgusted as we were by the selection of teachers for the fifth grade, formed a group to try to change things. We met for several evenings and wrote a letter to Mildred Doyle, the superintendent of schools for Knox County. The fourth time we met, the head of the PTA unexpectedly showed up. She was a bright and aggressive woman who had lived in Atlanta. She told us that she had heard that there were some "commie pinko" parents having meetings about the school. She smiled when she said it. Her daughter and our daughter were good friends. The good news was, she was on our side. She arranged for Mildred Doyle to come to our next meeting and hear our grievances.

Dr. Doyle listened and soon after hired Mr. Horn, a young Vietnam veteran, to take over Mrs. Morris's class for the second half of the year. Mrs. Morris was reassigned to another grade. Mr. Horn was the first male teacher Ellen had ever had. He was a committed, sensitive teacher and a wonderful person. This is sort of a happy ending, but one teacher doesn't change a school. Although I was always an outspoken believer in the public school system, for junior high and high school we sent Steven and Ellen to private school. I felt like a hypocrite, but as we say in the South, "My mama didn't raise no fool."

Both Steven and Ellen graduated from the University of Tennessee. Steven was top graduate in the School of Liberal Arts and Ellen graduated with high honors. Steven went to Columbia University Law School in New York and is now a partner with Goulston & Storrs. His wife, Belinda, grew up in Johnson City, Tennessee, a city much smaller than Knoxville. They met when they were both working for the World's Fair that was held here in 1982. (No kidding—there was a World's Fair in Knoxville.) Belinda is also a lawyer. She graduated from the University of Tennessee College of Law and is now a partner at PriceWaterhouseCoopers. They live in Boston. Obviously, being educated in the South was no detriment to their careers.

Steven was nine when we moved here but, remembering his experience at Mount Olive elementary school, sometimes tells people he's from New York. It's not a lie, but it's not quite the truth, either.

DR. X, MS, AND MY FORTIETH

I got my second ride in an ambulance on May 20, 1977, my fortieth birthday. I was taken to the emergency room of St. Mary's Hospital and examined by Dr. Ogden, the physician on duty. He said, "Young lady, you have Multiple Sclerosis." Dr. Ogden was rather old and I guess to him I was a young lady. I had already spent a month at St. Mary's, been given a lot of tests, and finally sent home only two weeks before to "see what develops." The reason Dr. Ogden could so quickly diagnose what the other doctors had failed to see in the previous month was that his daughter had MS and he was familiar with the symptoms. I had taken a hot bath, and if Stuart had not been at home to hear me yell for help, I think I would have drowned. My body had frozen into a grotesque position and I was slipping under the water. I would learn later that getting overheated triggers an MS attack.

It had been a strange month. I had been in the hospital before, of course, but that was to give birth to Steven and Ellen—not because I was sick. This time a feeling of helplessness overwhelmed me. Being Jewish in a Catholic hospital was also slightly un-nerving. The cross that hung above every bed didn't bother me especially, but I wasn't fond of the nun who woke everyone in the morning with a prayer delivered over the loudspeaker in a monotone that made the sound of water dripping from a leaky faucet sound like calypso. The nurses, though—all of them named Mary or Theresa or Mary Theresa—were very kind.

Here's how it started. In April I had gone to Winter Park, Florida, for a week to help Stuart with a sidewalk art show. He told me I would love Florida because the sky there is always blue. The sky was gray all the way there. Desolate Interstate 75, between Macon and Valdosta, Georgia, made me long for the chaos of a Brooklyn street. The show took place from 10 A.M. to 10 P.M. The temperature was actually chilly in the morning, but broiling hot for the rest of the day. The sky was indeed blue and sun beat down throughout the day.

I was not a good salesperson. Even after eight years of exposure to Southern gentility and hospitality, some of the people who came to the show brought out my innate New York hostility. A man and two women were looking at Stu's drawings. The man pulled a handkerchief out of his pocket, looked at me, and said with a sneer, "I bet you thought I was pulling out a big wad of money." I looked at him coldly and answered, "Actually, I didn't, because I saw the booger in your nose." (I never could resist a good zinger.) If I had actually been *working* for Stu, he would have fired me, but I was just along for the ride. The man bought three prints. He was visiting from New York.

I came back to Knoxville feeling very ill. My whole body had gone numb. My hands were tingling painfully, as if I had slammed my funny bones into a brick wall. I was exhausted and had to drag myself to work the next morning. I called Dr. Hakim, my GP, and told him what was happening to me. He gave me the number of a neurologist, Dr. Paulsen. When I called, Dr. Paulsen's nurse told me he could see me in a month. I said I might be dead in a month and hung up. (He eventually became my doctor and was wonderful.) Two days later I woke up in the middle of the night with severe pain in my legs and hands. I felt like I couldn't breathe. Stu called an ambulance and I was driven to St. Mary's emergency room. I was admitted to the hospital and began one of the worst months of my life so far.

I'd never had a lot of warm, fuzzy feelings for doctors. In my experience some doctors have misdiagnosed me and others have treated me remarkably shabbily, as when Ellen was born. Once a gynecologist had told me that I needed an emergency hysterectomy; it was fifteen years before I actually needed—and got—one. Another time, when I was at work, I started seeing large black spots in front of my eyes. I went to an ophthalmologist who told me there was nothing wrong with my eyes. I went to my internist (no longer Dr. Hakim), who told me he thought I had a clot at the base of my brain and should have an arteriogram, which I had heard was an invasive, painful, and dangerous test. I refused. So he wrote me a prescription for a blood thinner, to help get rid of the clot (which it turned out I didn't have). At work, before the advent of computers, I sometimes cut paper or mat board and used razor blades, X-Acto knives, and other sharp instruments to prepare layouts. I thought if I took a blood thinner and then cut myself I might bleed to death, so I threw the prescription in the garbage. About a week later the spots disappeared and never came back. It was enough to make you lose faith in the medical profession, and it became abundantly clear to me that you had to speak up if you thought the doctor was wrong.

After my first ambulance ride some good things did happen. The next day our neighbors started bringing food to our house and offering to help in any way they could. News travels fast in Knoxville and people look out for each other. By that afternoon everyone in the neighborhood had heard that I had been rushed to the hospital in the middle of the night. People began dropping off casseroles and prime rib, salads and homemade pies. Stu and the children were eating much better than they did when I was home.

A neurologist on the hospital staff scheduled a series of tests that would take place during the next four weeks: a spinal tap, a myelogram, and an electro-encephalogram. Multiple sclerosis does not necessarily make its presence known on any of those tests, so when they turned up nothing and I still complained of pain and weakness, it was time to send in the psychiatrists. (The MRI was not available in 1977; if it had been it would have saved me a lot of frustration, and Blue Cross a lot of money.)

One evening at eight o'clock, an old man sat down in a chair next to my bed. He had wild, bushy, gray hair that made me think Albert Einstein's barber was still on the loose. He didn't say a word. I looked at him for a while and finally asked, "Who are you?" When he said to me in a German accent, "I'm ze psychiatrist," I started to laugh. It was the best money Blue Cross had spent all month. Then he asked me if I hated my mother, and I laughed harder. When he asked me if I was in love with my father, I would have fallen out of bed laughing, but the bars were up for the night. He said, "For someone with a supposedly serious disease, you are certainly euphoric." I'm sure he wrote me up as a hysteric.

The second psychiatrist was a kind, mild-mannered, middle-aged man. I guess they needed a second opinion to have me committed. We talked for quite a while and he told me that I was probably the most well-adjusted person he had ever met. I thanked him. The next hurdle was with a psychologist who was going to give me more tests—Rorschach tests and the like. I had taken psychology in college. I wasn't going to tell him I saw monsters in the inkblots—I was going to tell him I saw butterflies. I had no faith in any of that anyway and thought Blue Cross was throwing away its money. However, after an exhausting battery of tests the psychologist said to me, "I think you have some kind of neurological disorder. You score very high on intelligence and many other things, but your coordination skills are so low they are off the graph." I was amazed that a discipline I had so little faith in—psychology—was the first to indicate that I had a neurological disease.

Dr. Hakim came to see me. He told me there was nothing wrong with me. I had been given every conceivable medical test, he said, and nothing had shown up. I guess he hadn't talked to the psychologist. Maybe he had spoken only to the German psychiatrist, who thought I was crazy. I didn't know. What I did know was that I understood my own body and I knew something was wrong. I fired him. (He has since quit medicine and is selling Oriental artifacts. I think he's found his true niche in life.) I called Stuart and said, "I just fired the Arab. Find me a Jew."

Stu asked our insurance man, who was Jewish, to recommend someone; he suggested Dr. X, a neurosurgeon, whose name I will not use because I don't want the son-of-a-bitch to sue me. Dr. X came to my room the next day. He was Jewish and from Brooklyn, just like me. What more could I ask for? He said I should go home and wait to "see what develops." He gave me no clue as to what was the matter with me. I couldn't walk without staggering. I couldn't use my hands at all. Stu had to feed me and dress me. I was too weak to stand up in the shower, which was why I took the hot bath that sent me back to the hospital.

After Dr. Ogden had me admitted back into St. Mary's, Dr. X came to see me. I asked him, "Do I have MS?" He said, "Who told you that?" I told him it was Dr. Ogden in emergency. He said, "What does he know? He's just a GP." My New York hostility reared its ugly head. I said, "Listen, all I want to know is, when can I go back to work?" He said, "You'll never work again as long as you live," and stormed out of the room. The nurse, who was standing by my bedside, said to me after his dramatic exit, "I can't believe the way he talked to you, but if it will make you feel any better, we call him Adolph Hitler around here." I wondered if she knew Dr. X was Jewish. She told me he was going through a messy divorce and was having a very bad time financially. I started to cry, but not for him. I called Stuart and told him that Dr. X had told me I'd never work again, and how nasty he had been to me. Stu went storming up to the doctor's office. Dr. X was very nice to my husband, but Stu told him to go back and be nice to me—I was the one who needed his kindness.

Dr. X returned to my room that evening. He told me he had known from the start that I had MS, but didn't want to tell me because I would be unemployable and uninsurable. (Both untrue; I had a job and Blue Cross.) Dr. X, oozing bedside manners, told me, "MS is a disease of the central nervous system—the brain and the spinal cord. Think of the nerves as electric wires, sending signals from the brain to the spinal cord, which then tells the body what to do." He told me about myelin, and said, "Imagine myelin as the rubber insulation protecting the wire. When a person has MS the myelin is destroyed in many areas, disrupting the signal. The message can't get through; it's like the power the brain has to communicate with the body is lost." After telling me there was no cure he asked if there was anything else he could do for me. I said, "Today is my fortieth birthday. Would you mind singing 'Happy Birthday'?" He looked at me as if the German psychiatrist knew what he was talking about and walked out of the room. I never saw him again.

Dr. X had told Stuart that I had progressive MS and that I would keep getting worse. He was wrong, but Stu didn't know that at the time. I have the type of MS that has long periods of remission and I worked for seventeen highly productive years after Dr. X told me I never would again. Dr. Paulsen became my doctor and still is. The treatment was twenty days of ACTH: steroid shots, deep in the muscle. At the hospital the nurse asked me if Stu could give me my shots. I told her my husband had fainted when a doctor cut his ingrown toenail. I couldn't give myself the shots, as my hands weren't functioning. Stu did do it, although it was a lot more painful for him to stick me with a needle than it was for me to get stuck. They used an orange to teach him how to give shots, sticking the long needle into the fruit, but Stu said an orange doesn't bleed.

The people in my department at the University of Tennessee were wonderful to me. They hired a freelance artist to do my work until I could return. After two months at home, I came back to work an hour a day until I built up enough strength to work a full day. It took four months. When I retired it had nothing to do with MS.

• • •

Almost twenty years later I started feeling much better. It was then that Stu told me that when he talked to Dr. X after my diagnosis, the bad doctor told him, "Your wife is a very sick woman. She's never going to get better. You're a relatively young man and you ought to think about making another life for yourself." I couldn't believe my ears. My doctor had virtually told my husband to leave me. I asked Stu what he said to that and Stu said he didn't say a thing. He thought Dr. X was speaking from personal bitterness toward women—he's been married five times—and felt almost sorry for him. I feel no pity for Dr. X. It's his patients I feel sorry for.

As I look back, I realize how many women have told me similar stories about their bad experiences with people in the medical profession. Being treated like a piece of meat has become a cliché. Too many male doctors treat perfectly sane women as if they are crazy when they have an illness that is difficult to diagnose. Maybe the same gene that prevents men from asking for directions when they're lost causes that attitude. Whatever the reason, it always seemed unfair that whenever I thought my doctor was the one who was crazy, I was the one who had to look at inkblots.

After I came home from the hospital I read up on my disease. Multiple Sclerosis is an autoimmune disease in which the body attacks is own tissue. No one knows what triggers it. The myelin is lost in many areas, leaving scars, or sclerosis. Not much more was known back then than what Dr. X had told me. Now, more than twenty years later, there has been a lot of research and there are some promising treatments. MS, though, is still called a "mysterious" disease. No one knows the cause, and there is no cure. Stu no longer has to give me shots for twenty days. The last time I got sick a visiting nurse came to the house and gave me massive doses of steroids intravenously, two hours a day for five days. All I have to do is take a painting off the wall and sit on the couch; the nurse hangs an IV bag on the picture hook.

In 1977 I was powerless to change what was happening to me, and possibly what was happening to Ellen. I was diagnosed with MS when Ellen was not quite fourteen, a vulnerable time for a young girl. I was forty, a vulnerable time for a woman. Steven was seventeen and left for France three months later. He had been chosen by the American Field Service to be an exchange student. He would be away from home for a year, living with the Benet family in Paris and graduating from a Catholic high school there. Steven had learned French at Webb School and by the time he left for France he was fluent in the language—enough to graduate first in his French high school class. Ellen missed Steven a lot—and she wrote long letters to him every week.

While I remained in the hospital waiting for a diagnosis, Stu came to visit me three times a day. He told me that as soon as he got home he wanted to come back, even though I knew he hated being inside a hospital. I didn't want Steven and Ellen to see me looking so sick so I talked to them on the phone. Ellen created an elaborate get well card that must have taken her hours. She cut pictures of women out of magazines, carefully cutting out their faces and positioning them over a photo of my face, which was pasted on the last page. Under each photo was a poem.

A GET WELL BLESSING FOR MOMMY

Why do I love my Mommy?
by Ellen Eichel

(A photo of woman holding a laundry basket)
Not because you do all the work
Including laundry and the dishes
And race around the community
To satisfy my wishes.

There are fifteen more pages between the first stanza and the last.

(A photo of a woman running in a race)
And not because you're always trying
To be the best that you can be,
For the real reason that
I love you . . .
Is that you're the
BEST MOMMY

Get well soon,
Love, Ellen

I called Ellen and told her that her card was the best thing I had ever seen and I only wished I looked like the women in the magazine photos. I had been in the hospital for two weeks. I realized that, although I had tried to protect them from the sight of their mother looking so terrible, Steven and Ellen *needed* to visit. They both looked shocked when they saw me. I was trying my best to look happy but I failed. I was not fun to visit. I felt awful, I was nauseated most of the time, my head hurt, my legs and hands hurt, and I could barely walk so I didn't get out of bed. I had lost a lot of weight.

Ellen baked a huge plate of "Meringue Surprises." She had gotten the recipe from a cookbook I had designed for the Knoxville Utility Board. (In the early '70s they were still encouraging people to use lots of energy.) Those cookies are really delicious. I used to love them but I couldn't look at food. The only thing I wanted to eat was cantaloupe and Stu brought me two melons every day. However, I forced down a Meringue Surprise. All that night I heard the nurses on duty coming into my room and helping themselves to some. By morning there were only three left. I was glad they'd eaten them so the next time Ellen visited me they would be gone and she'd think I'd eaten them.

I wonder now if Stu and I were so focused on my illness that we stopped paying enough attention to Ellen. After I came home from the hospital I didn't know if I would ever work as an artist again. At the time I couldn't even write my name. Stu said, "You like to tell stories. You could talk into a tape recorder and someone could write down what you say."

Ellen quit Webb the next year and went to Doyle High School with all her old friends from Mount Olive. Ellen said she hated Webb, the kids were snobs, the work was too hard, and the bus ride too long. It was while she was a student at Doyle that Ellen started dating Chuck and, as we would find out later, taking drugs and drinking. Multiple sclerosis means, literally, "many scars." Maybe the scars weren't all mine.

When she was six Ellen came running home crying, holding out her hand. She had run it along the top of an old wooden fence and had at least twenty splinters in her palm. I sterilized a needle, and with Ellen crying bitter tears, removed about fifteen of them. But there were at least five more embedded so deeply that I told Ellen we would have to go to the doctor to take out the rest of them.

The pediatricians were known as "the kid factory," because they were the best-known children's doctors in Knoxville (the ones recommended by *everyone* to a new mother in town) and there were always mobs of children in the office waiting with their mothers. This was the 70s, before the arrival of the "sensitive men" of the 80s, and there were never *any* fathers in the waiting room. The "sick" children who were coughing and sneezing, or throwing up were treated first. Splinters waited their turn. Ellen and I waited, and she had stopped crying because splinters hurt only when you touch them. Ellen held her hand on her lap, palm up, while I read her a story. When our turn finally came she was lifted onto an examining table and held down by a nurse while the doctor, with nothing to kill the pain, removed the deep splinters. Ellen, justifiably so, screamed for the entire time. I should have stopped them from hurting her, but I didn't know what to do, or didn't think quickly enough. In less than two minutes it was all over and I held Ellen in my arms and told her how brave she had been. She said, "I hope they die." A nurse came in and gave Ellen a tetanus shot; when she was finished Ellen bit her.

From that day on whenever we went for a check-up someone said, "Uh oh, better watch out. That's the little girl who bit the nurse." Ellen just smirked, never sorry for a minute that she had at least inflicted some pain on the person who had held her down while the doctor was inflicting such pain on her. I never told Ellen she shouldn't have done it, because I was so angry I could have bitten the doctor.

• • •

The day Ellen overdosed on drugs she was fifteen. I was at work. Stu came to my office, his face ashen, and said, "Now don't worry. Everything's going to be OK. Ellen's in intensive care, but they say she's going to be all right." I thought a car had hit her, but Stu said that apparently she had taken a drug overdose. She had taken all the leftover painkillers and tranquilizers that the doctor had given me when I was sent home from the hospital after being diagnosed with MS. Her boyfriend, Chuck, called for an ambulance after Ellen phoned him and said that she had "taken a bunch of my mother's pills and was feeling very funny." Chuck saved her life. The doctor told me later that Ellen was five minutes away from death when she was brought in. She didn't take enough of any one drug to kill her, but she'd had a reaction to all the drugs she had mixed. (It never occurred to me to throw them away.)

When Stu and I got to University Hospital Ellen was lying in bed in the intensive care unit with tubes in her nose and her mouth, and an IV in her arm. Stu had waited until after they had pumped her stomach to bring me to the hospital. I burst into tears when I saw her looking so ill, her eyes filled with fear. I held her hand. "Whatever it takes, Ellen, we'll help you. Daddy and I love you and you're going to get better," I said. She couldn't speak because of the tube in her mouth, but the next day, the first thing she said to me was, "The nurse is so mean to me." I wondered if Ellen had bitten her. I said it must be very hard for a nurse in intensive care, always seeing people so close to death, to see a beautiful young girl who was *trying* to die.

Ellen had been seeing a psychologist for the past six months. It was a time when her hostility toward us and her unhappiness had reached the point where we realized it was no longer "a phase" and we could no longer cope with her moods or her anger. Her psychologist didn't help her, and after her suicide attempt she never saw him again. Afterward, when all the doctors agreed it was not a serious suicide attempt but a cry for attention, she went to a psychiatrist, who suggested Stu and I try "tough love." He, and we, didn't seem to be able to help her either. Ellen, from the day she was born, went her own way.

Now she was on the fifth floor of the hospital, in the psychiatric ward. People who seem to have attempted suicide are always sent to the psychiatric ward for a week of observation before they are released from the hospital. There were bars on the windows, and the doors were all locked. We had to ring a bell to get in. I remembered the time when my mother was in the psychiatric ward in New York, while getting shock treatments for her depression.

When we came to see Ellen each night she acted as if she were the hostess at a party, wearing her hospital gown as if it were an evening gown and introducing us to her new friends on the ward. After she came home she still wanted to wear that gown all the time. We finally got tired of looking at her parading around the house in it and threw it away. I asked her why she had taken the pills. She said she was upset because Chuck was going to break up with her. She told Stu the real reason was she had sold the ring Chuck had given her. All the kids in school knew she had sold it and thought she was pond scum. Chuck's ring was the last one that Ellen would ever receive. One week after her death he wrote us this letter:

April 7. 1993

Dear Stu and Greta,

I am so sorry to hear about the death of your beautiful, darling daughter. It's hard for me to know what to say. There's nothing I can say to help I know, but I had to communicate my sympathy and sense of loss to you. When I learned of Ellen's suicide Saturday I wanted to come see you, but my mother told me you were not doing well and didn't want to see anyone. I hope it is O.K. that I have written you.

I don't know, nor can I imagine, the pain of losing a child. Especially one so special—who was always filled with joy and laughter. Ellen always had great potential—she knew it and the people who know her knew it. She fulfilled that potential in the lives of the people who were lucky enough to know her. I have such very very fond memories of Ellen. We were madly in love with each other when we were kids. At one time I knew her as well as anyone in the world—and now I realize how much richer I am for that. I will always be thankful that I knew Ellen, and I will always carry many, many beautiful and fond memories of your daughter.

I am sorry to have gone on and on. I hope you do not resent anything I have said. I am not trying to cause you more pain. I just wanted to let you know that Ellen was loved dearly by myself and many others. I am so sorry. I have always been very fond of both of you, and my thoughts and prayers will be with you for the days ahead. If there is ever anything I can do for you please call me.

Love, Chuck

Three years after Ellen's death I became friends with a new neighbor. She was a lot younger than me and asked if I was still working. I explained that I used to be a graphic designer but now I was writing a book. She asked if she could read the manuscript. Her husband is a surgeon.

The first time I met him he told me he had read my book and hoped I didn't mind. I replied that I was delighted that he had wanted to read it. He then said, "I have only one question to ask you and you certainly don't have to tell me. Who was Dr. X?" I was happy to tell him. He said, "Of, course. I should have been able to figure it out. Let me tell you something. If the medical community of Knoxville had its way, Dr. X would be at the bottom of the Tennessee River."

REACHING FOR LOW CLOUDS

In 1969, the year we moved to Knoxville, lithium released Mother from the prison of her mind. She had five happy years between the time she recovered from her profound depression and her death from cancer in 1974. She became the mother I used to know. After shoveling a mile of sidewalk snow she wrote:

> The low clouds seem to be within reach.
> It's as if I were a child again,
> The same impatience is in my blood

Mother had always been shy, but now, for the first time in her life, she started submitting her poetry to journals and loved seeing it in print. She won awards for her poetry. She learned Japanese brush painting and joined the Sumi-e Society in New York. Literally, Sumi-e, means nothing more than black-ink painting. But the technique is said to reflect the inner goodness of a person's heart. My mother's work was displayed in the society's annual show at the Japan House on West Fifty-seventh Street in Manhattan, which was attended by the consul general of Japan. I wondered if my mother had finally forgiven the Japanese. (From the end of World War II on, Mother would never buy any product that was made in Japan.)

She was asked to display her paintings in schools and libraries. She entertained her old and new friends for dinner and became a whirlwind of activity. Mother wrote me long, chatty letters once a week. After years of silence on what she was thinking about (except for her own misery), she told me in more detail than I ever wanted to know whom she had invited to dinner and everything she was preparing. She even told me whom she was putting on her shit list. She sent me an article called "Poison in the Backyard," which listed all the plants that could kill you if you ate them. I would never dream of tasting a plant, but my mother was always picking strange leaves and flowers and tasting them. She told me that after reading the list she was going to be more careful. At last she really wanted to live.

A man who had read her poetry in one of the journals started to write long letters to her, which she always answered. Her sad yet hopeful poems had struck a chord with him. After they had been writing to each other for about a year, exchanging poems they each had written, Daddy noticed the address on the envelope. He asked my mother if she knew where her new friend lived. She had no idea. He told her the address was the prison in New York that was called "the Tombs," where men accused of violent crimes waited for trial. Mother didn't stop writing to him.

She volunteered to work with mental patients at Pilgrim state hospital on Long Island, a dark, red-brick building with bars on all the windows. It sat in the marshes, isolated from everything and everyone. You could see it from ten miles away and know what it was (everyone's nightmare vision of a mental institution). A neighbor who was a volunteer at Pilgrim had brought her a poem by a patient. Mother read the man's touching poem and wanted to help him. She went to see the assistant director of the hospital and told him she wanted to try to help the patients there via poetry. He was happy to cooperate. He knew she would be a strictly nonprofessional therapist—she had gone to high school for only one year. He had a room assigned to her for the thirty or forty patients who attended her sessions. It was painted an ugly green color. Mother bought bright blue paint and repainted the walls herself, brought her paintings and hung them up, and hung drapes over the barred windows. She got people to donate comfortable couches and chairs and brought baskets of flowers from her garden. She turned the sterile hospital room into a living room where people, who might never see their own homes again, could feel at home. And she helped the patients to write poetry. They loved her. One of the patients, a twenty-seven-year-old man, wrote to her in a letter: "You believe me, ah my friend and I am glad you think so much of me. You are one of the nicest people I have met in my life." Another patient, a fifty-year-old woman, wanted to go home with my mother after each poetry session because she "wanted to be with my mama."

Once, on my yearly visit from Knoxville, Mother asked me to visit Pilgrim with her, not for her poetry session but for the celebration for patients who had birthdays that month. The patients were hollow-eyed and disconnected looking, dressed in virtual rags. Each one got a small gift. People sang "Happy Birthday." She introduced me to one of the patients and told him that, like him, I was an artist. He asked me if I would look at his work and showed me his sketchbook, in which he had copied every page of a *Life* magazine. The photos, the headlines, the small print. There were thousands of hours of work in that book. It meant nothing to anyone but him. When I was ready to leave, he asked me if I would come back and see him again. I said yes, knowing I never would, not only because I didn't live in New York, but also because the experience was so upsetting to me. (I had nightmares about it for months afterward.) After the party the chief psychiatrist of the ward met with the volunteers and I was invited to attend. He told us that some of the patients had not really been "insane" when they had arrived. They were problems for their families, who either didn't want them or could not deal with their eccentricities. So they had been committed. He implied that after the patients had been there for a while, their mental health had deteriorated. I cried all the way home and asked my mother how she could stand going there. She answered that they needed her.

The happiest I had heard Mother sound in years was the day she called and told me she had submitted a poem written by one of her students to a newspaper and it had been published. The man had been in Pilgrim for almost twenty years. They put his published poem up on a bulletin board, and he became an instant celebrity among the patients and the nurses. Everyone made a big fuss over him. He experienced a remarkable recovery soon after and my mother liked to think the acceptance of his poem by the newspaper had something to do with it. He was one of the very few long-term patients to be released from Pilgrim. It was a poem of his that my mother's neighbor had shown her that had made Mother decide to become a volunteer.

A small press, Bale of Turtle Press, in Armonk, New York, published *The Sound the Heart Makes,* a book Mother wrote on her experiences at Pilgrim; three essays were contributed by doctors, illuminating the procedures and goals of poetry therapy (a concept that had existed for some time, but was just now gaining acceptance in the medical community), and of the important role played by nonprofessional therapists. One of the doctors, Nathan Kline, was the psychiatrist who had started my mother on lithium. He believed writing poetry was a "healing balm." One section contained Mother's poems and another contained poems by the patients. Martin Tucker, the publisher, wrote in the preface of the book, "Hedda Friedman conceived of the idea of people who were searching for their voices, their persona, to find it in the journey of a poem's creation, and she, with the patients, began their travels."

The book was sold all over the world. Mother got letters from hundreds of people, including one from the White House. *Newsday,* the Long Island newspaper, wrote a long story about her and included a photo of her. It is framed and hangs on my wall. The reporter who interviewed Mother and wrote the story said, "Hedda Friedman is a youthful 62, with soft, short, blond hair and a rather elegant feel for clothes." That amused me, because if there was one thing Mother never cared about, it was clothes.

The publisher of *The Sound the Heart Makes* asked me to design the book and it was one of the happiest jobs I have ever done. I used Mother's Sumi-e drawings throughout. On the dedication page, pleading for more volunteers to work with mental patients, I showed two little birds Mother had drawn. A Chinese saying, quoted on that page, said, "Even a small bird leaves claw-marks in the snow."

Now, though, when I look at *The Sound the Heart Makes* and see those two little birds, I think of Mother and Ellen, both suffering from depression and both leaving their marks.

MAC AND SLIPPERY SAM

When Steven and Ellen were kids it was just like my mother's time—a very different time from today. There was no such thing as day care. If you had young children, you stayed home. I was one of the lucky women who had found a profession in which I could work at home.

In 1973, when I started a full-time job, my children were not very happy about it. I didn't get home until 5:15. Steven and Ellen were used to my greeting them with milk and cookies when they came home from school, even though they hated milk, and the cookies were "slice and bake."

When I went back to work, Steven was a seventh grader at Webb. He got home at 4:30 each day. Ellen, who was almost ten, still went to Mount Olive School. She got home at 3:30 and so had an hour to be alone.

A few months after I started working, Ellen told me that she had made a new friend on the telephone. She said her friend was a woman older than me who used to be blind but had had an operation, and now she could see. Ellen said they planned to rob banks together. She told me that she called her friend "Mac" and that her friend called her "Slippery Sam."

Ellen had always been an imaginative child and I didn't believe her. I told her I thought it was a very good story and that she might want to write it down. Ellen said if I didn't believe her, I should get on the other phone and listen in, because she was going to call Mac right then. I did, mostly to humor her. A woman answered the phone and I heard Ellen say in a very deep, altered voice, "Hello Mac," and to my astonishment, the woman said, "Slippery Sam, where've you been? I haven't heard from you in a couple of days and we have banks to rob."

When she got off the phone I asked Ellen how she got the woman's phone number. She said she had started to call her best friend, Dana, one day and then remembered that she was not speaking to Dana. So for the last digit, she dialed one number past Dana's. When a woman answered the phone, Ellen said, "I'm gonna do it." The woman, instead of hanging up or telling her she had the wrong number, asked her what she was going to do. Ellen said, "I'm gonna rob a bank." The woman said, "I've always wanted to rob a bank. Maybe we can be partners."

I told Ellen that the woman sounded very nice, but that she should not call her anymore. I thought Ellen might be bothering her. After a few days Mac called Slippery Sam. I answered the phone. I think she knew that Ellen was a troubled child years before we did and she was a very kind person. She told me she didn't mind Ellen calling her at all. In fact, she enjoyed their conversations. When my parents came for their Christmas visit, Daddy joined the club and became Frank the Forger, getting on the telephone extension for a three-way conversation among criminals.

After a few years Mac and Slippery Sam became Marie and Ellen, and they would talk to each other several times a week. They had changed their minds about robbing banks and just talked about whatever they felt like. I asked Ellen if she wanted to invite Marie and her husband to the house for dinner one night. I wanted to meet this wonderful lady. Ellen told me she didn't want to know what Marie looked like. It would spoil the illusion.

Marie sent her son Tim to our house every Christmas with a present for Ellen. They lived in Sevierville, the town next to Knoxville. Ellen always gave Tim a present to take back to Marie. The tradition went on for four years, until Ellen decided she was ready to meet her phone friend in person.

Marie and her husband came to visit one Sunday. Marie was an attractive woman, and her husband, Tom, a career military man, seemed to be right out of central casting for the French Foreign Legion. He was tall, his posture perfectly erect, and he was handsome, with gray hair and a handlebar mustache. Marie and Tom had been stationed all over the world. When Tom died, seven years later, Ellen was the first person Marie called, and Ellen rushed to her house to comfort her. When Ellen graduated from college and moved to Nashville, she drove the four hours to Sevierville each year to take Marie to dinner for her birthday. They wrote letters to each other. If Marie didn't hear from Ellen for a few months, she would call us to see if she was all right. Their friendship lasted for twenty years.

I was never jealous of Marie for her relationship with Ellen. I was happy that my daughter had a woman friend who truly loved her. Marie was deeply religious and was always trying to get Ellen to join the church. Ellen, in her way, liked teasing Marie into believing that some day she might. As long as Ellen lived, Mac never gave up on saving Slippery Sam's slippery soul.

The night the medical examiner called us from Seattle to tell us that our daughter was dead, one of the first things I said to Stuart was, "How will we ever tell Marie?" After several days I decided I would write to her, but I couldn't track down her address. I thought she might have moved to California, where her son Tim now lived. After Steven sent back Ellen's papers I found her address book and wrote Tim a letter. His address was in the book, but Marie's wasn't. I guess Ellen knew it by heart. I told Tim what had happened and asked him to please tell his mother for us. I sent him a picture of Ellen and a story I'd found among her things, called "Mac and Slippery Sam."

Six months later the phone rang, and it was Marie. She told me she hadn't heard from Ellen for a long time and wondered how she was doing. I asked her if Tim hadn't told her that Ellen had killed herself. He hadn't. I guess he couldn't. Marie wept violently when I told her. She asked me how Ellen did it. I told her that she shot herself. I listened silently while Marie cried for a long time. After a while she asked me, "How am I supposed to go on living without my Ellen?" I thought, "She's not really *your* Ellen, but at this moment I wish she was." Marie never called me again.

• • •

When Ellen was fourteen I got her a telephone for her bedroom. (She was the kind of teenager whom call waiting was invented for.) It freed me to nag her about things other than getting off the phone; cleaning up the mess in her room, doing her homework, setting the table for dinner. Ellen's bedroom had a light chartreuse carpet and pale yellow furniture with white Formica tops on all of the flat surfaces, which could be hosed down if need be. The doors on the hutch over her desk were covered with pasted-on frog pictures, and the shelves behind housed her collection of frogs. Ellen had glass frogs and ceramic frogs and pewter frogs and plastic frogs and papier-mâché frogs. For her eighth birthday we gave Ellen a large stuffed green-and-yellow frog, which, from that day on always accompanied us on trips.

That year, 1971, flying home from a visit with my parents in New York, there was an unoccupied seat in our row of six. Stu, Steven, and an elderly schoolteacher sat on the right side of the aisle with Ellen, the frog, and I, on the left (the frog in the middle). We all (including the frog) fastened our seat belts, and Ellen took the "for airline sickness" bag out of the seat pocket and tipped the frog's head into it. Everyone who passed by on their way to the bathroom laughed when they saw it. The stewardess smiled without fail, whenever she went by. When the plane landed in Saint Louis to take on more passengers, the pilot came out of his cabin to look at the frog still wearing its seatbelt and seemingly vomiting into the bag (the stewardess must have told him to). The pilot said in the most patronizing voice to both Steven and Ellen, "Isn't that cute? Is it a boy frog or a girl frog?" Ellen rolled her eyes, and Steven said, "It's a homosexual." The pilot wheeled around and walked back to his cabin without saying another word, and the elderly schoolteacher said, "When I was teaching school the students didn't know words like that." Steven was eleven.

Ellen's frog collection went with her to Nashville and later to Seattle. Her friend Tim sent some of them back to us after her death. They are now in a closet in Steven's old bedroom; it would make Stu sick to see them. Steven had sent back the framed picture of a frog that Stu painted as a gift for Ellen's thirteenth birthday. He signed the watercolor of the frog as if it were a print,

1/1. Ellen liked having the one and only copy. At the time Stu was on the road once a month for a week, selling the prints of his pencil drawings. When he went to the frame shops and galleries and did the sidewalk art shows, he always looked for different kinds of frogs to bring Ellen. Like so many daddies, though, he didn't understand that his little girl was growing up, and he continued to do this long after Ellen was interested in adding to her collection. By the time she was fifteen, Ellen was interested in collecting boys, not frogs. The watercolor remains in the closet with her papers. I don't think Stu could bear to look at that either, and that's where I have left it. On the program her friends from Seattle did for her memorial service, "Service to Celebrate the Life of Ellen Eichel," there is a frog motif.

When she was fourteen Ellen returned from a trip to Gatlinburg with her friend Dana and Dana's father. Ellen proudly showed me all the trinkets she had bought. Later that evening Dana's father called to tell us that he found out the girls had spent the day shoplifting in Gatlinburg. Stu went crazy. Honest to a fault, he started hitting Ellen with an anger that I had never seen before. I had to intervene to stop him. I remembered my brother screaming at my daddy to stop hitting me when I was seventeen and dating Jon Arista. My daughter and I each managed, at a certain point in our lives, to push our fathers' "I don't know what to do anymore" buttons. The difference was, Ellen never *stopped* pushing it, and I never pushed it again.

The next day Stu kept Ellen out of school, drove her to Gatlinburg, and told her to put everything she'd stolen back where she got it; if she did, he would not report her to the police.

Fourteen seemed to be the turning point in Ellen's life and it took us a while to notice it. That was the year I was diagnosed with MS, the year Ellen left childhood behind. And she left it behind with a vengeance. She quit Webb at the end of that year and started dating, smoking pot, and emptying the bottles in the liquor cabinet. We never thought of getting rid of the liquor, until the day when we tried to serve some to company. We found the bottles were almost empty and poured what was left down the sink. Stu and I don't like to drink liquor, but Ellen eventually became an alcoholic.

The first person to have sex with Ellen was Steven's French "brother," Georges, who returned with Steven after our son's year in Paris and spent six weeks living with us. When he got off the plane with Steven, Ellen, not quite fifteen, clutched my hand and said, "God, he's so cute." It was July, and Steven, Ellen, and Georges spent the days together listening to music, playing tennis, and going to the pool. When Georges said "bayzing zoot," Ellen pretended to swoon. The Commodores' "Three Times a Lady" played on the radio seemingly every ten minutes. Georges hated that song and pretended to throw up whenever he heard it.

Ellen had not yet started to menstruate. After Georges had gone back to France she told me that having sex with him was like trying to push a hot dog into a thimble. When she told me that she was afraid she might be pregnant, I bought a pregnancy self-test package from the drugstore and was relieved when the strip didn't turn the wrong color. Was it blue? Pink? I hoped Ellen hadn't become pregnant at exactly the point that she was about to get her first period. When I told Ellen she was too young to have sex, she told me Georges was her first. She felt much better now that she wasn't the only one of her friends to still be a virgin, she said. I found a story that she had written about Georges, called "My First Kiss," in the papers that Steven sent home from Seattle. So girlish. So innocent. So phony.

At fifteen, Ellen told me she was sleeping with her steady boyfriend Chuck. I sent her to my gynecologist. Dr. Kinlaw put her on birth control pills and Ellen said Dr. Kinlaw looked at her like she made him sick. I told her she probably did, but she would make him (and me) sicker if she became pregnant. After I became suspicious of *everything* that Ellen was doing I started listening in on her telephone calls. Once I heard her talking to Dana, who said, "If I have to fuck one more guy I don't think I can stand it. It's so *boring*." Ellen said, "I don't think it's boring at all."

Two years later on a Saturday morning I overheard her talking to someone on the phone. I was just passing by her room on my way to the kitchen to make breakfast. She sat cross-legged in her short pink nightgown on her pretty yellow bed and said, bubbling with excitement, "I'm dating the biggest drug dealer in East Tennessee." Helpless and hopeless, I stormed into her room and ripped the telephone that she had gotten for her fourteenth birthday out of the wall. She wouldn't tell me who the drug dealer was and I didn't know if she was telling the truth or showing off. The phone and my trust (what little was left), would never be replaced. At seventeen Ellen was seemingly beyond our control. We decided that she would not be allowed out with any*one* for the next month. (It's called spitting in the wind.) After she was grounded, Ellen went to school and came home and sulked. I felt a terrible coldness toward her and tried not to show it. I don't think I succeeded. I was still under the illusion that I could have an influence on her.

One evening Ellen came into my bedroom, all contrite. I was lying down because I was going through a period of MS problems and my energy level was almost nonexistent. She apologized for giving her father and me such a hard time and asked if she could take the car this one night and visit her girlfriend Mona. Ellen and Chuck had recently broken up. Ellen said she had finished her homework and was going nuts hanging around the house. I knew, and liked, both Mona and her mother and told Ellen she could go, but that she had to be home by ten-thirty. She hugged me good-bye—a rare occurrence. *Was this some kind of turning point?* I thought, deceiving myself yet again.

By eleven I was getting upset, and by eleven-thirty I was furious. But we didn't know what to do. Ellen was seventeen. It was too early to report her missing and too late to think she was up to anything good. It was too late to call Mona's mother and I was so tired. We went to bed but couldn't sleep. At midnight we heard the sound of something crashing into the garage and bounded out of bed. It was my car, of course, and Ellen came staggering into the house bleary eyed, very drunk.

"Where have you been Ellen? You lied to me and you're drunk," I cried.

"I'm not going to tell *you* where I've been," she slurred, looking at me as if I were the enemy.

Stu and I were livid, and Stu said to her, "Maybe you'll tell the police." Then he said, "Greta, do you want to come with me while I take Ellen to the police station? I want to know what shit hole served her liquor." So I got dressed and at one in the morning we drove Ellen to the police station. She sat in the back of the car without saying a word to us. I thought she might have fallen asleep.

When we got to the police station I said to the officer, "This is my daughter. She's seventeen and she's drunk. We want to know which bar served her and we think you should shut them down." I spoke before Stu because I didn't want him to say he thought they should put Ellen in jail. We were escorted into a small room and waited about fifteen minutes for a detective to come and speak to us. He asked Ellen her name and said, "What have you had to drink, Ellen?"

"Five Long Island teas," she slurred.

"That's a pretty strong drink," he said. "Where did you get it?"

"I'm not going to tell you."

"Do you think you'll tell someone after you spend the night in jail Ellen?" he said in a very kind voice. Ellen told him the name of the bar on "the Strip," and he said to us, "They're known for serving liquor to minors. We'll send someone out to shut them down, but I can guarantee you that tomorrow night they'll be open again." I wondered, in spite of the officer's kind manner, who was getting paid off, but hesitated to ask, under the circumstances. "Why don't you just take Ellen home and put her to bed," he said to us.

She slept like a baby, but she was my baby no longer. I think I hated her that night, and at that time I only wanted her to graduate from high school, try to function in college, and get out of the house.

Nothing changed between us when Ellen went to college. In her first year at the University of Tennessee she moved out of the dorm and into her boyfriend Erik's apartment. This was against the rules for freshman, but Ellen never played by the rules. I suspected Erik hit her, but she never talked about it. When she came to my office, usually for money, she sometimes had bruises. When I asked her about them she told me things like "I fell down the stairs." After six months she tired (or became frightened) of Erik and moved out of his apartment. She called us one night at eleven o'clock and told us she wanted to come home. Erik was visiting his parents in Nashville. Stu went to get her and she quickly packed up her clothes and her books. When she got home she said that Erik didn't know she had left, and she wanted to know if I thought she should call him in Nashville and tell him? I told her it would probably be the decent thing to do. (Don't ask me why.) When she called Erik he said, "You'd better be back there by three o'clock tomorrow. If you're not, nothing is safe. Not your car. Not your house. Not your parents." Stu immediately called Erik's father in Nashville and told him what his son had threatened to do. His father said, "I'll talk to him. That boy is as mean as a snake."

We ultimately had to get a court injunction to keep him away from her (and us). We took Ellen out of school for fear that he would hurt her and sent her to live with Stu's mother in Detroit until Erik graduated. At the end of that semester he would move home to Nashville. To our disgust, Ellen called him from Detroit to "let him know she was OK." We felt Stu's mother was also in danger, but Eric never bothered Elizabeth. After Ellen graduated she moved to Nashville. She assured us she wasn't seeing Erik. I hoped not.

I always wondered if Ellen had moved to Nashville after she graduated to be around Erik. When it came to Ellen, we never understood her motivation. Years later Erik called me in Knoxville to tell me that Ellen was a stripper in a nightclub. I told him that I didn't know if she was or she wasn't, but in either case it was none of his business and to please never call me again. I told him not to forget the injunction, which said he would be put in jail if he ever made contact with us. But I called

Ellen and told her what Erik had said, and she told me that it was ridiculous. I sensed she was lying but didn't tell her that. Then she called me back a short time later and said it was true. She needed the money because she had been arrested for drunken driving, and after spending the weekend in jail she had to pay a $1,200 fine.

Ellen told me she was moving to Seattle because she "needed a change of scene." After her death one of her friends told me she moved as far away as possible because an old boyfriend was stalking her. I wonder if Erik, whose own father had called him "mean as a snake," was the stalker.

When we sent Ellen to live in Detroit to get her away from Erik, she fell in love with Jason, the maintenance man of Elizabeth's condominium, a divorced religious fanatic in his thirties (Ellen was nineteen) who wanted to marry Ellen and travel around the country with her, preaching the gospel. Jason said he had his own ministry. When we met him he gave us his card.

Steven was getting married to Belinda that August. I was having some MS problems and felt numb and exhausted. Belinda's mother said I needed to wear a long dress for the wedding, but I didn't own a long dress. Stu took me shopping, but I was too weak to try anything on or even look for a dress and asked Stu to just drive me home. I called his mother and asked her if she had a long dress. Elizabeth said she had one, but had just cut off the bottom. I asked her if she would please sew it back on and send it to me. She did. It was the kind of flouncy pink dress that I would never buy, but beggars can't be choosers. I couldn't stand to shop for matching pink shoes and it *was* a long dress, so I wore canvas sandals. They kind of looked like sneakers and I hoped nobody would see them beneath the long dress.

Jason was driving Ellen back from Detroit so she could be a bridesmaid in the wedding. He was going to stay at our house for the weekend. I was nervous about Ellen coming home with Jason because she had told him we were atheists. As it turned out we liked Jason a lot—for a weekend. He was one of the best-looking men I had ever seen. He was bright and articulate, and if he weren't as crazy as a loon I would have been delighted for Ellen to marry him (as if I had a choice). I think Ellen was distressed that we seemed to like him, as she made a point of dating men that she knew we wouldn't approve of. After Jason went back to Detroit, promising to write, Ellen lay on her bed for hours and listened to the religious tapes he had given her of him preaching. I'm sure she did it to bug us, but when she went back to school she forgot all about her supposed religious conversion. Jason scrawled "Jesus is love" all over the envelopes of the letters he kept writing to her.

Years after Ellen graduated and had moved to Nashville I got a phone call from Jason:

"Hello, Mrs. Eichel. This is Jason. Do you remember me?"

"Jason, I will never forget you as long as I live."

"You thought I was crazy."

"But, Jason, you are crazy. That doesn't mean I didn't like you. I'm very fond of a lot of crazy people."

"Do you think you could give me Ellen's phone number and tell me where she's living?"

"I don't think so, Jason. She's deeply involved with another man and I don't think it would be right for you to call her."

The other man, a would-be songwriter, called me recently not knowing that Ellen was dead.

FINISHING THE CHINESE DINNER

Mother died at the end of a bitter cold February day. She had entered the hospital only the day before at the insistence of a visiting nurse. We sent out for Chinese food that night. The white cardboard containers of chow mein, fried rice, and shrimp in lobster sauce sat on the table like tombstones while we picked at our food. We didn't talk. We had just finished eating when the phone rang. It was someone from the hospital saying death was imminent and we should come as quickly as possible. Daddy said, "Isn't it just like your mother to let us finish eating our dinner before she dies?"

Charles Werner was our doctor during the four years Stuart and I lived in Huntington Station. Dr. Werner was a kind man and a good doctor. Like Mother, he had once suffered a nervous breakdown, and he had that faraway and distracted look typical of someone who has. His shoulders stooped and he was as skinny as Daddy. He liked to take photographs of flowers and they were beautifully framed and hung in his office. I told him I was an artist and when I went for my annual checkups he liked to talk to me about art. He always asked me if I liked his new photos and I told him I thought they were beautiful. (They were sensitive and vulnerable looking, like he was.)

Dr. Werner became Mother and Daddy's doctor too, after they moved to Huntington Station in 1968 to be close to their children and grandchildren. None of us had any idea at the time that Stuart would be offered a great job in Tennessee and we would be leaving the next year. My parents understood, though, having lived through the Great Depression, that people have to go where they can get the best job.

When Mother and Daddy came to Knoxville for their Christmas visit in 1973, Mother told me she didn't feel well. She was tired and had pain in her stomach. She had always been afraid she would die of cancer, as she had seen her own mother die at the age of sixty-seven. She said, "I've probably got cancer." She had lost weight and looked gaunt. I told her that she looked wonderful.

When my parents got back to New York, Mother went into the hospital for exploratory surgery to see what was causing her pain. That day Daddy called me at work. "Mother has cancer," he said. "They just opened her up and closed her back up again." He started to cry and hung up. I shared an office with two other artists and there was no privacy. I always hated for anyone to see me cry. Jim Kelly was both my boss and my friend, so I ran into his empty office, shut the door, lay my head down on his desk and sobbed. After a while, Ted, one of the other artists and also my friend, opened the door, came in, and put his arms around me. I cried into his blue-and-white striped shirt, smearing it with mascara. I said, "My mother is going to die." He called Stuart at his office to come and take me home.

Daddy had asked Dr. Werner to call me in Knoxville. When he called later that day, he said, "Greta, I'm sorry to have to tell you this. Hedda has cancer of the pancreas and has about one month left to live. My own mother had the same type of cancer and your mother is lucky to be able to die so quickly."

Daddy never told Mother she had cancer and forbade me to discuss it with her. He said she would not be able to deal with the thing she had always feared. I believed my mother knew she was dying but did not want to talk about it.

By the time we got to the hospital, after having just finished our Chinese dinner, Mother had lapsed into a deep coma. The nurse told Daddy and me to keep talking to Mother until she died. She said that a person's hearing is the last thing to go, and that even if it didn't seem like Mother could hear us, there was a good chance that she could.

Daddy and I took turns whispering in Mother's ear. I said, "I love you Mommy. Spring is almost here. Your pink hyacinths will soon be blooming." I don't know what private things my daddy said. We were still talking to her when the nurse came in and gently told us that my mother was no longer breathing. Daddy and I went into a little room to wait for Dr. Werner to come and sign the death certificate. I was sitting on a shabby, brown leather couch when he arrived and sat next to me. Daddy said, "Dr. Werner, I talked to Hedda until the moment she died. Do you think she heard me?" Dr. Werner started to say, "Well, John, I don't . . ." when I jabbed him hard in his ribs with my elbow and hissed coldly to him, "Say yes." He paused for just a moment, then said, "Yes, John. I'm sure she did." Daddy smiled for the first time that day.

On the way out of the hospital, Dr. Werner touched my arm and said, "You're some tough cookie." I answered, "You bet your sweet ass." I couldn't tell him that I was not quite as tough as I seemed. I could not allow myself to break down yet. I was almost thirty-six the night my mother died, but I felt very old. I had to get Daddy, who was moving as if in a trance, out of the hospital.

We went straight to the funeral home to pick out a coffin. The cheap ones all had shiny white satin lining, pink or blue ruffles on the pillow, phony bronze handles, and ornate scrollwork on the sides. They disgusted me. The expensive ones were wonderfully simple. Even at a time like that I couldn't help saying to the Italian salesman, "The Mafia must have good taste." We bought a medium-priced coffin that was a compromise between gaudy and simple.

I chose a long, black wool skirt and a white silk blouse for my mother to be buried in. I would not give whoever would prepare her body for burial the earrings Mother had always worn, that had been Grandma's, to be buried with her. I wanted to give them to Ellen. I gave them a pair of turquoise earrings that Mother sometimes wore.

The following day the rabbi called and asked me to tell him some things about my mother that he could use in the service. I asked him to please not act as if he knew her. She had not been in a synagogue once since Peter's bar mitzvah, almost twenty years earlier. "My mother was a poet and we'd like it if you would read some of her poems" I said. I picked out ones she had written about her garden. When the rabbi read them, everyone but me broke down and wept. I sat there dry-eyed and numb, clutching Stuart's hand.

Daddy had gone to the funeral home the night before the service to say good-bye to Mother by himself. He came back and said she looked beautiful. When I saw her body the next day I didn't think she looked beautiful at all. I thought she looked dead. Worse, the person who had prepared her body for burial had not put the turquoise earrings through the pierced holes in her ears, where they belonged, but, shockingly, had stuffed her earlobes through them. I wish I hadn't looked, because that is the image I remember to this day.

The funeral was held in Huntington Station and almost a hundred people came. Mother and Daddy had a lot of friends. A snowstorm had started during the night and by morning the ground was covered with about six inches of wet snow. The burial, however, was in Clifton, New Jersey, almost 100 miles from Huntington Station, and only a small group of us made the long trip. As they lowered Mother's coffin into the frozen ground I heard Daddy whisper, "Good-bye darling." It was freezing cold and windy, the falling snow blew harshly in our faces. I was shaking violently and Stuart and his mother held me as tightly as they could. I wasn't crying however, I was shivering from the cold.

I thought when I got back to Knoxville the numbness would fade, it would all become real, and I would finally break down and cry. I never did. On March 15, three weeks after Mother's death, I received a letter from Daddy thanking me for helping him during the darkest hours of his life. He said he went through my mother's files and found a letter written to him in January. It read:

Dear John,
Perhaps I can say now what is so hard to talk about calmly. I would like the following Indian poem, which I so love, to be carved on my grave:

NIGHT CHANT
In old age wandering on a trail of beauty,
lively may I walk.
In old age wandering on a trail of beauty,
lively again, may I walk.
It is finished in beauty.
It is finished in beauty.

Ever yours, Hedda

Ah, so she knew all along, I thought.

. . .

Sixteen years later I was back in Huntington Station to stay with Billie after my father underwent a triple coronary bypass. Less than three months later he died, never having left the hospital.

The day of the operation Stu and I were still in Knoxville, where we waited all day for news of how my father had come through the surgery. Billie called us much later in the evening to say that after the surgeon had closed my father's chest, following the "successful procedure," they found that his blood wouldn't clot, so they had to open his ribcage again to try and stop the bleeding. Billie sounded calm, but was clearly holding back tears. After I hung up I sobbed to Stuart, "My daddy's going to die." I didn't believe that my father, who had looked so frail on his eightieth birthday four months before, could survive being cut open twice.

We drove to New York the next day. Daddy was in intensive care; he had a large tube down his throat and smaller tubes in his nose. A machine showed the beating of his heart and we could hear the air being forced in and out of his lungs. He never opened his eyes, and although his heart was pumping away just fine, he looked as if he had already died.

It was early in January and it was freezing cold in New York. Every day we walked through deep, dirty slush to get from the parking garage to the hospital. Because Stu and I both had jobs we couldn't stay for very long. After four days we drove back to Tennessee. In Knoxville I bought a winter coat. It sometimes gets cold in Knoxville, but you can drive everywhere, practically right up to any door, so I had given my winter coat to Goodwill many years before. But I thought, superstitiously, that if I bought a winter coat, Daddy would at least live through the winter and maybe get better in the spring.

Three weeks later, we drove back to New York and stayed with Billie a second time. This time I remained there for a week, but Stu drove back to Knoxville the following day. Daddy never spoke. There was a feeding tube in his stomach. The tube that was previously in his throat had been removed, but they'd given him a tracheotomy, so now there was a tube in his neck. He was attached to machines by wires.

Billie said my father was angry with her for letting him have the operation and that she could tell by the look in his eyes. I told her that *he* was the one who had wanted the surgery. He had seemed so optimistic about the outcome. The doctor had told him that he might get to play tennis again. Daddy answered, "That would be great, if I could just see the ball." Although he didn't speak or acknowledge our presence in any way, I too thought he looked angry. But who wouldn't be, hooked up to all those tubes and wires? Over and over again I told him I loved him. When Billie left the room for a while I whispered in Daddy's ear the poem he had written to my mother during their courtship.

A few weeks later, on our third trip to New York, Daddy was sitting in a chair in his hospital room. He thought he was in a restaurant and complained about the shortage of waitresses—how could they serve all his guests with so little help? He drew a picture showing perspective—which he used to draw for me when I was a child—train tracks and telephone poles receding into the distance. I thought that a miracle had occurred and he was going to get better after all. Billie was ecstatic.

We talked about the events that were unfolding so quickly in the world— events that, if Daddy had been able to read the *New York Times* for the last two months, he would have explained to me. East and West Germany had reunited and the Soviet Union seemed to be collapsing. Stu and I drove back to Knoxville feeling some hope for my father, and even some for the world.

Two weeks after our third visit, however, Daddy went into a coma. The doctor told Billie that there was no hope for my father—all his organs were "shutting down." Stu and I flew back the next day because the doctors said he had only a few days to live.

The first day we got there a nurse from the hospital called. She wanted Billie to come to the hospital and sign a "code blue," which was a do-not-resuscitate order. I told Billie I wanted to sign it too, so that she wouldn't be the only one who had to take responsibility. I wasn't allowed to sign it, though. Only the wife can give this permission, the nurse said. Billie started to cry, saying she felt like she was signing his death warrant. Saint Francis is a Catholic hospital and the nurse said to Billie, "We're doing everything we can to keep him alive, dear." I said, "I wish you weren't." The nurse gave me a withering look and replied, "Only God can take a life." I wanted to ask her if God wanted to have my father hooked up to machines and to have all those tubes in his body when there was no hope for him to recover, but I restrained myself. My father survived for ten more days, never awakening from his coma.

Stu stayed for the weekend. On Friday I flew home to Knoxville. Five days later Stu and I flew back to New York for Daddy's funeral.

Steven came down from Boston and stayed with us whenever I came from Knoxville to visit. Billie didn't drive and I had been out of New York for so long that I couldn't stand the trauma of driving in hostile New York traffic. Steven drove Billie and me to the hospital every day.

On our third visit, Billie got sick. She was under a lot of stress and, of course, was not a young woman herself. Dr. Werner was her doctor, too. I hadn't seen him since my mother's death, sixteen years before, and the last thing I had said to him was "You bet your sweet ass," so I was embarrassed going to his office. I wondered what he would say to me, or if he would speak to me at all. When he saw me walk in with Steven and Billie, he looked embarrassed too, whirled around, and left the room without saying a word to us. He was gone for about ten minutes and we stood there stupidly, not knowing what to do. When he came back, he put his arms around me and said, "Greta, I'm so sorry about John. I know this is a tough time for you all. John told me you had MS and I always ask him about you. You seem to be doing just fine and I see you're still beautiful." He asked me how I liked the new photos of the flowers he had taken, which were hanging on his walls. They reminded me of Mother. I told him they were lovely. When I left his office I cried, I think for my mother, for the first time.

STU COOKS THE LAST SUPPER

I was still working as a freelance artist and staying home with the children when Stu decided he wanted to go into business for himself and sell prints of his pencil drawings. Each original took about three months to do, and most people could never afford to buy them; besides, Stu couldn't bear to part with them. Stu needed to travel around the country and do sidewalk art shows and visit frame shops and galleries to make a living as a fine artist, but he had a full-time job with Lavidge.

One of my clients was the University of Tennessee. The people there had been asking me to work full-time since I had started freelancing for them, three years earlier. So, Stuart and I decided to switch our roles. I said I would support us in half the style to which we were accustomed until he could get his business started (my salary would be exactly half of what he had been earning).

I was in the habit of going back to sleep in the morning, after Stu and the kids left, and doing things at my own pace and in my own time. I took a nap in the afternoon. I sat outside and read a book if it was a nice day. I sat in the sun and worked on my skin cancer. Then I would start doing my work after dinner and usually worked until one in the morning. I always heard the "Star Spangled Banner" playing on TV before the station shut down for the evening. (This was before the curse of cable television.)

Now *Stu* would stay home with the children, shop for food, take Steven to tennis tournaments, Ellen to dancing lessons, and *cook dinner*. He had never done anything in the kitchen before except boil water for tea, but I told Stuart that his planning the meals was part of the deal. I left for work at eight in the morning and didn't get home until after five in the afternoon. I wasn't used to getting up at six in the morning and staying up and working all day. It was a shock to my system.

A bigger shock awaited me. The evening I got home from my first day at work I was very tired. When I opened the door an awful odor greeted me. It smelled like the house had been in the process of burning down and that someone had beat out the fire using a rubber mat. I tried to smile and play the supportive wife. I said to Stu, "Hi honey, what did you fix for dinner?" He said, "Hamburger Helper," which I, far from a gourmet cook myself, wouldn't feed to the dog. I stared at the sink, which was filled with burned pots and pans. I thought Stu must have burned every cooking utensil that we had. The supportive wife pretense was heading quickly for the window. I said, "Isn't Hamburger Helper a one-pot meal?" Stu said that's what it said on the box, but he put the stuff in a pot and it burned, and so he put it in another pot and it burned, so he put it in another pot and it burned, and . . . I guess I should have taught him how to work the stove, but for some reason, I thought he knew that there was high heat and medium heat and low heat and all those increments in between.

The supportive wife bit had gone down the toilet, and I said, "You know, Stu, at least you could have cleaned the fucking pots before I got home." Looking abashed, he said, "I did. You should have seen them before."

Now, if you didn't know Stu, you might think he was faking this stupidity. But the man can't even work the thermostat. The circuit breakers, located in the garage, have always been flipped back and forth by me when the power went out, even in the middle of the night in winter when it's freezing cold. Stu has never learned to play records on the stereo. So what could I possibly have been expecting with the stove?

I have come to accept that there are some people in this world who are hated by machines. I am married to one of them. Stuart's car hates him. The stereo hates him, too. I took full responsibility for the disaster of Stu's first dinner and we ate out that night. We had no choice. There was just a tiny pile of revolting, burned, chopped meat on a plate, hardly enough for four hungry people, even if their taste buds had been surgically removed. After that I was willing to break the covenant we had made. Although Stu did the shopping and the other motherly chores, I always cooked dinner. He fixed the salad, though, since you can't burn lettuce.

By the time Steven and Ellen grew up and left home, Stuart and I were both working. He had gone back into advertising and got home later than I did. I no longer was willing to do *any* cooking. Steven, thinking he could make our lives easier, sent us a microwave oven. He said we could pop something in and in four or five minutes we could have a delicious dinner on the table. I bought five microwave dinners. Three times I put one on the table, took one bite, and said, "I can't eat this shit." Stu didn't seem to mind them, but I think he was faking it. When we had two dinners left I would sweetly ask each night when Stu got home, "Honey, would you like the chicken tetrazzini or the vegetable lasagna?" Stu would say, "Fuck it, let's eat out."

We ate dinner in restaurants every night for almost fifteen years. Now, more than twenty years after the Hamburger Helper fiasco, since I have retired I'm cooking dinner again. Sometimes I even do breakfast. The other day I was preparing an omelet. I said to Stuart, "You know, before you die, I think you should have the experience of cracking an egg." Stu said, "I don't think I can do that." I said, "Sure you can. I'll crack the first one and then show you exactly how to crack the second one." As detailed a lesson as the one I wish I had given on using the stove that first day, so many years ago. Stu was very brave. He cracked the egg successfully and then said, "That was really disgusting. Please, don't ever ask me to do that again." I never will

THE EICHEL & EICHEL
BAR MITZVAH COMEDY TEAM

When Steven was twelve-and-a-half, his grandfather Eichelbaum asked when his grandson was having his bar mitzvah. Stuart and I were never interested in joining religious groups of any kind and were not part of the small Jewish community in Knoxville. Rather than give our children a religious education, we gave Steven tennis lessons, He also learned to play the saxophone at Mount Olive School. Ellen took dancing lessons.

Whether you are Christian, Jewish, or Greek Orthodox, Knoxville is a very religiously oriented community, and Steven and Ellen felt the pressure of not being part of a group. We sent them to Sunday school at the local temple, so they could say they belonged to something. We told the rabbi that we wanted our children to go to Sunday school, but that none of us would be attending services. He said that was OK with him.

One Sunday, when Steven was ten, we went for a walk in the Great Smoky Mountains, less than an hour's drive from our house. Steven, a normally talkative child, was very quiet. It took a long time for him to tell us what was bothering him. The teacher at Sunday school had told him to sit down when the other children got up to sing, because our family never attended services. We didn't send him or Ellen back. He became an excellent tennis player. Ellen continued dancing.

We used that event to try to explain to his grandfather why Steven would not be having a bar mitzvah. Grandpa Eichelbaum insisted that his first grandson was going to have a bar mitzvah and said this is what we were going to do: we would hire a tutor, who for the next six months would teach Steven everything he needed to know to get through the ceremony, then we would have the bar mitzvah in Detroit, and he would take care of everything. He said we didn't understand how important this was to him (we didn't). No argument was given. None would have been accepted.

We hired a tutor. Joseph Spector was a kind and gentle man who came to our house three times a week for six months. He taught Steven Hebrew and the Hebrew songs he would sing at the ceremony and Steven had a good time. It was fun to learn a new language and he loved to sing. (At the time, he wanted to be a rock singer when he grew up.) Ellen, who was nine years old, sat in on all of the lessons and learned every word of Hebrew that Steven did, and all of the songs. They formed what they called the "Eichel & Eichel Bar Mitzvah Comedy Team." Ellen, lifting her thin arms to the heavens, would mouth the words to the songs while Steven, hidden behind the door, would robustly sing them for us. The Hebrew words in Steven's deep voice really did sound as if they were coming out of Ellen's mouth. It was funny to watch, but would not have been a hit on Broadway.

The bar mitzvah, however, was a smash. Friends and relatives—250 of them—came from all over the country. Grandpa said proudly that there were people from twenty-two states. Steven got all his lines right and my father-in-law said no one would have guessed that he had not been studying for this day from the time when he should have begun. A little dig, but who could blame him? I had never seen my father-in-law look so happy.

After the event all 250 people were invited to a sit-down luncheon. No buffets for a first grandson's bar mitzvah. There was a live band and a master of ceremonies who was so corny he made our skin crawl. In an unctuous voice he spelled out *bar mitzvah* by starting with, "B is for the boy you used to be. A is for..."

Grandpa Eichelbaum said to Grandpa Friedman, "Now I can die. I have lived to see my first grandson's bar mitzvah." Since he was only sixty-six at the time, that seemed a bit dramatic to my father.

Steven got a lot of presents; cash in envelopes, an enormous and gaudy Old Testament Bible with gold filigree on the cover, and two silver ceremonial cups for drinking wine. The day after we came home from Detroit, Steven and Ellen were in Steven's room with the door closed for an unusually long time. Stuart knocked before he went in and found them in a secret ceremony of their own, drinking grape juice from the silver cups. Stu said he felt like the Gestapo.

One week later Stu's brother called and told me that their father had died. When Stuart came home with Steven and Ellen after picking them up from some event at school and saw me weeping, he rushed over to ask me what was wrong. I couldn't speak. Ellen simply said, and I have no idea how she knew, "Grandpa is dead." People from twenty-two states came to his funeral.

FIDDLER IN BIG STONE

Big Stone Gap is nestled in the mountainous coal country of southwest Virginia, with a population of about 5,000. It is completely surrounded by the mountains. Its houses are neat. Everything looks clean. After the Civil War, the Union soldiers, some of them engineers, headed back north through Virginia and later returned to open the first coal mines. Eventually the owners of the mines went west: no unions and flat land.

Nobody in Big Stone Gap had ever seen a Jew, my friend Joan Boyd Short told me one night in November. She had called to ask if Stu and I would visit Powell Valley High School, where Joan taught English, and talk to her students. The chorus was putting on a production of *Fiddler on the Roof* in February and Joan thought it would help them a lot if they could talk to some people who were Jewish. I laughed. I told her she had asked the wrong Jews. I said she *knew* we were atheists, were not religious in any way, and wouldn't be able to give good answers to the questions the students might ask. I told her, however, that we would love to see the performance, thinking it would be a hoot, as we say in the South, to see a bunch of mountain kids who had never seen a Jew portray impoverished Jewish peasants in Czarist Russia. I wondered which boy could possibly play Tevye, the pious old dairyman who had five daughters to marry off.

I suggested Joan contact the rabbi at the synagogue in Knoxville and ask him if he knew someone who would come to the school and talk with the students. The rabbi gave Joan the name of a young couple in Johnson City, a middle-size town in Tennessee seventy miles east of Big Stone Gap. They said they'd be happy to come talk to the Powell Valley students about Judaism and they went to one of the rehearsals.

I guess I should tell you something about my friend Joan besides the fact that she is one of my favorite people on earth. I met Joan Boyd, who grew up in Chattanooga, in February 1974 when we both worked in the Publications Service Bureau at the University of Tennessee. She was an editor. She loves Shakespeare and Faulkner and Robert Frost, and now teaches all three to her classes. She writes poetry. We became instant friends, even though we are quite different.

Joan gave me a genuine Southern iron skillet for my birthday one year and a recipe for cornbread using cornmeal, eggs, buttermilk and bacon grease. She said I was the only Jew to whom she would give a recipe that included bacon grease. When I told her I had added honey she looked appalled. She laughingly told me I had desecrated the skillet, apparently what I had made is called "Yankee cornbread." In spite of my culinary faux pas, she taught me to make iron skillet biscuits, cider beef stew, and lemon mousse. She gave me her mother's secret recipe for date-nut torte. Before Joan gave me her recipes, I had considered cracking open a tube of Pillsbury crescent rolls, rolling up the little triangles of dough, bending them into half-circles, and baking them on a greased cookie sheet to be making homemade rolls.

Joan stayed at the Publications Service Bureau for two and a half years before getting married and moving to Big Stone Gap with her husband, Ron Short, an Appalachian storyteller who needed to get back to his roots. Six months later, after I was diagnosed with MS, Joan wrote me a letter saying, "I know you're an atheist, but I'm praying for you anyway."

Joan wanted to become a minister but chose teaching English in a little town in the middle of nowhere. Well, she didn't exactly *choose* it, but she has made a wonderful life for herself there. She told me that being a schoolteacher is definitely a ministry. "I think of my school as a place where every day my students can spend an hour in my class and learn about themselves—if not much about English," she says with a laugh. Every year she "adopts" one of her students, taking a special interest in helping him or her get a scholarship to college or get through a personal crisis. She *adores* adolescents and her mission is to help them survive those complicated years. They bond with her and love her.

Joan met my daughter when Ellen was a skinny, self-conscious eleven-year-old. It was mutual love at first sight. Ellen wrote poems for Joan and gave her little gifts that she made herself.

Ron Short grew up south of the mountains in tiny Big Branch, part of Dickinson County, Virginia. He is a storyteller with the Roadside Theater and has sung songs and told stories all over the world. He also writes plays and can play the fiddle, guitar, mandolin, button accordion, Indian flute, saxophone, penny whistle, piano, and harmonica. "His voice though, is truly his instrument. He cannot read one word of music," Joan says. Ellen went to see Ron perform in Seattle shortly before she died, and he is the last person that *we* know to have seen her. Ron told me the only memory he has of that concert is talking to Ellen in the aisle, and that she looked so happy and bubbly.

In February 1980, when Powell Valley High School put on its performance of *Fiddler*, Stu and I drove through the winding mountain roads, checked into our room at the Trail Motel, dropped off our stuff, and went right to the high school, where the PTA was serving a traditional Jewish dinner on long tables in the cafeteria. (Don't ask, as they say in the North.) There were flowers on the tables and the fresh-faced students served the food and entertained the diners with songs from the play. The people from Big Stone, whom we ate dinner with, made us feel right at home.

The auditorium was packed and had that smell peculiar to high school auditoriums everywhere—even in Brooklyn. The parents, students, and their little brothers and sisters in the audience were excited and expectant and the feeling was tangible in the air. Almost everyone in the crowd knew someone in the play and became nervously quiet when the lights went down, probably hoping that no one would flub their lines. Ron was the fiddler standing on the roof and playing the mournful Jewish melody, while Tevye intoned: "A fiddler on the roof. Crazy, no? But in our little village of Anatevka, you might say every one of us is a fiddler on the roof, trying to scratch out a simple, pleasant tune without breaking our necks." Then the students walked on stage, dressed in peasant garb, singing "Tradition," and Stu and I sat back in our reserved seats in the fifth row center and smiled. I should say that we had seen the original production of *Fiddler* on Broadway, with the famed Zero Mostel playing Tevye. We had seen the movie. We had seen the University of Tennessee production. But *Fiddler on the Roof* at Powell Valley

High School, in Big Stone Gap, Virginia, was the most moving of them all. At the end of the play, when the students walked off the stage singing the lament "Anatevka," after the Jews of that town have been forced to leave their homes by order of the Russian Czar, Stu and I were weeping.

Jim Daugherty was the choral director. Joan was his assistant and also the production coordinator. At the end of the play, after many curtain calls for the wildly clapping and cheering audience, a student in the cast came forward to make a little speech about how they never could have done it without Mrs. Short's help. He called Joan out from backstage and presented her with six long-stemmed red roses. The love between Joan and the students, who at that point were both clapping and crying, was something that any teacher on earth would envy.

Joan introduced us to the cast. Barry Poff, who played Tevye, was an incredibly talented high school junior. He was almost as convincing at playing the old Jewish dairyman as Zero Mostel. Barry had even mastered the accent. He said to me that the students felt a great connection with the Jewish people, a oneness. As children of Appalachia, he said, they have also suffered from discrimination; they are called hillbillies, looked down upon, and many have been forced to leave their homes through no choice of their own because the mines shut down.

Stu and I went back to Big Stone every February for the next ten years, sometimes with Ellen, who would drive home from Nashville to see "The Play," whatever it was. *The Post*, Big Stone's weekly newspaper, wrote a story about the people who drove 140 miles to Big Stone Gap every year, from the city of Knoxville, just to see the performance at Powell Valley High School. Joan told us that the students always peeked out the curtain at the beginning to see if we were there.

Stu and Ellen and I were there in 1989, the next time Powell Valley High did *Fiddler on the Roof.* At intermission, Jim Daugherty came out on stage to tell the audience about this couple, who every year came all the way from Knoxville, Tennessee, to Big Stone Gap to see the play. He asked the couple to come up on stage, because the chorus had a gift for them. Suddenly Stu realized they were talking about us and was embarrassed, because we didn't do anything but *attend*, and he said, "Oh shit," loud enough for many people to hear him. Ellen and I scrunched down in our seats when Stu refused to go up on the stage. (Stu can't even stand for people to sing "Happy Birthday" to him, because he had nothing to do with his own birth.) The chorus was going to give us a poster of *Fiddler* that the whole cast had signed and two blue sweatshirts with "L'CHAIM" printed on the front in white letters and "FIDDLER/PVHS" on the back. (We accepted the gifts after the play was over.)

Now, I never knew what *l'chaim* meant until I saw my first *Fiddler on the Roof,* on Broadway. "L'chaim" is a toast that my daddy always made before downing his Scotch-on-the-rocks or his foaming glass of Pabst Blue Ribbon. I don't think Daddy knew what it meant either, when he raised his glass high in the air before drinking. L'chaim means "to life."

Three weeks after Ellen killed herself, Joan sent me this letter:

April 18, 1993

Dearest Greta and Stu,

We will not try to talk to you until you are ready to talk to us. We will not come until you are ready to see us. That leaves us only this piece of paper, and how can we write what there are no words for? We can only hope and trust that you are in some tiny measure sustained by the length, the depth, and the endurance of our friendship which is never diminished by separation or long silences.

Every now and then when I am rummaging frantically through old papers looking for this or that letter or insurance policy or notes on Frost or the extended warranty on the lawn mower (all of which are filed under "P" for papers), I run across a little folded note with JOAN, JOAN, JOAN, JOAN stamped all over the front in big black letters made from an eraser cut with childish love and care into the letters of my name. There's a funny poem inside which mentions my name several times, each time in big, black letters—JOAN. It lurks there waiting to surprise me and make me smile even when I am the most frustrated. I'll not look for it now. I'll wait for it to do its job when I least expect it, like a child crouching behind a door, waiting to jump out and yell BOO!!!

And in its place of honor in the dusty china cabinet, beached between the Zuni fetishes and the mushroom sculpture made by deaf, dumb, and blind children from the Orange Grove Center, is a little clay shark painted bright blue with a smile that is closer to funny than sinister and a broken fin, lovingly reglued. In almost faded crayon on its chalk white belly are the words TO JOAN. In place of a signature is a little red flower.

Having not had my own children, even the briefest soul connections I have made with the children of others glisten in my memory and take on an exaggerated importance to me that neither the child nor the parent would ever suspect nor possibly understand. At the end of Camelot (since we have a long tradition of quoting bad musicals to one another), Arthur sends Tom off to tell the story of Camelot. When Pellinore asks who that was, Arthur replies: "One of what we all are, just one tiny drop in the great rolling motion of the sea. But some of the drops sparkle, some of them do sparkle." Ellen sparkled. If only she could have seen what we saw. She will be one of us forever. I wish she had known that. Maybe she did.

Ron, who saw her in Seattle and felt good about her there, wept with me and sends his love to both of you.

I love you, Joan

That same day I found a seven-page letter from Ellen to us among the papers that Steven had sent to Stu and me from Seattle. Ellen had written it five months before she killed herself, but never mailed it. This was the last paragraph:

I love you. Hey, maybe I could fly to Knoxville in February to see Joan Boyd's play, being that we're not going to get together at Christmas. Just a thought. Or maybe you could fly here for my wedding, if there ever is one.

Arrrgh

POWERLESS IN KNOXVILLE

On March 13, 1993, a blizzard paralyzed Knoxville with sixteen inches of snow. Our house is at the bottom of a hill and we were unable to leave it for five days—that's how long it took for the roads to be cleared. Trees had fallen across the roads and power lines. Huge old trees lay strewn in our front yard. Large branches, laden with snow and ice, had snapped off and crashed to the ground.

Being snowed-in might not have been so bad if the temperature had not been thirteen degrees outside and if we'd had electricity. Or food. Or if Stuart hadn't had the flu. Or if we'd had wood for the fireplace. Everyone knows that Jews don't make fires. We had pretended to be Christians our first winter in Knoxville and Stu had fumbled with fires every night until he finally got the hang of it. The first time he tried to make a fire he rolled up an entire newspaper and tried to light it with a match. Never having had a fireplace before, we didn't know about crumpled paper and twigs and things like that. We had never gone camping. Stu was a Boy Scout but never learned anything. I was never a Girl Scout nor ever had any desire to be one. I doubt if I would ever sleep in a tent, even if it were heated or air-conditioned.

1993 was my twentieth year working for the University of Tennessee and we had been eating all of our lunches and dinners out for the last twelve years. I stopped cooking the day Ellen moved into the dorm at the university. Sure, there were Pop Tarts for breakfast, but if you can't toast them, what good are they? We also had two cans of tuna fish and some crackers and cheese. They went fast. Then I remembered the canned ham that Peter had sent us five years before in one of those Christmas no-thought cop-outs, when you send a huge box filled with little bitty packages of cheese and nuts and cookies and jam and, *ta da!* a canned ham. I hate canned ham and kept meaning to contribute it to the annual drive for the homeless that the University of Tennessee held. I would *buy* stuff for the homeless and drop it in the collection box, but I could never remember to bring the canned ham that was languishing in the back of a cabinet. After three years I decided that I did not want to poison the homeless, so I just left the ham in its home in the cupboard. (I, unlike Stu, with his affection for the chocolate bunny that had lived with us for twelve years, felt no love for the ham.) After five years I didn't think Old Mother Hubbard's dog would eat it either, but we were getting down to the bare bones. Peter's ham saved our lives. We ate it, cold and disgusting as it was, for the five days we were trapped in the house.

If I had suspected the power would be out for so long, I would have taken a shower that first cold morning, when we still had hot water. Instead I quickly put on thermal underwear, a sweat suit, my winter coat and a hat. The coat was the one I'd bought when visiting my father in the hospital three years before. This was the only other time I'd worn it. During the day I didn't take the coat or my woolen hat off. I took them off only when I went to sleep, leaving on the thermal underwear and sweat suit. We once bought a kerosene heater, but gave it away because we were afraid we would asphyxiate ourselves with the fumes. All that stuff is too scary for people like Stu and me, who are dumber than dirt when it comes to survival by any means that takes understanding directions to use. The five days we spent freezing in 1993, however, should have made us get another one. Instead we bought Sterno. We have not had to use it yet and would probably find a way to screw it up anyway. Jews don't do Sterno, either.

I must admit I felt very sorry for myself those five days, even though I knew that at the time, Sarajevo was being bombed out of existence and the people there had nothing to eat and were chopping up their furniture to burn for heat, since they had run out of wood. We didn't have any wood either, but our Christian neighbors weren't bombing us either, who actually saved us from freezing by supplying us with wood. (Some people who *did* have electric power those five days were pissed off that their cable TV was out, so I guess it's all relative.)

Edna Pridemore, who lives up the hill, called (at least the phone was still working) and told me that Joe, her husband, had just cut up a bunch of wood. She asked if Stu wanted to come up and get some. Even though he had the flu, Stu walked up the hill to their house and brought back two logs. Edna called again and told me that the logs Stu had taken with him would have lasted for about twenty minutes. She said Joe had brought down a wheelbarrow full of wood and left it at the top of our driveway. So we managed to keep a fire going for five straight days and sat in front of it with our eyes burning from the smoke, trying to read. While sitting in front of the fire the second night, Stu suddenly said, "Oh God! We forgot about the frozen yogurt and it's probably melted all over the freezer!" We caught it just in time to drink it and it tasted delicious, even though it was cold.

Later I was dying for a cup of tea and I figured I could hold a pan of water over the fire until it boiled. I squatted in front of the fire, feeling like I should get a merit badge from the Girl Scouts. When the water boiled, I got so excited that I lost my balance and spilled it all over my thigh. I refused to take off my clothes, however. The burn lasted for weeks. There went the merit badge.

Our new next-door neighbors, Ann and Bill Ransom, called one night during the power outage and asked if we wanted to walk over and have dinner with them. They had cooked some sausages and potatoes over their fire. I said, "Oh yes, oh yes, I would love to, and I'll ask Stu." Stu said we couldn't go over there because he didn't want the Ransoms to catch the flu for their kindness. It never even occurred to me to go by myself. So I called.

"Hello, Bill?"

"Yes?" the man answered.

"We won't be able to accept your offer of dinner because Stu has the flu, but thanks anyway," I said.

"What are you talkin' about?" he replied.

"Is this Bill Ransom?"

"No, this is Bill Lowry."

Oops, wrong number. I asked him if he had any food and he said he was finishing his last jar of peanut butter. He told me he was 76 years old and couldn't get out of his house. I probably should have called the police to go check on him, but there were so many people in the same situation that I doubted if I could get help for

Bill Lowry. I didn't try to get help for us either, although Stu wanted us to try to walk to University Hospital, about three miles away. I told him we'd never make it through the snow and since he had the flu it might kill him. I called Bill Ransom, and after regretfully declining their invitation, I told him that now I had to worry about Bill Lowry also.

Stu and I finished the ham right before the power came back on.

THE BAD DAY

I wish I could jump in the seven seas
But to do that I'd need six more me's.
I think I'll draw six more me's
So I can jump in the seven seas.

And when I did I drowned.
The drowning me was never found.

I am haunted by Ellen's childhood poem "The Bad Day" and must have had a premonition on what was to become the worst day of my life. I was meeting my friend Jane Garron for our weekly Tuesday lunch. The Great Blizzard of 1993 was over. The power had come back on two weeks before. That Tuesday some workers were coming to clear our yard of the trees that had fallen during the storm. At lunch, Jane, who knows me well, said, "What's the matter with you? You're wired." I was feeling fine. I assured Jane that I wasn't having an MS attack. *My* wires were working again, too— after fifteen years, my frequent attacks had grown further and further apart. Now my electrical system was functioning almost as well as it did before I got sick. Jane said, "But you're jumping out of your skin."

Stuart and I were going out to dinner that night with Bill and Ann Ransom. Bill teaches computer graphics at Pellissippi State, a community college, and Ann is an artist. I had just done something on the computer that I was quite proud of and I decided to bring it home that night to show Bill. It had to be shipped to the printer the following day and while I was driving home with the printer's proofs of the artwork in the car, I thought maybe I shouldn't bring them with me. What if I couldn't go to work on Wednesday? But I felt fine and dismissed the thought.

When I came home from work that evening the yard workers were cutting up the trees downed in our front yard and the sound of the chain saw was deafening, so instead of taking a nap before dinner, as I usually did, I decided to take a walk. I first looked at the mail and there was the Easter card from Ellen.

I left for my walk and by chance met Nancy, who lives at the other end of our street, and we walked together. I told her we were going to dinner that evening with our new neighbors and she asked me about them. I told her that Ann's first husband had committed suicide. Nancy spent the rest of the walk telling me about all the people she knew who had killed themselves and how they had done it.

After dinner I invited Bill and Ann into the house to see Stu's paintings, which were now hanging everywhere. We were in the process of removing most of the art that we had been collecting for the last thirty-six years and replacing it with Stu's work. I loved what he was doing and wanted his paintings in every room. I had grown tired of the things we had displayed for so many years. They had become invisible, like wallpaper.

Ann and Bill stayed for a long time, being artists themselves, and enjoyed seeing and talking about the work. Just before they went home I showed Ann a picture of Ellen. I have no idea why I did that, because I wasn't in the habit of showing people pictures of my children. She said, "My, what a beautiful girl." I said, "She used to be really screwed up." When they left I said to Stu, "I've never been so tired in my life."

As soon as Bill and Ann left, the phone rang. At first Stu sounded really annoyed. (He told me later he thought it was a mutual fund salesman.) Then his voice turned to horror and he said, "Get on the phone. Ellen's dead." The phone felt like ice in my hand. My whole body was turning numb, the way it does when an MS attack is beginning. The man who called said his name was Jerry Webster. He was the medical examiner on the Seattle police force and he told us that our daughter had died of a self-inflicted gunshot wound. I became hysterical for the first time since I had seen the movie *A Child is Waiting* when I was pregnant with Ellen and almost lost her. I wonder now if it would have been better if I had. Jerry Webster said, "I know how hard this is for you. Children aren't supposed to die before their parents." He gave us his phone number in case we wanted to call him.

I said to Stu, "How will we ever tell Marie?" We held each other and took turns crying and making cold decisions. Stu said he couldn't go to Seattle and walk into her apartment, because we had never been there when Ellen was alive. I said we would have her body cremated, but I didn't want the ashes. I remembered bringing Grandma's ashes home from Pennsylvania in a little cardboard box and couldn't think of bringing Ellen home that way. Stu promised me we would get through this. I didn't see how.

The only two people we called that night were Steven, who already knew, and Stu's mother. It was the third time I had heard Elizabeth cry in thirty-seven years. She kept sobbing, "No no no no," and when she said she wished she had died first, I thought, *I wish I had too*. We asked Steven to notify close relatives, but to please ask them not to call us, because we weren't able to discuss it yet. Steven said, "Don't ever blame yourself. You were a wonderful mother," and I thought what a sweet thing for a son to say at a terrible time like that, when he was devastated as well. I took two sleeping pills and went to bed, but they weren't strong enough and I couldn't sleep.

Ellen's best friend in Seattle, Tim Wilson, called Tuesday night. Tim was her hairdresser and used to be a social worker. He loved Ellen and had helped her from the first week she moved to Seattle. I wasn't able to speak to him that night, although I would talk to him many times afterward. That week, and the next, Stu took all the phone calls. A lot of our friends from Knoxville called to ask if there was anything they could do to help us, but I couldn't talk to them yet. Some of Ellen's friends from Seattle called. They were stunned.

Ellen's boyfriend, Brian, called. Stu came into the bedroom, where I was shivering under the covers, hoping the sleeping pills would knock me out. Stu said I should get on the phone because Brian was crying and wanted to talk to me. Brian said he and Ellen had gone out Friday night and that he loved her so much. He said they were planning to come to Knoxville that summer because Ellen wanted him to meet us. He was the only person I spoke to besides Jerry Webster, Steven, and Elizabeth that night. I needed to tell Brian he should never feel any guilt for Ellen's death, as Ellen was a very unstable person and didn't seem to like herself very much. Brian said, "I wish she could have seen herself through my eyes." He asked me if I would send him some pictures of Ellen, maybe include some pictures of her when she was a child. He said he would like to visit us.

Stu brought the proofs of the artwork that I had brought home to show Bill Ransom back to my office early the next morning. He walked into Jim Kelly's office, handed him the proofs, and said, "Greta can't come to work today. Ellen killed herself," and walked out.

Stu called Dr. Paulsen and told him that our daughter had killed herself. He said I had taken two sleeping pills Tuesday night but they didn't work. Dr. Paulsen sedated me with a lot of Xanax—one every hour—and I slept fitfully for the next 24 hours. I stayed in bed all day Wednesday and then on Thursday got up and looked at myself in the bathroom mirror. I looked like I had died myself and I told myself I had to make a decision. Was I going to go on with my life, or was I going to die too? Stu and I drove to the mountains.

I called my office on Friday and told Jim Kelly that I didn't know when I would be coming back to work—if ever, that when and if I did, I didn't want anyone to hug me or touch me or say anything about Ellen. I didn't want to find a terrarium on my desk the day I came back, as the people in my office had chipped in for and bought after my mother died, or a contribution to the Multiple Sclerosis Society, as they had done after my daddy died. I didn't want to have to thank anyone for anything.

The following Monday I went back to work. When I got to my office everyone looked away because of what I had said to Jim Kelly. I told them I was going to be OK, that they didn't need to walk on eggshells around me, that I'd probably cry sometimes, but they should understand it would take me some time to be myself again. And I went through the motions of living for the next year. Stu continued going to school.

On Friday Steven flew out to Seattle with their cousin Dennis to go through Ellen's belongings and to be there for the service that her co-workers were having for her on Sunday. Steven was amazed when he saw her apartment, partly because it was so neat and clean. Ellen had always seemed to relish chaos in the past. (Steven used to clean up her room when they were children, because he couldn't bear to look at the mess as he walked down the hall to his own room.) He said her apartment was beautiful and filled with art, much of it ours. Steven said it looked like Ellen had gotten her life—or at least her apartment—together. She had albums of photographs she had taken. Stories she had written. Steven stayed up most of the night reading a book of jokes she was writing for her act, which he said kept him laughing even though he was grief stricken and in shock. He told us the memorial service was beautiful.

Steven also found the receipt for the gun, bought in November, and lots of bullets under the bed. The police had taken the gun. Stu said he wanted to kill the pig-fucker who sold it to her.

Back in November I had been trying to call Ellen every night, leaving messages on her answering machine: "Ellen, this is Mommy. Please call me." But she wasn't returning my phone calls. Later that week, I came home at 11:30 P.M. after having dinner at a friend's house, and on my way to the bedroom I noticed the red blinking light on our answering machine. I thought of waiting until the next day to check it because I was so tired, but I then thought it might be from Ellen. It was Dr. Frank, Ellen's doctor. He said she was in a deep depression and if she got much worse he would have to commit her to a mental hospital. I hate to admit that my first thought was, "Oh fuck. Not her again." The doctor left a number to call. I called him back at midnight and told him about Ellen: her intermittent depression, her overdosing on drugs when she was fifteen, my mother's depression, and that my mother took lithium every day. I asked him to tell me what was really happening with Ellen. He said he couldn't tell me anything about her; she was an adult and he was not able to divulge any information.

We probably should have flown out to Seattle to see for ourselves, but Dr. Frank had put her on antidepressant drugs and Ellen improved very quickly. She called us and sounded all bubbly and fine—better than usual—and so we didn't go. Stu said later that nothing we could have done would have prevented what she did, it might only have delayed it. Once Ellen bought a gun, he said, her death was inevitable. We'll never know. When we called Dr. Frank after Ellen killed herself he was as upset as a doctor could have been. He said she had seen him March 25th (four days before her death) and she was so much better that he suggested she no longer needed the drugs. She was taking Prozac.

The people from INCA, whom Ellen had made fun of in her comedy act, had a memorial service on Sunday, April 4th, at the University Presbyterian Church: "Service to Celebrate the Life of Ellen Eichel." (Stu thought there was nothing to celebrate. His anger at Ellen has never abated.) Although Ellen told us she had a very hard time making friends in Seattle, there were almost a hundred people who went to the service who, Steven felt, really cared about her. Stu and I just couldn't go, nor did we have any sort of service in

Knoxville. We felt it would be too painful for us and for our friends. For Ellen's service in Seattle, the people from INCA printed a program with her picture on the cover and a short history of Ellen's life. People who wanted to say something about her got up to share their memories. They played "The Wind," by Mariah Carey. A man named Nick Roberts, who must have worked at INCA and whom we had never heard anything about from Ellen, wrote out his feelings and they were inserted in the program. This is just a small part of what he said:

ABOUT ELLEN

This was a special soul which transformed itself in many different ways. If you are the type that mines people's souls to find those flashes of humanity, you wouldn't have to wait too long to find those flashes with Ellen.

This sensitive soul walked hand in hand with an unquenchable spirit. A spirit that displayed itself in the way she took life on so energetically and unblinkingly. With this spirit she looked at things humorously and gave the gift of laughter to those who knew her and even sometimes to a public who didn't.

Ellen was captivated with people and captivated with life. This spirit of hers was so contagious. I can remember coming home exhilarated after spending time with her.

But there was a troubled side of her that she kept masterfully away from view. There was a lonely, hurt side of her that needed to come out and never did around me. Ellen's passing hit me hard because I was just beginning to sense a gradual invitation to those troubled waters and an opportunity to help her deal with what she needed to deal with. But the dam broke open much too soon.

But I'm writing this to celebrate who Ellen was to those who knew her, not to brood over what could not be seen. I'll remember her smiles, her laughs, her Woody Woodpecker faces, her jokes, her warm hugs, her sensitive soul and lively spirit. She was a wonderful human being and will be missed.

Stu and I called Ellen's friend Tim the next week. He told us he had done her hair the Saturday night before she died, that she was going to a rock concert and looked gorgeous, dressed all in black. He said she showed no signs of what was to come and was making all kinds of plans.

On April 16th I wrote a thank-you letter to the people at INCA. They had made a contribution to the Lifeline Institute, a suicide prevention organization in Seattle, and they had all signed a card telling us how much they cared about Ellen and how much they would miss her. Stu called me at work, weeping, after he had read the card. He sent them a framed print of one of his drawings, signed, "from Ellen's daddy." I wrote that Steven had told us the memorial service they gave for Ellen was beautiful and belatedly thanked them.

In June I finally was able to write Brian a letter and send him the pictures he had asked for.

June 12

Dear Brian,

Stu and I have thought of you many times over the past two months and we're happy that Ellen had a wonderful friend like you. We really would like you to visit us in the fall if you feel like it. It is beautiful here at that time of the year. We will all be stronger by then, although I know it will be very emotional for all of us. I am sending you these pictures in the hope that you still want them and will not be upset by getting them. You are young and I hope your life has moved on by now. Don't feel you have to answer this letter unless you want to keep in touch. We'll understand.

I'm sorry it has taken so long for me to write to you. I'm tired by the time I get home from work. I try to walk three miles every night but the weather is now getting too warm. We must have gotten about 100 letters from people about Ellen, but I haven't been able to answer any of them yet or to call people back when they leave messages.

I hope you are doing OK. I love you for loving Ellen. Please take care of yourself Brian, and write or call if you feel like it.

Love,
Greta

Tim Wilson sent us a message on a series of three postcards in August. The first is of a scene in the San Juan Islands showing sunset over Puget Sound. The second is the view from Mt. Constitution, the highest point in the San Juan Islands; it shows a man and a woman looking over the sound. The woman has long hair the same color as Ellen's. There is a view of Mt.

Washington in the distance, which Ellen told me she could see from her office window. The third is of Orcas Island. I believe Tim sent them so I could picture where he had scattered Ellen's ashes.

August 3, 1993

Hi Stu and Greta,

I took the 12:20 a.m. ferry to Orcas Island two days ago. The moon was full and reflected against the Puget Sound and San Juan Islands. Orcas Island is one of many islands on the inlet. This time of year it's God's country. The air is pristine and fresh. Hikers, bikers and runners enjoy the camping and total beauty.

Ellen and our friends had come here to camp. We would set up camp on a small bluff overlooking the other islands. We always picked the June, July, or August full moons. We would sit up most of the night, talk and watch the sea kayakers howling while they paddled by the moonlight.

At 6:30 a.m. I spread Ellen's ashes in the sound. It was beautiful. The Orca whales spawn in these waters. Ellen's spirit will be watched and loved by the whales and sea mammals.

I miss her, but I hide my hurt by keeping it to myself. Don't want friends to feel that there is an obsession with anguish, but there is a pain inside and I still shed tears at the loss. Hope this mends itself

Stu, I have sent and insured Ellen's camera. Greta, how's your health? You're in my prayers. Hope all is well. I think about you often.

Love, Tim

Brian called us in August, on Ellen's birthday. He said he had been thinking about us all day. He then told us that he'd had a terrible week. His best friend had shot his wife in front of their two-year-old daughter and then killed himself. His friend owned the restaurant where Brian worked. I thought, *Oh God, poor Brian. First his girlfriend and then his best friend.* I never heard from Brian again. I hoped he was OK, but didn't call him. I don't think I can deal with any more pain.

Six months later I read the letters addressed to Ellen that were in the old shoeboxes that Steven had sent home. I suppose that was an invasion of privacy, but I didn't care. I was looking for clues to her death. She had saved every letter that anyone had ever sent her, just like my daddy had saved every scrap of paper that was sent to him for his entire life. (When we went through Daddy's papers after his death in 1990, we found a letter from his boss, dated September, 12, 1931, that gave my daddy permission for a half day's leave from the post office.) The same day that I got Joan Boyd Short's letter to me about Ellen's death, I found this letter:

Oct. 17, 1992

Dear Mom and Dad,
Hi! I don't know what there is to tell you, but I wanted to send you this photo a friend took at the Fair. It's kind of neat with the clouds in the background.
Steven (our Steven) called me at work last week. That sure was nice, I screamed (squealed with delight) when I figured out who was calling. He's not the greatest at keeping in touch. Wouldn't it be funny if I turned out to be a

famous comedian and he turned into some Amway zombie? No, I guess that wouldn't be funny to you, him, or Belinda. Or me, actually. I want us all to be happy.

I wrote "happy" about half an hour ago. I was trying to think of more stuff to write, and probably thought about twenty pages worth. It was actually "deep" stuff, not funny stuff. But I think I'd rather make you laugh than make you cry. I've cried twice in half an hour. I cried last night in a restaurant talking with my friend James about rejection and self-doubt. "I feel like I'm a mess inside," I said. "Everybody's a mess inside," he said. I don't know if that's true, (are y'all messes inside?) but apparently I'm not the first one to experience self-doubt.

I went to a 4-hour one-day class at University of Washington called "Conversation Skills your Mother Never Taught You." It was basically a room full of very good-looking people (one geek) who probably came to the class if their conversations are less than sparkling. Of course I don't have that problem, I just went to gawk. We did all kinds of fun role and game playing. Topics such as fears, conversation openers (That's my forté, it's after that that I have trouble), good conversation patterns. One of my fears is that I offend people by saying fuck, etc. Mom, you probably don't care if people give a fuck. Have you ever had someone not have interest in you for a friend, and wondered if you said something that offended them? Fuck 'em.
Anyway, it looked like a fun class in the schedule. I got a $30 complete refund for the

guitar class. My fingers seemed too small to do what they said and I decided I wouldn't practice 30 minutes a day, etc., etc. Plus, that low frustration tolerance I was "diagnosed" with almost half my life ago causes me to quit things that are hard. Isn't it weird that those things are what is most satisfying when completed? I guess I've never worked very hard at anything, except trying to be happy and at peace with myself (it can be a full-time job). My relationship with you guys is very important to me. I love Daddy more than ever and Mommy I've always loved you even though I remember you saying you thought I didn't. I wonder if our love for each other could get even deeper. My friend James was telling me about how his mother was one of his best friends until she died last year. It was sweet.

I want to tell you things like friends do, but Bob Kronick told me not to tell you things that were going to make you mad. That all honesty is not good. It's easier to be honest than dishonest. I'm tired of hiding things. But maybe our relationship is fine the way it is. Do you like it or do you think I'm a mess? Because I don't know how to talk about politics or Palestine. I just don't give a shit, but maybe some day when I get done with my self-absorption, I will be interested in world events.

Anyway, next topic. Please don't ask me what are these "things" I'm toying with letting you in on so you would better know who I am. I might cry and you might not like me as much. I keep feeling the compulsion to tell you I was raped by the exterminator when I was 16, but I don't think I would be taken seriously because I was wearing a nightie in front of a man and I smoked a joint with him before, and I didn't want you to know I smoked pot. I was afraid if I told on him, he'd tell on me. I never really thought about it for years. I keep wondering why I get repulsed when a man with a mustache kisses me, but it could go back to that. Who knows, maybe mustaches could just be disgusting. I just want to let go of the baggage that the moving company packed with my furniture bound for Seattle.

Anyway, wish me luck. And I wish you luck too, that Daddy finds a new passion like painting and that Mommy's not in too much physical pain, and that I get my shit together. (I don't want to say up to your high standards, but I think I just did. My standards for what constitutes a good person are pretty fucking high though.)

Well, I'm kinda tired. Enough for this weeks installment from the "daughter that . . . " nevermind.

I love you. Hey, maybe I could fly to Knoxville in February to see Joan Boyd's play, being that we're not going to get together at Christmas. Just a thought. Or maybe you could fly here for my wedding, if there ever is one.

> *Arrrgh*
>> *Love & hugs,*
>> *Ellen*
>> *(Daddy, hug Mommy for me*
>> *Mommy, hug daddy for me)*

I would not look at the rest of Ellen's things for five years. They had become radioactive, and whenever I opened the closet door where I had put them, I closed it immediately, afraid of being poisoned

GRETA EICHEL IS ALIVE AND WELL (SORT OF) AND LIVING IN KNOXVILLE

Just before my fiftieth birthday, on May 20, 1987, I asked Daddy and Billie to give me a birthday party. Although I had been living in Knoxville for the past eighteen years, I wanted my party to be in New York, the place where I was born and grew up, met Stuart, and gave birth to Steven and Ellen. I wanted to invite my old friends to help me celebrate half a century of life.

Stuart stood directing traffic on Route 110 (a heavily traveled highway) wearing Bermuda shorts, a T-shirt, a little pointed hat, and a huge sandwich board, and he was blowing one of those party favors that curl out and back as you breathe.

The front of the board said:
GRETA'S BIRTHDAY PARTY
TURN HERE

The back of it said:
YOU MISSED THE PARTY
TURN BACK

Our friends said, "Nothing's changed."

They all asked how I was doing and if I still liked living in the South. This was my answer: "I'm still working for the university, where I'm involved as a witness in a case of sexual harassment committed by a paraplegic. Stuart, after years of working for other people, is now a partner in his own advertising agency and hates his partner. Steven wants to quit law and become a comedian. Ellen [who was twenty-four] is living with a thirty-seven-year-old divorced and penniless illegal alien." My friends thought I was trying to be funny. I wished I was.

Steven *did* quit law and start his own business (he didn't become a comedian—Ellen did), but he went back into law after a year because it's hard to live on Beacon Street in Boston and not make a lot of money. Steven said his daddy and I had ruined him for the working world. As a result of Stuart and myself always loving what we did, Steven grew up thinking work was going to be fun, and it wasn't. We told him we hadn't lied to him. You were supposed to enjoy what you did and if you didn't you should find something that you would enjoy. Now he is a partner in one of Boston's oldest law firms and has found out that it *is* possible to love your job. In the winter he and Belinda go skiing most weekends in Vermont. They called me once from the phone in their new Lexus on the way to their ski house. As an old knee-jerk liberal from the sixties it's not easy to be a yuppie's mother, but I'm glad they're happy.

Stuart quit advertising in 1992 and became an art student at the University of Tennessee. Because he was so much older than they were, the students thought he was the teacher. He loved school and said the only problem was finding a place to park his car on campus. I was still working for the university and had a reserved parking spot. Stu sometimes showed up in my office and asked, "May I borrow your car and do you have any money?" Déjà vu. Both Steven and Ellen did the same thing.

The first sculpture he ever completed was accepted into a show in Alabama called "Art with a Southern Drawl." I wondered if they knew he was born in New York and grew up in Detroit. He now thinks of himself as a Southerner anyway and has been accused by our friends in the North of having a Southern drawl, so maybe it's OK. Now he goes out every day and paints landscapes. He's still running his cute ass off and winning some of his races.

In 1995 I grew tired of dealing with bureaucracy, got pissed off, and quit my job at the University of Tennessee. What instigated this seems so dumb now, but at the time it seemed important to me. I was told to use a photograph that I thought was unprofessional on the cover of a publication that I was designing—a photo that was the idea of a senior vice-president, which he wanted me to use. I refused. I had spent twenty-five years designing publications for the university and was not willing to compromise my standards. (Talk about pompous!) Jim Kelly said I had no choice. I said, "Of course I do. I quit." I felt it was both a personal and a professional betrayal. I took what was called "early retirement" (I was able to get a pension and keep my medical insurance), and I think leaving was the best thing I ever did. (In case you're wondering, the paraplegic was allowed to retire early on full disability three years after molesting countless women. "Early retirement" covers a lot of ground.) I'm still friends with Jim Kelly because I can't carry a grudge for more than a little while.

Stuart had been asking me to retire for two years before I quit. He said he didn't want me to drop dead there. But I loved my job and the work I did. I was good at it and winning awards meant a lot to me. I told Stu that I was afraid that if I retired I would turn to shit. I could imagine myself sleeping until noon every day, sitting around all the time, getting fat—be careful what you wish for—and getting bored. When I finally quit, people asked me what I was going to do, and I told them I was going to do lunch.

Bill Ransom immediately asked me to teach a class at Pellissippi State. I was asked to freelance. I was asked to do lunch. I taught the class for five months, a good transitional experience for me. It was a professional seminar and all I had to do was talk to advertising students twice a week for an hour, show my work, tell them what I knew about the field they were going into, and answer any questions they asked me. It was fun and I enjoyed it. When the school asked me to do it again, I realized I didn't want to. I didn't even know that until one of the students in my class told me, "You were the best teacher I ever had. When are you going to teach your class again?" I surprised myself when I answered, "Never."

I bought a lot of computer equipment, because I thought I would start freelancing at home again. When people started asking me to design things for them, I said no. I realized that after thirty-five years as a graphic designer, I'd had enough. I had no idea I felt this way about my lifetime profession until I had time to stop and think about it. I finally understood what other people meant when they said they had burned out. I love staying home. I get up early in the morning and take long walks. It used to be that at six in the morning

I was always getting ready to go to work, except on the weekends, when I slept late. The day I retired was the first time I'd seen the sun rise in thirty-six years, when we went to Europe after we graduated from Pratt and I threw up into the early morning Atlantic Ocean.

Ted came over for lunch one day and told me something I hadn't thought about before. He said, "You had to get angry to leave. If you didn't get mad, you'd still be there." But perhaps getting angry wasn't the reason I quit my job at all. Maybe it was simply an excuse. Ellen's death, two years before, had made me fragile, vulnerable, and unwilling to spend time working things out with people. In the past I had usually been able to talk my clients into understanding why I was being so insistent on not using their idea if I thought it was awful, and then trying to show them a better way to get what they really wanted. Sometimes I could be really obnoxious, using my New York abrasiveness to wear them down. Now I had lost the patience, the will, and the energy to fight. Maybe I needed time to be alone for a while, so that I could heal.

Then I began to understand myself in ways that I never did before I quit my job. I found out that I enjoyed my own company and didn't mind being alone for most of the day. Previously people had always surrounded me. My office was like Grand Central Station. I found out that I wanted to write. Writing this book has been therapy of a sort and has helped me to cope with Ellen's death. And Stu is home every night.

CLOSURE: I HATE THAT WORD

Some people told me that because we didn't go to Ellen's memorial service in Seattle, we could never have closure. Stuart said he *couldn't* go; he couldn't walk into her apartment. I agreed. I didn't think I could stand it either. Stu said he would not cry in front of strangers, so we did our weeping at home, holding each other and talking of her death for perhaps the last time. As I sat writing this on what would have been Ellen's thirty-fourth birthday, I know that there is no such thing as closure—only time passing.

On August 15th, 1997, Stu and I were guests at Steven and Belinda's ski condo in Vermont, there to escape the Tennessee heat. When I got up that morning I said to Stu, "Today's Ellen's birthday," although I have never mentioned it since the first birthday after her death in 1993. On that hot August day Stu cried for such a long time that I finally suggested we go to the track club picnic (an event I've always detested), even though Stu said it would be too hot for me. So we went and stayed for less than a minute, but it broke the tension of the day. On her birthday in 1997, Stu went out to take pictures with Ellen's camera. Of all her things, it was the only one he wanted.

Ellen used to take pictures of her stuffed monkey in unlikely places and mail them to us, so we could see where she'd been. Ellen was disarming and could usually talk her way past guards, who would let her go for a moment, beyond areas cordoned off with a rope. She took a picture of the monkey sitting between Lincoln's white marble feet at the memorial in Washington, DC; looking at the real monkeys at the Central Park Zoo in New York; hanging off a cliff on a mountain she had climbed in Mexico; with a lei around its neck in Hawaii.

Steven sent home Ellen's papers and some little things he thought we would want. We gave her friend Tim her car, her furniture, her artwork, and anything else he wanted. We told him to give away her clothes and anything he *didn't* want. But three weeks after her death, Stuart asked Tim to send him Ellen's camera. The camera arrived in a large carton, its gunmetal gray, heavyweight canvas carrying case surrounded by wadded-up newspapers. Stu couldn't bring himself to open it and when I arrived home from work he was sitting at the kitchen table, staring straight ahead, unable to speak, as he'd been the day he had to put Stella to sleep. Stuart looked as if the camera case held a coiled snake about to strike. I put the unopened case in the back of my closet so he wouldn't stumble upon it by accident.

When Stu enrolled in a photography class at the University of Tennessee, two years after Ellen's death, he needed a good camera. Early one morning, he said he was going out to buy one. I said it was time either to use Ellen's camera or give it away. He sat mutely on the bed and I took the case, which said "LeMans" on the side, out of the back of my closet and opened it for the first time since I'd hidden it away. I put the camera on the bed and said, "Touch it. It isn't going to bite you."

The case had a soft, velvet-padded strap that once rested on Ellen's shoulder and now would rest on Stuart's. In the case were neat compartments, separated by Velcro-tipped straps to hold each thing in its proper place. (It was the exact opposite of Ellen's childhood room, where she had developed chaos into an art form.) A brush for cleaning the lens was tucked into a netlike holder in the lid of the case and a bottle of lens cleaner in the zippered pocket on the front.

The camera, a Nikon 4004s, with all its numbers and dials intimidated Stuart. The manual was safely tucked under the camera, but Stu never read manuals, because he couldn't understand a word they said. There was a Sigma zoom lens that would take him two more years to learn to use with instructions all in Japanese—a comfort to him, since he couldn't be *expected* to read them. There were new Duracel batteries in their bright yellow and black package looking strangely harsh and aggressive amid all the dull gray and black. A roll of Kodak TMAX film, whose expiration date had already passed; a $1.00 off coupon from Target for developing and printing any roll of film; and another coupon for a free second set of prints were all tucked under the manual.

When Stuart finally picked up the camera and pushed the shutter release button, a click made him jump, as if the snake he knew was there had struck. When he pressed the film rewind button he heard that whirring sound, as if a roll of film was still inside. Would we develop it? "Absolutely not," he said. He thought, crazily, Ellen might have set the self-timer to take a picture of her killing herself, since there was no suicide note. (I wonder if Ellen's unsent letter to us was a kind of suicide note? I never showed it to Stuart because he couldn't stand looking at Ellen's things.)

Stuart was afraid to look inside and he took the camera to Thompson's Photo so they could see if there was film in it. He breathed a sigh of relief when they told him there wasn't.

For so many years Stuart and Ellen didn't get along. Sometimes they seemed to hate each other. He thinks, to this day, that her successful attempt at self-destruction was an unsuccessful attempt at his. I disagree and tell him she was sick and that I have bad genes. He says that I'm entitled to my opinion. I always thought the crazy gene came from Stuart, but now I realize it came from my side of the family.

Stu thinks Ellen killed herself because it was the only way to attract our attention. I tell him I think that's insane—she knew that we loved her. He said she never showed *us* the side that made so many people love her (in some ways that's true), but he just doesn't want to think about the good times. Stu said he never wants to look at our home movies, showing Steven and Ellen as babies, their first steps, the chronicle of their growing up years. He won't look at any pictures of Ellen. But I know it's because they make him sad. I love the photos because they remind me that there were good times as well as bad. Stu and I will never agree with each other about Ellen.

Last summer Steven visited us in Vermont. We talked about Ellen and he read the manuscript for this book and cried. When he got back to Boston he wrote me a letter:

> *I don't think I get so sad because I feel sorry for Ellen, but rather because of how Dad suffers because of what she did. I think you and I can deal with our feelings about it pretty openly, but*

you know how Dad internalizes that stuff and probably suffers at least twice as much as we do as a result. While Dad may have his own set of idiosyncrasies, I think he probably has the biggest heart on the planet, and it kills me to know the effect of Ellen's death on him. He just didn't deserve to have anything like that happen to him. Not that any of the rest of us did, but somehow I feel the tragedy hit Dad the hardest deep down, if not on the surface.

When Stuart reluctantly started using the camera and nothing on it seemed to work for him he said wryly, "Ellen must know that I'm using her camera." However, two years after he began taking pictures with it, his photography teacher at the university, who knew nothing of Ellen's death, because Stuart never talked about it, said to him, "Sometimes a photographer will have a very special relationship with his camera . . . you have that with yours." Stuart is now at ease with a camera whose complexities he never thought he'd understand.

The day that would have been Ellen's thirty-fourth birthday, after Stu left to take pictures, I went to the swimming pool at the condo. I was sitting on a chaise lounge, my back to the pool, looking at a small pond (about fifty feet wide) stocked with rainbow trout that people seemed to feel good about catching. I couldn't understand why. Perhaps since most of the fish have lived in that pond for such a long time they seldom get caught because they're too smart to bite.

I was watching a mother and her two children. The little girl and boy reminded me of Steven and Ellen when they were small. The girl, a toddler of around eighteen months, had hair the same color as Ellen's—

reddish blond. However it was straight, not curly like Ellen's. The boy, about five, was serious looking, like Steven, his brow wrinkled in concentration and his jaw set with purpose. He was going to try to catch a fish. He dumped his worms, now dead, on the grass and screamed, "Yech! It's just a bunch of worm guts." He searched through the pile (Steven would *never* have done that) looking for a live one to bait his hook. His mother cried, "They smell awful. I can smell them from here," and she scooped them into their plastic container and tossed them in the trash.

The girl was laughing and threw her bottle toward the pond, racing around on the moist, prickly-feeling grass, her sturdy little legs pumping fast (Ellen's legs were much thinner), but when she was caught up in her mother's arms and whirled around, I had a sense of déjà vu and my eyes filled with tears.

When we were in Vermont, Steven asked me if he could read the poems I had written about Ellen. But when I gave them to him he burst into tears. I snatched them away and said I was sorry and hugged him. He didn't argue. That spring I had taken a class at the University of Tennessee called "Dreamworks," where I kept a journal of my dreams and wrote poems about them. Although I said I felt no guilt when Ellen shot herself, my dreams were oozing with guilt. The symbolism was so obvious that even I, an art school graduate who had only taken Psych 1, could read their hidden meaning. So maybe my friend was right when he said, from the very beginning, that I *had* to feel guilt. He also said it would take something like a dream search to even get at it.

If I do feel guilt for Ellen's death, I'm trying not to blame myself for it. I see now that she took after my mother, and that depression ran in my family, and even though we had tried to help her, we couldn't. I wonder if it's possible to stop a person who is bent on self-destruction from carrying out that plan.

I can't let myself think about how I might have stopped her. I have to go on living. But I wonder if it is sufficient to explain what happened to Ellen by simply saying that depression was in her genes or that heredity is the reason she took drugs and became alcoholic?

Evidence suggests that recurrent depression is often hereditary, that depressives are particularly at risk to commit suicide, and that many of them turn to drugs and alcohol as a way of calming themselves, of coping with feelings of isolation, hopelessness, and the fear that they will never get better. I have also heard that despite all the advances in psychology and medicine in the understanding and treatment of mental illness, many general physicians are still relatively ignorant of how to diagnose and treat depression.

Could Stu and I have done more as her parents? I read one book on child development asserting that parenting has little long-term effect on the development of a child's personality, that peer groups and influences outside the home are critical factors. But whenever I feel tempted to believe that argument, "cop-out" keeps clanging around in my mind.

Then again, a friend of mine, a minister and teacher who has worked with troubled adolescents for decades, agrees with the book's assessment. He said, "One thing is clear to me and that is that usually a child's troubled behavior has nothing to do with his or her parenting. After the kids go to school, peers, school environment, and the general culture outside the home have more to do with their behavior than anything else. That any kid gets through adolescence unscathed nowadays is luck or a miracle."

I still don't know if any answers or resolutions have surfaced in the telling of this story, or if what I've learned about depression and addiction holds true for Ellen, or if nurture can ever triumph over nature. When I started writing down my memories I had hoped to discover the secret—a way to understand what events led to my daughter's suicide. Now I think of March 29, 1993, as the day Ellen decided to escape from despair—that she saw death as her only way out.

When we came back from Vermont I looked at all the things that Steven had sent home from Seattle in 1993. There was an envelope packed with papers on how to quit smoking, a story titled "My First Kiss," a thick folder labeled "Rejection letters to save and treasure," her driver's license, her season pass to the Knoxville World's Fair, a wallet-size copy of her diploma from the University of Tennessee and a book of jokes she was writing for her act: "Now girls, beware of guys who call their dicks their weenie—they might be right." There was a music box with some trinkets inside—the pin we had given her with "Good fish/Bad fish" (the bad fish was smoking) and my daddy's gold medal from Commerce High that had "John Friedman/100 WPM" engraved on the back. When I turned the key on the music box and heard the tinny sounds of "Sunrise, Sunset. Sunrise, Sunset. Is this the little girl I carried?" from *Fiddler on the Roof,* which is always played at Jewish weddings, I broke down and wept. Why was there still music coming from that box? I thought, stupidly, that when I turned the key there would be no sound. There should not have been any sound.

There were five years' worth of "Pocket Pal" organizers, with plans for each day. I was drawn, as if by a magnet, to look at the one for 1993—her last year of life. Then I was repelled, fearing what Ellen had planned for March 29th. But I looked. The Pocket Pal thoughtfully included the last week of 1992, and there was a notation to see Dr. Frank at 5:30 on December 29th, exactly three months before Ellen's suicide. On New Year's Day there was a date with "Nick" at nine o'clock, and I wondered if it was the same Nick who wrote "About Ellen," which was inserted in the program for her memorial service. I supposed it was. For the first three months of the year Ellen had dates for movies and dinner and skiing. Dates for going to the theater. A day to bake Vinnie a cake. Lots of dates with Brian. She had noted her grandma's and Belinda's birthdays.

There were dates for people whom she had invited to her apartment for dinner. Dates to play tennis with Tim Wilson. Dates to play Ping-Pong with Dan. A date to baby-sit for Andy on January 17th. I remembered a letter that Ellen had written to us about baby-sitting for Andy. I looked for it and found it right away, at the top of the hundreds of letters I'd saved:

1 /19 / 93

Dear Mom and Dad: I survived Sunday night. I baby-sat for 6 hours a 3-year old and a 15 month old. I got to say things like "finish your fish sticks" "make nice to the kitty" and "wave good-bye to the poo poo." Nothing like wiping somebody else's kid's crap off his butt to make me appreciate my freedom. Andy and D'nece (the same couple who had me over for Xmas) came home an hour early @ 10:00 P.M. from the symphony. They asked if I wanted a glass of their homemade wine. I said I'd love to, but I had an early morning appointment to get my tubes tied.

. . .

Now it's February 1999, and I think about going to Big Stone Gap, Virginia every February to see the play at Powell Valley High School, and about the time we saw Fiddler on the Roof with Ellen. And I look at the letter that my friend Joan Boyd Short wrote me after Ellen died and stop at the part where Joan said Ellen sparkled and that she wished Ellen could have seen what the rest of us saw.

In the winter, when I take my morning walk, sometimes I wear my blue-and-white sweatshirt from Powell Valley High with L'CHAIM on the front and whisper to myself, "to life." And I think of Tevye's words: "Every one of us is a fiddler on the roof, trying to scratch out a simple, pleasant tune without breaking our necks." Stu and I are still scratching out our tunes, but Ellen fell off the roof. I think of all the times, after her suicide, that I wished Ellen had never been born, and then I tell myself that in spite of everything, Ellen's life did matter. She did sparkle.

L'chaim. To life.